Alive in

A STUDY OF SALVATION

by David D. Duncan

AN INDEPENDENT-STUDY TEXTBOOK

Developed in Cooperation with
the ICI University Staff

Instructional Development Specialist:
Juanita Cunningham Blackburn

Illustrators: Bill Stewart and Brenna Olsen

ICI University Press
6300 North Belt Line Road
Irving, Texas 75063
USA

Address of the local ICI office in your area:

First Edition 1981
Second Edition 1996 7/96 3M LR

S3231E-90

1-56390-027-0

TABLE OF CONTENTS

THE ICI CHRISTIAN SERVICE PROGRAM

This is one of 18 courses (subjects) that make up the ICI Christian Service Program. The symbol at the left is a guide for order of study in the series, which is divided into three units of six courses each. *Alive in Christ: A Study in Salvation* is Course 3 in Unit II. You will benefit by studying the courses in the proper order.

Study materials in the Christian Service Program have been prepared in a self-teaching format especially for Christian workers. These courses provide a student with Bible knowledge and skills needed for practical Christian service. You may study this course in order to receive credit toward a certificate, or for personal enrichment

ATTENTION

Please read the course introduction very carefully. It is important that you follow these instructions so you can achieve the goals of the course, and be prepared for the student reports.

Address all correspondence concerning the course to your ICI instructor at the address stamped on the copyright page of this study guide.

COURSE INTRODUCTION

You are about to study a very important subject: salvation. Salvation includes all that was purchased for us at Calvary. In addition, it meets our every spiritual need. Salvation includes forgiveness of the sins of the past, deliverance from the power of sin in the present, and even protection against sin's aggression in the future (Jude 24).

Salvation is both a future expectation and a present source of joy. Yet many Christians know little or nothing about salvation as a present enjoyment. They think of it only as a way of getting to heaven. But, as we shall see, the Word makes clear that those who partake of the gift of salvation are 1) enlightened, 2) share in the Holy Spirit, 3) savor the goodness of the Word of God, and 4) experience a foretaste of the coming age (Hebrews 6:4-5). Christians thus experience an earnest or down payment of the unlimited, future joy of heaven as they walk with the Lord on earth.

After careful examination of the background of salvation, you will consider the chain of events that begins as the sinner turns away from sin (repentance) to God (faith) and makes an about-face in his life-style (conversion). You will evaluate the results of the new birth as the new believer receives a new nature (regeneration), a new standing before God (justification), and a new position in God's family (adoption). And finally, you will examine the believer's responsibility to begin to grow spiritually just as soon as he experiences salvation. For an immature Christian is no credit to Christ and His power to save. Such a person obviously lacks spiritual development because he lacks spiritual nourishment (1 Corinthians 3:1-3; Hebrews 5:11-14).

You will learn that ignorance and indifference hinder spiritual growth and development. Ignorance can be overcome by reading the Word of God and understanding the value of salvation. Indifference, however, can be overcome only by the work of the Holy Spirit in your heart as you surrender to Him and receive the hunger and thirst for righteousness that characterize a healthy spiritual appetite.

As you consider the work of the Holy Spirit in the heart of Christians, perfecting their spiritual life and bringing them to productive maturity, you will learn about His method and purpose. This will enrich your life. My prayer is that, as a result of this course, you will appreciate your salvation more, understand it better, and be able to communicate it more effectively.

Course Description

Alive in Christ: A Study of Salvation concerns the doctrine of salvation. It presents salvation as both the will and work of God which rest upon the atoning work of Christ. Preliminary consideration is given to the grace of God as the source of salvation. The biblical teaching on election and foreordination is examined as background for consideration of the respective roles of God and man in salvation. Care is taken to avoid the extremes of emphasis on either the initiative of *God* or the initiative of man in the process and progress of salvation. Included in this study are the biblical teachings of repentance, faith, conversion, regeneration, justification, adoption, sanctification, and glorification.

Course Objectives

When you finish this course you should be able to:

1. Discuss the respective roles of God and man in salvation.
2. Put in sequence the logical steps of salvation.
3. Explain the biblical basis for the assurance of salvation.

4. Contrast the method of salvation presented in the Bible with any nonbiblical approach.
5. Appreciate more deeply the love, grace, and wisdom of God which is revealed in His salvation.

Textbooks

You will use *Alive in Christ: A Study of Salvation by* David Duncan as both the textbook and study guide for the course. The Bible is the only other textbook required. Most of the Scriptures. quoted in this course are from the *New International Version,* 1978 edition. In a few instances we have quoted from the *King James Version* (KJV) or *Today's English Version* (TEV).

Study Time

How much time you actually need to study each lesson depends in part on your knowledge of the subject and the strength of your study skills before you begin the course. The time you spend also depends on the extent to which you follow directions and develop skills, necessary for independent study. Plan your study schedule so that you spend enough time to reach the objectives stated by the author of the course and your personal objectives as well.

Lesson Organization and Study Pattern

Each lesson includes: 1) lesson title, 2) opening statement, 3) lesson outline, 4) lesson objectives, 5) learning activities, 6) key words, 7) lesson development including study questions, 8) self-test (at the end of the lesson development), 9) answers to the study questions.

The lesson outline and objectives will give you an overview of the subject, help you to focus your attention on the most important points as you study, and tell you what you should learn.

Most of the study questions in the lesson development can be answered in spaces provided in this study guide. Longer answers should be written in a notebook. As you write the answers in your notebook, be sure to record the number and title of the lesson. This will help you in your review for the unit student report.

Do not look ahead at the answers until you have given your answer. If you give your own answers, you will remember what you study much better. After you have answered the study questions, check your answers with those given at the end of the lesson. Then correct those you did not answer correctly. The answers are not given in the usual numerical order so that you will not accidentally see the answer to the next question.

These study questions are very important. They will help you to remember the main ideas presented in the lesson and to apply the principles you have learned.

How to Answer Questions

There are different kinds of study questions and self-test questions in this study guide. Below are samples of several types and how to answer than. Specific instructions will be given for other types of questions that may occur.

A *MULTIPLE-CHOICE* question or item asks you to choose an answer from the ones that are given.

Example

1 The Bible has a total of
a) 100 books.
b) 66 books.
c) 27 books.

The correct answer is *b) 66 books*. In your study guide, make a circle around *b)* as shown here:

(b) 66 books.

(For some multiple-choice items, more than one answer will be correct. In that case, you would circle the letter in front of each correct answer.)

A *TRUE-FALSE* question or item asks you to choose which of several statements are TRUE.

Example

2 Which statements below are TRUE?
a The Bible has a total of 120 books.
(b) The Bible is a message for believers today.
c All of the Bible authors wrote in the Hebrew language.
(d) The Holy Spirit inspired the writers of the Bible.

Statements **b** and **d** are true. You would make a circle around these two letters to show your choices, as you see above.

A *MATCHING* question or item asks you to match things that go together, such as names with descriptions, or Bible books with their authors.

Example

3 Write the number for the leader's name in front of each phrase that describes something he did.

..1.. **a** Received the Law at Mt. Sinai	1) Moses
..2.. **b** Led the Israelites across Jordan	2) Joshua
..2.. **c** Marched around Jericho	
..1.. **d** Lived in Pharaoh's court	

Phrases **a** and **d** refer to Moses, and phrases **b** and **c** refer to Joshua. You would write **1** beside **a** and **d**, and **2** beside **b** and **c**, as you see above.

Ways to Study This Course

If you study this ICI course by yourself, all of your work can be completed by mail. Although ICI has designed this course for you to study on your own, you may also study it in a group or class. If you do this, the instructor may give you added instructions besides those in the course. If so, be sure to follow his instructions.

Possibly you are interested in using the course in a home Bible study group, in a class at church, or in a Bible school. You will find both the subject content and study methods excellent for these purposes.

Unit Student Reports

If you are studying independently with ICI, with a group, or in a class, you have received with this course your unit student reports. These are to be answered according to the directions included in the course and in the unit student reports. You should complete and send your answer sheets to your instructor for his correction and suggestions regarding your work.

Certificate

Upon the successful completion of the course and the final grading of the unit student reports by your ICI instructor, you will receive your Certificate of Award.

Author of This Course

David Duncan has served as a missionary on the Instructional Development Staff of ICI University, Irving, Texas (USA).

Mr. Duncan earned his bachelor of arts degree at California State University–Fullerton. He also holds a masters of arts in social science from the same institution. And be has completed course requirements for the doctor of ministry degree at the California Graduate School of Theology.

Your ICI Instructor

Your ICI instructor will be happy to help you in any way possible. If you have any questions about the course or the unit student reports, please feel free to ask him. if several people want to study this course together, ask about special arrangements for group study.

God bless you as you begin to study *Alive. in Christ: A Study of Salvation.* May it enrich your life and Christian service and help you fulfill more effectively your part in the body of Christ.

Additional Helps

Other materials are available for use with this Individual Study Textbook, including supplemental audio cassettes, video cassettes, an Instructor's Guide, and an Instructor's Packet (for instructor's use only). Consult the Evangelism, Discipleship, and Training Manual.

Unit 1

WHAT GOD REQUIRES

LESSON 1

Man's Salvation Prepared

In recent years much has been written and said about salvation. The term *born again* has appeared in many newspapers and magazines, some of which have worldwide circulation. The theme of the *new birth* and the idea of *salvation* have thus come to occupy a prominent place in the public mind. Nevertheless, the experience of the *new birth* and the *doctrines of salvation* rest upon some very important and basic concepts which are often misunderstood. It is these basic concepts that provide our subject matter in this lesson.

The structure of salvation rests upon God's provision. In this lesson you will consider God's provision of *grace* which made possible the *plan of salvation.* You will see that salvation stems from the grace of God, expressed through the atoning work of Christ. Planned in eternity and put into effect in time, God's plan of salvation meets the needs of all people. Then in Lessons 2, 3, and 4 you will consider the biblical teaching concerning the activity of man in salvation.

As you examine the biblical teaching on salvation in depth, you will appreciate more deeply the love, grace, and wisdom of God that brings salvation to all people. And you will marvel at the great care He has taken in framing salvation's plan.

lesson outline

Salvation Stems From God's Grace
Salvation Proceeds From the Atoning Work of Christ
Salvation Meets Man's Needs

lesson objectives

When you finish this lesson you should be able to:

- State the source of salvation and explain its significance.
- Explain the relationship between your salvation and the death of Christ as a substitute for individuals.
- Explain that salvation rests upon the atoning work of Christ and fully meets the needs of persons such as you.

learning activities

1. Carefully read the preliminary section in this study guide.
2. Study the lesson outline and lesson objectives. These will help you identify the things you should try to learn as you study the lesson.
3. Read the lesson and do the exercises in the lesson development. Most of your responses can be made in this study guide. However, where longer responses are required, write your answers in a notebook. Check your answers with those given at the end of the lesson.
4. Check the glossary at the end of the study guide for definitions of any key words you do not understand.
5. Take the self-test at the end of the lesson and check your answers carefully with the answers given in the back of this textbook. Review any items you answer incorrectly.

key words

appease
atonement
belittle
compassion
concept
exalt
incarnate
penalty
predicament
propitiation
ransom
rebellion
reconciliation
redemption
righteousness
sacrificial
sovereign
unmerited

lesson development

SALVATION STEMS FROM GOD'S GRACE

Objective 1. *Define grace and explain its relationship to salvation.*

When we consider salvation, we begin with a very basic truth: that a sovereign, loving God, without any apparent reason, chose to show His kindness toward undeserving people by forgiving their sins. This act of forgiveness is an expression of the grace of God.

The story is told of a small underfed orphan boy who attended a large one-room village school. The children were required to leave their lunches and coats in the entryway, where they could be picked up at lunchtime. One day a lunch was missing. The teacher sternly asked, "Who took the lunch?" At last the small orphan boy raised a thin and shaking hand. Taking a cruel whip out of his desk, the teacher ordered the boy to come forward to receive his punishment. As he stood there, guilty, alone, weeping silently, with bowed head and trembling body, a hush fell over the other children. Suddenly a husky boy came forward and said to the teacher, "I'll take the whipping in his place!" And in front of the class he bared his back *in place of* the guilty orphan boy and paid the penalty for the broken rule. Compassion and sympathy caused him to suffer the punishment of the hungry, uncared-for, and unloved orphan boy. It was a much greater love that caused God to give His Son to take the punishment for people. Paying the penalty by taking the punishment of another is a way of showing what the Bible calls *grace.*

Grace is simply unearned favor. In salvation grace is the kindness with which God grants favor to undeserving people. Those who have sinned deserve only judgment and punishment. They do not deserve to receive pardon for their disobedience to God. But God showed His love for them by sending Christ to die in their place. In love He sent His Son to pay the penalty for their sin, release them from its control, and consider them as if they had never sinned. This is grace!

GOD'S MERCY

HE DOESN'T GIVE US
WHAT WE DO DESERVE

GOD'S GRACE

HE DOES GIVE US WHAT
WE DON'T DESERVE

Grace does not mean that God excuses sin. God's Word says that the wages of sin is death (Romans 6:23). And God cannot set aside His righteous attitude toward and judgment against sin. However, Christ's sacrifice on Calvary completely satisfied the righteousness of God. The penalty for breaking His law was thus paid. Grace does not *overlook* sin, rather it *removes* it.

1 Using your own words, write in your notebook the definition of grace and explain the relationship between grace and salvation.

Grace, then, originates or has its beginning in God. He is the source of grace. It proceeds from Him in an unlimited supply and through His favor it is extended to every person.

...tiate between examples of common grace and saving grace.

We see two kinds of grace in God's relationships with people: common grace and saving grace. ***Common grace*** is the kindness which God shows to all people, even though they are sinners. It helps to keep people from evil acts and encourages them to do what is right and orderly. It enables individuals to act somewhat decently, and it helps them to live together in a degree of social harmony. It is God's grace which provides the blessings of the natural world (rain, fruitful seasons, food, and many other social and material blessings).

2 Read Matthew 5:43-48. Which of these verses gives an example of common grace?

....

In addition to the blessings of the natural world, common grace provides the presence and influence of the Bible, the Holy Spirit, and the church. Common grace in itself is not sufficient for salvation, yet it reveals God's goodness to all people. It makes them conscious of God's provisions for life. And it creates a favorable climate for further revelation and undoubtedly makes them ready for salvation. Common grace also gives to the sinner the ability to make a favorable response to God. Through grace God makes it possible for all people to be saved.

3 Read Romans 2:1-11. Which one of these verses indicates that God's favor (grace) is related to salvation? also Romans 3:24

....

We have seen that common grace makes it possible for a man to respond favorably to God. However, it is God's saving grace which brings people to Christ (John 6:44), renews their hearts, and frees them from sin. The saving grace of God is uniquely demonstrated in Christ. In his gospel record, John says that "grace and truth came through Jesus Christ" (John 1:17). This does not mean that there was no saving grace before Christ came. All Old Testament saints were *saved*, that is, accepted before God on the basis of their faith in God's provisions which includes obedience to His commandments. John simply means that Christ is the full revelation of ***saving grace***, and the only person through which saving grace may be received since He came.

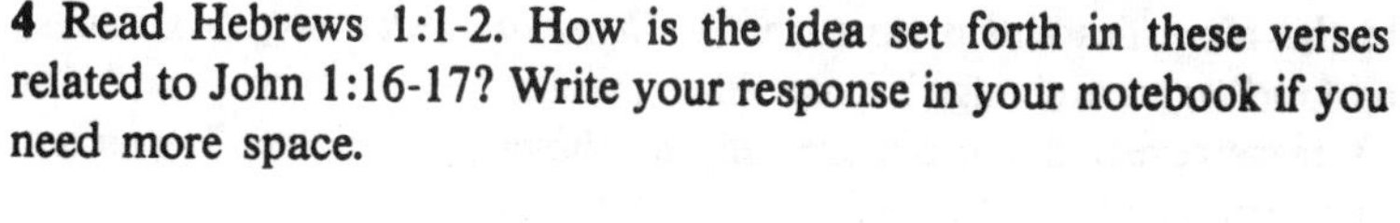

4 Read Hebrews 1:1-2. How is the idea set forth in these verses related to John 1:16-17? Write your response in your notebook if you need more space.

....

5 In front of each of the following items indicate whether it is an example of common grace or special grace by writing either 1) for ***common grace*** or 2) for ***special grace***.

.... **a** The sun shines on the evil and the good alike.
.... **b** The sinner is drawn to God.
.... **c** Conditions exist which make it possible for man to respond favorably to God.
.... **d** The blessings of nature rest upon all men.
.... **e** Man is enabled to respond to the call of God and to be set free from sin.

1) Common grace
2) Saving grace

Grace in the Bible

Objective 3. ***Appreciate the importance of grace in the Bible by noting its frequent use in both the Old and New Testaments.***

The word translated grace is used 166 times in the Bible. It is used 38 times in the Old Testament and 128 times in the New Testament. Grace is most often used of God, since He is by nature gracious (Jonah 4:2). God expressed His grace in: 1) giving good things to all people (Matthew 5:45), 2) desiring that all people be saved (2 Peter 3:9), 3) offering His riches to those who believe (2 Corinthians 8:9), and 4) keeping the Christian during times of trouble (1 Peter 5:6-10). And as the apostle Paul emphasizes in Romans 5:20, the grace of God has no limit. It is sufficient for all the needs that sinful people bring to the cross, and more. It is a vast supply.

6 Grace is used in the Old Testament, but it is much more prominent in the New Testament because
a) God's grace changed from time to time.
b) Jesus revealed grace more fully as shown in the New Testament record.
c) the Old Testament emphasized judgment and the New Testament emphasized only liberty.

7 To see how frequently grace is used in the Epistles (all of the New Testament books from Romans through Jude), look at the first chapter of each Epistle. In how many do you find the word *grace* at the beginning of the letter?

....

8 Now examine the last verses of each of the Epistles. How many of them do NOT end with the word *grace*? Name them.

....

9 Grace is mentioned throughout the Bible, but in the New Testament grace is mentioned
a) about twice as much as it is mentioned in the Old Testament.
b) nearly four times as much as it is in the Old Testament.

Did you notice in the endings of the Epistles that *grace* is connected with Jesus Christ? You have probably come to realize that *grace* is highly important in the teachings of the New Testament and that Christ is the fullest expression of God's grace. Indeed, it is by His *grace* that our hearts are drawn.

Consider the story of Tigranes, a powerful king of Armenia, who was taken captive by an invading Roman army. The defeated king, his wife, and all his children were brought before the commanding general to receive the sentence of death. Tigranes threw himself at the feet of the victor and pleaded for the lives of his family. He begged, "Do with me whatever you like, but spare my wife and children." His plea so moved the Roman general that he set the entire family free. As Tigranes and his family travelled away from the Roman camp, the grateful king turned to his wife and said, "What did you think of the Roman general?" She responded, "I never saw him." Her husband exclaimed, "You were in his presence. Where were your eyes?" She said, "They were fixed on the one who was willing to die for me. I saw no one else." When we look at God's salvation and the cross we see only Jesus, the one who was willing to die for us. The death of Christ is the greatest expression of God's grace.

SALVATION PROCEEDS FROM THE ATONING WORK OF CHRIST

Objective 4. *Identify statements which describe the relationship between man's sins and the atonement.*

If we are to understand the nature of salvation, we must consider the *atonement*. *Atonement* is a word which gives the idea of enemies being brought together to make peace. It refers to *reconciliation*, the change from a state of enmity to one of friendship. In salvation it speaks of the action by which the sinner is reconciled, or brought back, to God. Another meaning of *atonement* is to cancel or cover. As a result of Christ's sacrificial suffering and death, people's sins are covered over by His blood and the penalty for their sin is cancelled.

To fully grasp the importance of the atonement and its place in the plan of salvation, think of the following scene. A father and his son had a violent argument. As a result the son left home, vowing never to return as long as the father lived. The mother suffered greatly, for she dearly loved both her husband and her son. After many months the son received an urgent message to return home, since his mother was seriously ill and not expected to live. As the son walked into her hospital room, he saw his dear mother pale and wasted on the bed. Both father and son looked silently at their loved one, knowing she was very near death. Summoning her last reserves of strength, the mother reached out with one hand and took the hand of the father;

with her other hand she took the hand of her son. As a final act of love, she brought the hands of father and son together on her breast . . . as she died.

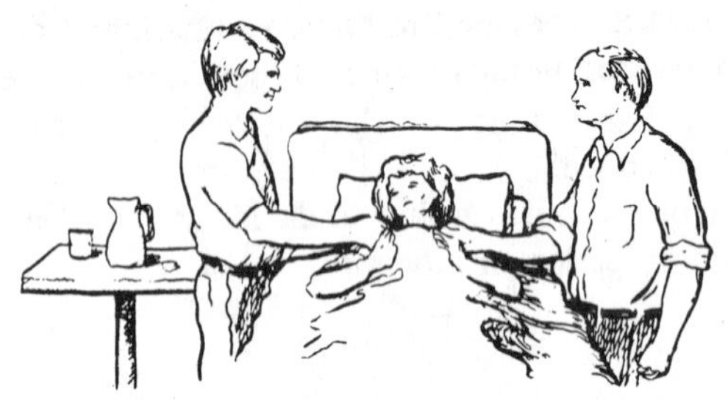

Christ's death on the cross was the means of bringing a holy God together with sinful people. Through the cross we have atonement for sins; that is, sins have been covered by the death of a substitute, the penalty has been paid, and God and people have been brought together.

10 Which statements below are TRUE and show the relationship between man's sins and the atoning work of Christ?

a Our sins have separated us from God, but the atonement restores the relationship.

b Sin speaks of disobedience, which separates God and man, but the atonement brings a covering of sin and removes the cause of the separation.

c The sins of man, while serious, are not fatal; the atonement is a means of showing man's good intentions. . . even if he will not, or cannot, live in obedience to God's law.

Necessity of the Atonement

Objective 5. *Recognize why the atonement was necessary.*

Some may wonder why God didn't just abandon people in their sins, or else simply declare them good and make them upright. Scripture, however, shows that God is holy and loving as well as righteous. He was not willing that any person should be lost, but He could not excuse people's guilt or accept them in their sin. In order to restore people to Himself, therefore, God provided a solution through the atonement. The solution lay in the person and work of Jesus Christ. In Christ all the requirements of righteousness were met, both in His life as He kept the Law perfectly in our place and in His death as He died under the penalty of the broken Law.

In atonement the purpose of perfect justice and divine love was accomplished. People were set free from the power and guilt of sin and restored to fellowship with God.

That the atonement was necessary is shown clearly in the Scriptures. First, God's holiness cannot overlook sin (Exodus 34:6-7; Romans 3:25-26), it must be covered, cancelled. Second, God's law, which reflects His very nature, made it necessary for Him to require satisfaction of the sinner (Deuteronomy 27:26). Then, the truthfulness of God requires atonement (Numbers 23:19; Romans 3:4). God had plainly said to Adam and Eve that they would die if they disobeyed His commandments. (Compare Genesis 2:16-17 with Ezekiel 18:4 and Romans 6:23.) God's truthfulness demanded that He uphold His word and required that this penalty be carried out on either the offenders or their substitute. And finally, the great cost of the sacrifice suggests that the atonement was necessary. Surely God would not have required the death of His Son unnecessarily (Luke 24:26; Hebrews 2:10; 9:22-23).

11 Read the above scriptural passages which relate to the necessity of the atonement. Which one, in your opinion, helps most in understanding how the atonement was necessary because of the nature of God?

....

12 Which statement or combination of statements explains why the atonement was necessary?

a) God's holiness, justice, and truthfulness demand atonement for sin.
b) The great cost implies that the atonement is necessary.
c) Divine law, which reflects God's nature, made it necessary for Him to require satisfaction for sin.
d) All of the above explain why the atonement was necessary.

The Biblical Doctrine of the Atonement

Objective 6. ***Identify statements that give the biblical doctrine of the atonement.***

The Bible teaches that man fell into sin by ***disobedience***, and that Christ by *obedience* in the sinner's place paid the penalty which the sinner had brought upon himself (Romans 5:12-19). This means that Christ died as our substitute—He died in our place. His sacrifice for sins makes God favorable toward us. This act of paying the ***penalty*** for our sins and dying as our ***substitute*** is referred to as ***penal substitution.***

The penal substitution of Christ is basic to the Bible teaching of atonement. In Isaiah 53:5-6 we read:

> But he was pierced for our transgressions, he was crushed for our iniquities; the punishment that brought us peace was upon him, and by his wounds we are healed. We all, like sheep, have gone astray, each of us has turned to his own way; and the Lord has laid on him the iniquity of us all.

These verses (as well as 53:4) teach quite clearly the atonement by substitution.

Jesus said concerning Himself, "For even the Son of Man did not come to be served, but to serve, and to give his life a ransom for many" (Mark 10:45). In Galatians 3:13 the apostle Paul writes that "Christ redeemed us from the curse of the law by becoming a curse for us." These words can only be interpreted to mean that Christ, the sinless one, took upon Himself the penalty that sinners should rightfully have borne. And in Romans 3:21-26, Paul, who wrote at length on this subject, insists that the atonement through the death of Christ shows God to be both just and merciful.

13 Identify the statements below which are TRUE and give the biblical doctrine of the atonement.

a Man by his disobedience deserves to pay the penalty for sin.
b Christ by His obedience has paid the penalty for all people.

c Christ died first for His own sin and then for those of other men.
d Christ died as a *substitute* for the sins of all mankind.
e Christ came to earth to give His life as a ransom for sin.

Aspects of the Atonement

Objective 7. *Identify definitions of five aspects of the atonement.*

When we speak of *aspects* of the atonement, we simply acknowledge the fact that no one term is able to include and explain all of the greatness of the atonement. The following terms are given to help you understand Christ's saving work more fully.

Obedience. Of the various aspects of the atonement, the one which most unifies the whole concept is Christ's obedience. Since it is the *general* aspect on which all the others depend, we shall consider it first.

In providing salvation for us, Christ became our obedient sacrifice. He did not assume His own rightful status of equality with God but willingly took the form of a servant (Philippians 2:7-8). It was thus necessary for Him to become, for a time, limited as we are (Hebrews 2:14). John described this by saying, "The Word became flesh and lived for a while among us" (John 1:14)—as a man. Luke records that during His youth Jesus was obedient to His parents (Luke 2:51). And Jesus Himself testified that His mission on earth was to do God's will obediently (John 6:38).

As the Son of Man, Christ obeyed the demands of the Law. He kept the civil law as one born a Jew and observed the ceremonial law as well. He also kept the moral law, fearing God and keeping His commandments. And, in addition, He submitted to all the penalties which resulted from man's disobedience to the law of God.

14 Circle the letters of the TRUE statements which follow.

a From our discussion of the atonement to this point, we can conclude that the word *atonement* includes a number of important concepts (ideas) which relate to Christ's saving work.

b The general concept (notion) of the atonement upon which all others rest is obedience.

c Jesus' example of obedience related primarily to His ministry, not to His personal, domestic life.

In addition to the *general* aspect of the atonement, obedience, there are four *specific* terms which describe what God did in Christ's death: *sacrifice, propitiation, reconciliation,* and *redemption.* Each term describes the provision of God which meets a specific need of sinful man. These words are especially important because they are the ones used in the New Testament.

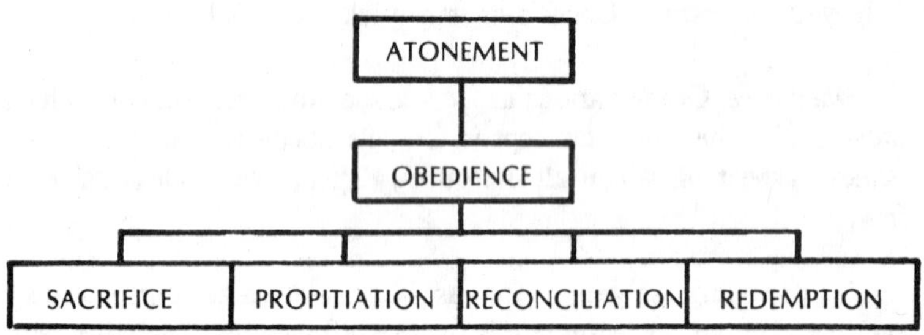

Sacrifice. This is a broad term and includes all that Christ did to provide salvation for us. His sacrifice covers the sins of man. It is directed to the need created by our guilt. Paul tells us that "Christ loved us and gave himself up for us as a fragrant offering and sacrifice to God" (Ephesians 5:2). Nothing is clearer in the New Testament than the use of sacrificial terms to describe the death of Christ. When Scripture describes Him as the Lamb of God, says that His blood cleanses from all sin, and teaches that He died for our sins, we clearly see that Christ's death was a real sacrifice for sin (John 1:29; 1 John 1:7-9; 1 Corinthians 15:3). His death is described as a death for sin, as a bearing of sin (2 Corinthians 5:21). God made Him a sacrifice for sin (Isaiah 53:10). He paid the debt we could not pay, and blotted out (erased) the past which we could not undo. He is our sacrifice, for His death is set forth as an act of perfect self-giving (Hebrews 9:14; Ephesians 5:2). His one sacrifice was sufficient to turn away the wrath (anger) of God and to remove all barriers between God and man (Hebrews 9:28; 1 Peter 3:18) that interrupt fellowship.

15 Circle the letter in front of the statements which are TRUE concerning Christ's sacrifice.

a It covers the sins of man.
b This supreme sacrifice has resulted in the possibility that at least some men can be saved.
c Sacrifice was a means of turning away divine wrath (anger).
d Christ's sacrifice was offered on a once-for-all-time basis.
e Christ's death was not murder; it was sacrifice. He accomplished the will of God in order to make an atonement for man's sins and to reconcile him to God.

Propitiation. Propitiation meets the need that arises from the anger of God. To propitiate is to appease (satisfy) the righteous anger of God by an atoning sacrifice. Christ is described as such a propitiation (Romans 3:25; 1 John 2:2; 4:10). The concept of God's anger is found throughout the Bible, but especially in the Old Testament. It emphasizes the seriousness of sin. By the suffering of the sinner's atoning substitute, Jesus Christ, the divine anger is propitiated (appeased), and as a result of this propitiation the punishment due to sin is not placed upon the sinner.

Because some people misunderstand the love of God, they reject the idea of God's anger. But His anger is not like ours. We become angry because we have been hurt or offended, and we strike out in a fit of rage. But God's anger is judicial and is directed against sin and sinful people. He does not lose His temper.

16 Circle the letter in front of the TRUE statements.

a The wrath (anger) of God is not an uncontrolled fit of passion but rather a constant burning anger against sin.
b The idea suggested by the word *propitiate* is to appease one.
c Propitiation provides for the removal of divine displeasure, which sin creates, by the punishment of each individual sinner.

Reconciliation. Reconciliation meets the need which is created by God's separation from sinful persons. The Bible tells us that sinners are enemies of God (Romans 5:10-11; Colossians 1:21; James 4:4). The broken relations between God and man were caused by man's sin (Isaiah 59:2). But Christ died to remove our sins which were the cause of the hostility and separation. In restoring fellowship between God and man, God took the first step to correct the problem: "While we were still sinners, Christ died for us" (Romans 5:8) and "God was reconciling the world to himself in Christ" (2 Corinthians 5:19). Reconciliation, then, refers to the adjustment of differences between God and man. It makes things right.

17 Have you ever sinned against or offended a close friend and later been reconciled to him? What were your feelings? What were his feelings? Now read the 15th chapter of Luke. What do you learn from this chapter about God's feelings? Answer these questions in your notebook.

Redemption. Redemption answers the need created by man's bondage to sin. Redemption speaks of deliverance from certain evil by the payment of a price. In order to set us free from sin and its penalty, a price was paid. That price was the atoning death of our Savior. The writer to the Hebrews declares that "he has died as a ransom" (Hebrews 9:15) to set us free from sin and Satan. Also, "Christ redeemed us from the curse of the law by becoming a curse for us" (Galatians 3:13). Without this deliverance from the curse we could not have salvation. In addition to deliverance from the curse of the Law, we have been set free from bondage to the Law, and from keeping the Law as a condition of acceptance with God.

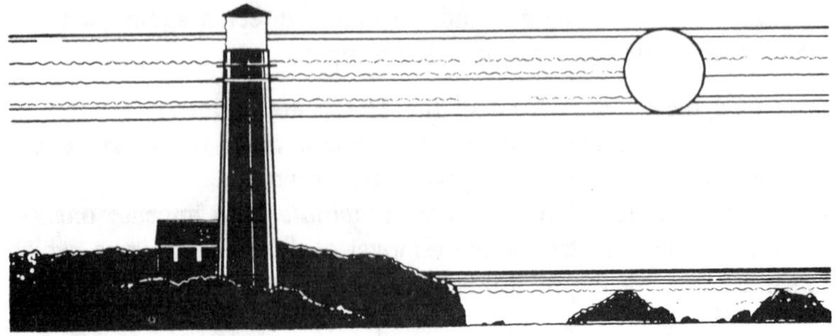

18 Match each need or description in the left column with the proper aspect of the atonement in the right column which meets that need or completes the thought.

.... **a** Speaks of appeasing God's wrath	1) Christ's obedience
.... **b** Covers man's guilt and atones for his sin	2) Sacrifice
.... **c** Adjusts differences between God and us	3) Propitiation
.... **d** Secures release from bondage by payment of a price	4) Reconciliation
.... **e** The one aspect which underlies and unifies all the others	5) Redemption

Extent of the Atonement

Objective 8. *Describe the extent of the atonement.*

When we discuss the *extent* of the atonement, we must consider these questions: Was it God's intent for Jesus to die for all people? Or did He intend that Christ should only die for a select few?

19 Read the following representative Scriptures: 1 Timothy 2:4, 6; 4:10; Hebrews 2:9; 2 Peter 3:9; 1 John 2:2. In your own words state the theme of these passages and tell how this theme affects our view of the extent of the atonement. Use your notebook, please.

The value of the atonement is *unlimited*, but its application is *limited*. The atoning death of Christ is *sufficient* for all, but it is *efficient* only for those who believe. God so loved the (whole) world (mankind) that He gave His Son to provide salvation, but as we shall see in a following lesson, *each person* must respond to God's provision (John 3:16).

SALVATION MEETS MAN'S NEEDS

One of the basic reasons for studying about salvation is that salvation meets man's needs. Our responsibility as Christians is to share the good news with all people. However, if we are to be effective in showing them how Christ can meet their needs, we must know what their needs are.

Man's Sin

Objective 9. *Define sin and list two ways in which all people are sinners.*

Two things stand out in the Bible concerning the nature of man: man's sin and his predicament (or condition). Sin is failing to live according to the law of God, or else openly breaking the law. Sin is more than disobedience, however. It is also the exalting of self and the belittling of God. Since we are reasoning, thinking creatures, we know that when we do what we should not do, or do not do what we ought to do, or are what we should not be, or are not what we should be, we are guilty of sin.

Every person is a sinner in two ways. One is that he is born into sin, and the other is that he chooses to do sinful acts. Adam's sin has been charged to all people because he was the representative head of the human race (Romans 5:12). When Adam fell, therefore, the race fell, and all people inherited a sinful nature, which is responsible for attitudes of stubbornness and rebellion toward the law of God. In addition, people are responsible for their own sinful acts (Galatians 5:19-21).

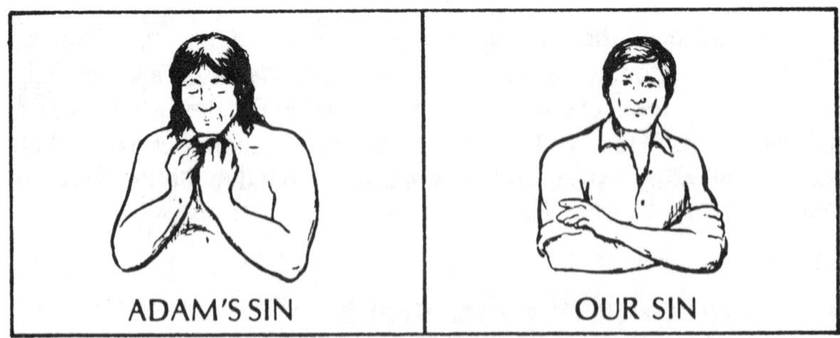

BOTH CAN CONDEMN US!

20 Define sin in your own words, and list two ways in which all people have become sinners. Write your response in your notebook.

Man's Predicament

Objective 10. *Recognize true statements which show the predicament of people and how salvation meets their needs.*

The result of people's sin is separation from God and their fellow persons. Because of the sinful nature which resulted from the Fall, people are totally evil. Every part of their nature has been affected: their intellects, emotions, and wills. Because of this they are completely incapable of saving themselves. Their minds have become so darkened by sin that they cannot understand spiritual things (1 Corinthians 2:14). To them spiritual things are foolish. And since they are without spiritual insight, they cannot understand the truth of the things of God. Their natural minds cannot grasp these issues; they need information which is made available only by the work of the Holy Spirit.

People's wills are bound in slavery to sin. Paul says this is so "because the sinful mind is hostile to God. It does not submit to God's law, nor can it do so. Those controlled by their sinful nature cannot please God" (Romans 8:7-8). We can draw a number of conclusions from these facts:

1. Fallen persons cannot think, will, or do what is truly good.
2. They may, on occasion, do good deeds because of common grace.
3. Their ability to choose and act is limited by their slavery to sin (Romans 6:17, 20).
4. The only deliverance from this bondage to sin is God's redeeming grace.

It is thrilling to know that people's wills are free to turn to God, to repent, and to believe. This is the teaching of Scripture.

21 Read Matthew 3:2; 18:3; Luke 13:3, 5; John 6:29; Acts 2:38; 3:19. What do these verses show us about one's freedom? Use your notebook for this response, please.

We see then that sinful persons are commanded to repent. And if they were not free to respond to these commands, they would be without meaning or real force. With the help of God, people can will and act according to God's good purpose: repenting of their sins, believing in Jesus, and accepting His salvation (Philippians 2:12-13). Salvation through Christ is the *only* solution to people's sin.

22 Select the TRUE statements which show the predicament of people and how salvation meets their needs.

a The problem of sin is that it affects the mind of man, and thus, it tends to ruin his thought life, and, in time, his whole life.
b The result of sin is separation from God and fellowmen.
c Sin has affected every part of man so that in his natural state he is totally evil: intellectually, emotionally, and volitionally.
d Salvation gives one a new nature and restores the ability and desire to live according to God's law.
e The only deliverance from sin is the intention of each individual who recognizes his need to repent of sin and believe on the Lord.

self-test

After you have reviewed this lesson take the self-test. Then check your answers with those given at the back of this study guide. Review any items you answer incorrectly.

1 Salvation stems from the grace of God. Which ones of the following statements are TRUE of grace?

a Grace may be defined as the expression of God's love to undeserving people for no apparent reason.
b Simply stated, grace is undeserved favor.
c Grace is the favor of God which overlooks sin.
d God's grace does not tolerate sin. Instead grace provides a way to remove sin.
e Common grace is that grace which is common to all men, bringing them to salvation.

2 Salvation proceeds from the atoning work of Christ. Which ones of the following statements are TRUE concerning the atonement?

a The atonement was necessary because God's holiness and man's sinfulness demanded it.

b The central theme of the atonement is the *hiding* or *ignoring* of sin.

c In atonement there is a sense of bringing enemies together.

d Penal substitution refers primarily to the penalty that was paid for man's sins through the offering of a substitute, Jesus Christ.

e Propitiation is a term which refers to appeasing one who is offended.

f The one aspect of the atonement which most unifies the whole concept is *sacrifice*.

g The atonement is sufficient for the salvation of all people, but it is limited only to those who believe.

3 Salvation meets man's needs. Circle the letters of the TRUE statements which relate to man's sin and predicament.

a Sin includes failing to keep God's law as well as openly breaking it.

b Man, according to the Bible, has no part in or connection with Adam's sin.

c Sin makes man feel "self-sufficient" and "scornful of God."

d Man's predicament is that he is separated from God by sin and is totally evil; therefore, his only solution is salvation through Jesus Christ.

e Man's problem is great, for he is a victim of fate. He cannot turn to God of his own free will, since he can only do what God wills.

f The many biblical commandments to repent let us know that man is not directed by the uncertainties of fate. He is capable of turning to God as the Spirit of God draws him.

answers to study questions

The answers to your study exercises are not given in the usual order, so that you will not see the answer to your next question ahead of time. Look for the number you need, and try not to look ahead.

12 d) All of the above explain why the atonement was necessary.

1 Your answer. You probably said that grace is unearned or unmerited favor. Grace is the basis on which God grants forgiveness to undeserving people.

13 **a** True.
b True.
c False.
d True.
e True.

2 Verse 45 gives an example of ***common grace.***

14 **a** True.
b True.
c False.

3 Verse 4 shows that it is God's goodness that leads people to repentance.

15 **a** True.
b False.
c True.
d True.
e True.

4 The Old Testament gave a partial revelation of God. The New Testament gives a more complete revelation of God in Jesus, through whom we have received the full revelation of God's grace.

16 **a** True.
b True.
c False.

5 **a** 1) Common grace.
b 2) Saving grace.
c 1) Common grace.
d 1) Common grace.
e 2) Saving grace.

17 Your answer. We learn that God has great joy when we return to Him.

6 b) Jesus revealed grace more fully as shown in the New Testament record.

18 **a** 3) Propitiation.
b 2) Sacrifice.
c 4) Reconciliation.
d 5) Redemption.
e 1) Christ's obedience.

7 Sixteen.

19 Your answer. Clearly, Christ died for the sins of the whole world. This biblical fact convinces us that God's provision of salvation is unlimited.

8 Five. James, 1, 2, and 3 John, and Jude.

20 Your answer. We have noted that sin is failure to obey God's law or even breaking it openly. It is the exalting of self and the belittling of God. Sin comes from our own sinful nature, which we inherited from Adam, and our own sinful acts.

9 b) nearly four times as much as it is in the Old Testament.

21 Your answer. They are all directed to man, urging him to do something. If man were not free to respond, then these commands would be meaningless.

10 **a** True.
b True.
c False.

22 **a** False.
b True.
c True.
d True.
e False. (Good intentions do not save us. The act of accepting Christ is all-important.)

11 Your answer. In my opinion, Romans 3:25-26 is very helpful in explaining the necessity of the atonement based on the nature of God. Luke 24:26 is a very forceful statement on this issue.

LESSON 2

Man Changes His Course: Repentance

There was a small boy who had a great appetite for sweet foods. He was especially fond of candy and cookies. One day his mother baked some cookies. She told him, "Son, I don't want you to have any cookies until after dinner."

He really wanted some of those delicious, tempting cookies. And as the day passed, his hunger and desire grew. Finally, he went very quietly into the kitchen and opened the cookie jar, taking only two or three cookies. But as he hurriedly replaced the lid, he overturned the jar and broke it. As his mother entered the room to see what had happened, he realized that he was going to be punished. He pleaded, "Mother, I'm sorry. Please don't spank me. I'm sorry." She was understanding and sympathetic, but firm, as she said, "Yes, I know you are sorry—but not because you disobeyed and took the cookies. You are sorry because you were caught."

In this case, the boy was not repentant; rather, he was sorry for the consequences of his actions. In this lesson you will examine the difference between true *repentance* and concern over the ***consequences*** of sin. You will marvel at the nature of true repentance as you see how it begins the process of bringing together a loving and holy God and sinful people. And you will learn to appreciate more fully the sweet and gentle moving of the Holy Spirit that brings man to repentance.

lesson outline

Nature of Repentance
Aspects of Repentance
Relation to Restitution
New Testament Emphasis
Experience of Repentance

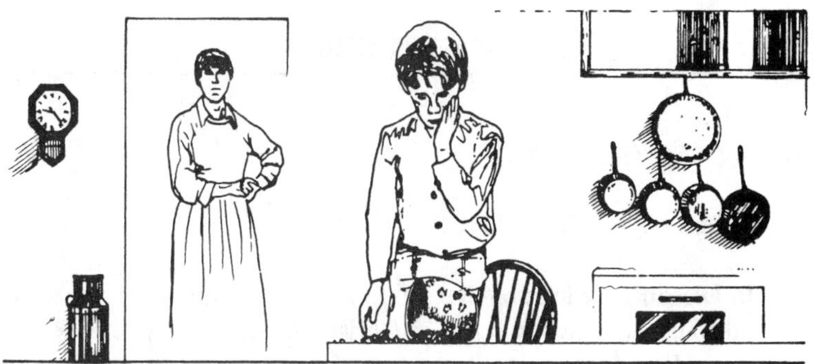

lesson objectives

When you finish this lesson you should be able to:

- Explain why repentance is a necessary part of the process of salvation.
- Analyze the aspects of repentance and explain the importance of each.
- Describe the experience of repentance and its results.

learning activities

1. Study the lesson outline carefully and read all of the lesson objectives.
2. Read Luke 15:11-24 through carefully several times.
3. Learn the meanings of key words that are new to you.
4. Study the lesson development and answer the study questions according to the procedure given in Lesson 1.
5. Take the self-test at the end of the lesson.

key words

consequences	idolatry	sovereignty
forsake	merit	yoke
grief	repentance	zeal
grieve	restitution	

lesson development

NATURE OF REPENTANCE

In Lesson 1 we learned that God provided salvation for all people. And through the atoning death of Christ, He made a way for them to come to Him. Also, we saw that the salvation He offers meets every spiritual need. And it leads to abundant life, great peace, supreme joy, and finally, eternal life. But for the wonderful process of salvation to begin, man must respond to God's offer. Man's response begins with repentance.

The title of this lesson suggests that repentance produces change. To some people, repentance suggests an uncomfortable change, because they are content to live on in their self-centered ways. To others who are without hope and purpose, the light of the gospel offers a refreshing change: péace of mind, freedom from fear, and an unending hope. If they are to know the grace of our Lord Jesus that can change the hopeless, shake the careless, and produce changed lives, then repentance must be proclaimed. Repentance is an absolute condition of salvation (Luke 13:2-5). Repentance combined with faith produces conversion.

Definition of Repentance

Objective 1. *Recognize the meaning and identify examples of repentance.*

A small boy has defined repentance like this: "It is being sorry enough to quit." Repentance, like a coin, has two sides.

1. It is the act in which one *recognizes* and *turns* from sin, confessing it to God.
2. It is *more* than just turning away from one's sins—it means to leave them completely!

Repentance also includes the idea of feeling pity, suffering grief (sorrow), and comforting oneself. In addition, to repent means "to turn back, change a course of action." In this sense, *repent* indicates a change of mind or purpose.

1 In the following question circle the letter of the statement that gives the most complete definition of repentance. Repentance may be defined as

a) feeling sorry about one's sins.
b) turning from one's sins because they are causing someone to grieve.
c) recognizing one's sins, feeling sorry about them, turning from them, and giving them up completely.

As you study the concept of repentance, you will notice some Scriptures which say that God "repented" of some action. Let's examine what is meant by this expression.

2 Read the following Scriptures and explain why God "repented." Notice the words used to describe His "change of mind."

a Genesis 6:5-7 ....

b Exodus 32:7-14 ....

c 1 Samuel 15:11 ....

These Scriptures show that God was grieved over the attitudes and actions of His people. Their sinfulness, disobedience, and rebellion against God's revealed standard of conduct called for change.

3 Examine the following Scriptures closely: Psalm 147:5; Proverbs 15:11; Isaiah 46:10; and Hebrews 4:13. What do they teach us about God?

....

We have learned that God knew in advance how people would respond to His grace and His revealed plan. But their free, though sinful natures, under the deadly influence of Satan, could not produce the righteous and holy character which God requires and longs for in His people. When He created man, or chose Israel, or selected Saul, He did not determine how each would respond to His grace, although He *knew* what the outcome would be. Each had the opportunity to respond positively, but did not do so. (We will consider the subject of God's foreknowledge in greater depth in Lesson 5.)

Let us remember that God's nature is unchanging. Everything he does is consistent with His nature. Thus, when God said to Nineveh, "Forty more days and Nineveh will be destroyed" (Jonah 3:4), we recognize His unchanging justice and righteousness. But when Nineveh repented, His other unchanging qualities—mercy and long-suffering—became evident as He "repented" and spared the city. God, in this example, did not change; the people of Nineveh did. All Scripture which refers to God's "repenting" can be understood in this way.

4 Repentance, as seen in God's response to those situations mentioned in this lesson, may be explained best as the
a) action God took based upon His authority alone.
b) response God made to man's failure.
c) unchanging purpose of God to judge, punish, and destroy man.

In the New Testament we see examples of repentance that show clearly what this word means. In Matthew 21:28-31 Jesus gives the Parable of the Two Sons. In this parable, the Father asked his older son to go and work in the vineyard. The son responded, "I will not," but later he *changed his mind* and went. The Greek word translated *changed his mind* (repentance) also means "to feel regret, experience a change of feelings, remorse." Other words used for repent and repentance give us the meaning of one who has arrived at a different view of things. This person has had a change of mind and heart. He has recognized his errors and shortcomings, is sincerely sorry for them, and is willing to forsake them. The person who repents, then demonstrates a different attitude toward sin and God.

Repentance may include a spirit of grief (Luke 18:13) and a broken spirit (Psalm 51:17). As one confesses his sins, he may be greatly moved by their awfulness. Some, like Peter (Luke 22:62), may weep bitterly. But regardless of the extent of grief that one feels or expresses, the important thing is confessing the sins and deciding to forsake them. No amount of emotion will make up for confessing and forsaking sin.

5 Repentance, as seen in the New Testament words which explain it, represents

a) the emotional response of a sinner to a sense of guilt.
b) regret for sins committed and a change of mind toward sin and God.
c) primarily a change of mind and attitude, but not a change of behavior.

Repentance includes a godly sorrow for sin. The regret of the truly repentant person involves a deep sadness of heart, not because he will

be punished but for the terrible wrong he has done to the holy, loving, and gracious God. Paul speaks of this kind of sorrow to the Corinthian believers: "Godly sorrow brings repentance that leads to salvation and leaves no regret, but worldly sorrow brings death" (2 Corinthians 7:10).

While it is all-important for you to recognize sin and confess it, it is equally important that you turn away from sin, forsaking it completely. You will remember the illustration of the boy's *sorrow* over disobeying his mother and breaking the cookie jar. His *sorrow* was not true repentance. Why? He had no intention of turning away from future temptations to satisfy his desire for sweets. *To repent is to turn away from sin.*

6 Read the following Scriptures and list the things that people *turn away from* when they repent.

a 1 Thessalonians 1:9 ....

b Acts 14:13-15 ....

c Acts 26:18 ....

Repentance is not just feeling sorrowful about your sinful actions. To be true repentance, there must be a turning away from sin. For example, Maurice is caught cheating on his examination. The instructor punishes him by giving him a zero. Maurice regrets being caught and failing his test, but he is not at all sorry about the times he cheated and was *not* caught. He is *sorrowful* but not *repentant.* In fact, he is ready to cheat again at the first opportunity. Mary also cheats on an examination, but her conscience bothers her. She goes to her instructor, confesses her dishonesty, and offers to accept the penalty. She is truly repentant, because she has decided to stop cheating. Someone has said, "Heaven is full of repentant people who were once sinners; hell is full of regretful people." Regret or sorrow for one's actions is not enough; repentance is required if one is to be forgiven and is to know the joy of having sins forgiven.

7 Distinguish between an example of true repentance and an example of what is incomplete repentance (or just regret alone).

a) A father, after becoming drunk, drives his car onto a busy highway, where he has a serious accident. His only child is killed, and two other people are badly injured. He is filled with sorrow and blames himself for the tragedy. He decides to forget about it by again getting drunk.

b) Alonzo runs with a very rough gang of street fighters. His gang beats a young man to death. Alonzo's conscience bothers him. He recognizes the awfulness of his crime and confesses his part in it to the police. He breaks away from the gang also. He is required to report regularly to the police and follow their instructions for a year, and he begins a new life as a law-abiding citizen.

In Question 7, you saw that there was a difference between Alonzo and the father. The father was deeply sorrowful for his error, but he continued to do the thing that caused the tragic accident. Alonzo, however, was more than sorrowful. He recognized his errors and then made a decision—he had a change of mind and heart—and broke away from his life of crime.

In Luke 16:19-31 we see the rich man in hell crying out for pity. He was full of sorrow, but it was too late for him to repent. Those who do not repent now will some day weep and wail in sorrow (Matthew 13:42, 50; Luke 13:28), but not in true repentance. One day they will cry for the rocks and mountains to fall on them to hide them from God's judgment (Revelation 6:16-17) *because* they were unwilling to turn from their sin.

Sorrow without a genuine change of mind and heart leads only to despair. But true repentance, which is the godly sorrow that leads to salvation (2 Corinthians 7:10), involves a change of mind and heart. Sorrow over our failures, shortcomings, and errors (without the change of heart and mind), makes us place our attention on our own weakness and sins. This kind of sorrow even makes us hate ourselves—even though we may love sinning. But repentance opens wide the door of God's mercy and pardon. True repentance helps us to see beyond our unhappy, miserable condition to the cross of Christ—where there is freedom, and light, and life.

FREEDOM FROM SIN

8 Choose the statement below which best describes the meaning of repentance (as it is presented in the Word of God).

a) A person finds himself overcome by weakness and failure. He is guilty of either breaking the laws of God or of failing to observe them. Finding himself miserable, guilty, filled with sorrow and hating himself because of his weakness, he decides to work harder and perform good works, to make up for his sinful ways.

b) A person recognizes that he is guilty of breaking God's laws or of not keeping them. He sees the awfulness of his sins and is deeply sorrowful. He confesses his sins and determines to stop sinning.

In answer a) we see a tendency that has led some people to completely misunderstand the nature of repentance. That is the idea that one can gain the favor of God by doing good works. As we have seen, repentance, when it is united with faith in Christ, produces conversion, while doing good works is part of an unscriptural plan to gain merit before God. There is nothing that can be added to Christ's work of atonement. Moreover, a person might do good works without ever forsaking his sins, and he might mistakenly believe that as long as he does good deeds, he can continue in his sins. But in repentance a sinner *must* recognize his sins, *turn away from them*, confess them to God, and forsake them completely. It is only in this way that his sins will be forgiven; only in this way will he enjoy the benefits of God's great salvation.

ASPECTS OF REPENTANCE

Objective 2. *Identify the three aspects of repentance and explain their significance.*

Scriptural repentance has three aspects or ideas: the intellectual, the emotional, and the volitional (which we will refer to as "an act of the will"). To illustrate these aspects of repentance, let us consider the following example. Suppose you were travelling on a bus and suddenly realized that you were on the wrong bus and travelling in the opposite direction from your desired destination. This knowledge corresponds to the *intellectual aspect* by which a person recognizes, through the ministry of the Word, that he is not right with God. You are disturbed when you discover that you are travelling to the wrong destination. You become anxious, maybe even fearful. These *feelings* illustrate the *emotional aspect* of repentance, which is a self-accusation and genuine sorrow for having offended God (2 Corinthians 7:9-10). You leave the bus at the first opportunity and find the right one. This decision illustrates *an act of will*: to make a complete turn-about and to begin travelling in God's direction. This simple illustration shows that true repentance affects the intellect, the emotions, and the will of the repentant sinner.

9 Identify each of the three aspects of repentance by matching the number of the aspect on the right with its correct definition on the left.

.... **a** Involves a decision to change directions	1) Intellectual
.... **b** Deals with recognition of the fact that one is not right with God	2) Emotional
.... **c** Involves the change of feelings one has in relation to sins he has committed	3) An act of the will

The cost of turning from our sins is high: "Any of you who does not give up everything he has cannot be my disciple" (Luke 14:33).

Repentance involves every part of our life. It means not merely recognition of sins and sorrow over the past, but also our intentions for the future. It is the forsaking of our own way to go God's way in obedience and fellowship with Him.

Often we hear messages which stress the appeal of Jesus, "Come to me, all you who are weary and burdened" (Matthew 11:28), but he who says "come" to the burdened sinner says also, "Take my yoke upon you" (v. 30). We cannot "*simply* accept Jesus and be saved," with no strings attached. It is impossible to accept the Lord Jesus as our Savior without involving our intellect, emotions, and will, which include every aspect of life: our affections, desires, and intentions. There must be a total surrender to the Lordship of Christ and a heartfelt acceptance of His yoke.

10 Explain how each of these is involved in repentance.

a Intellect ....

b Emotions ....

c Will ....

RELATION TO RESTITUTION

Objective 3. ***State the relationship between repentance and restitution.***

In Luke 3:3-18 John the Baptist preached the Good News to the people and urged them to change their ways. In verse 8 he urged them to "Produce fruit in keeping with repentance." Here John was asking for evidence which would prove that their repentance was genuine. Paying back what we have wrongfully taken, or making right a wrong we have done, is called *restitution*.

Restitution is a principle which is introduced in the Old Testament Law (Exodus 22:1; Leviticus 6:5; Numbers 5:6-7). Although the custom of making restitution for the wrong we have done is biblical and time-honored, we must understand that in itself, it does not save a person.

11 Read Luke 3:8-14 and 19:2-10, and circle the letter of each TRUE statement.

a From Luke 3:12-13 and 19:8 we learn that Zacchaeus was reluctant to recognize his sins.
b In Luke 19:8 we see that Zacchaeus had truly repented.
c By comparing Luke 3:8-14 with 19:2-10 we learn that restitution is a declaration to God and man that we have turned from our old way of life.

Restitution is a visible evidence of our decision to turn from sin to Christ. It backs up our testimony that we are following a new master. Although restitution is not a means of salvation it is a healthy indication that we have experienced God's saving grace.

12 State the relationship between repentance and restitution.

....

....

NEW TESTAMENT EMPHASIS

A Continuous Message

Objective 4. *List four New Testament persons who preached repentance and state the emphasis of each.*

The Bible declares that repentance is the first step in the soul's return to God (Ezekiel 14:6; 18:30; Malachi 3:7; Luke 13:3, 5). Without repentance no one can be saved. Thus, the plea to repent is primary in God's call to people in both the Old and New Testaments. The compelling and urgent plea of Old Testament prophets, ending with Malachi, was revived in the powerful message of repentance proclaimed by John the Baptist (Matthew 3:2, 8, 11; Mark 1:4; Luke 3:3, 8).

There is a definite development of the use of the word *repentance* in the New Testament. In the New Testament alone the words *repent* and *repentance* occur 64 times. From a desert of Judea John the Baptist sounded the warning to the Jewish people that they should repent in view of the coming of the Messiah (Matthew 3:1-12). His message of repentance produced great results among the people, and multitudes repented and reconsecrated their lives to God. Undoubtedly many of these people who sincerely responded to John's preaching were among the thousands who came into the church on the Day of Pentecost and following.

Jesus began His public ministry in Galilee, and like John He declared "Repent, for the kingdom of heaven is near" (Matthew 4:17; compare with Mark 1:15). In Matthew 4:17 (TEV), the definition of *repent* is: "Turn away from your sins, because the Kingdom of heaven is near." Repentance continued to have an important place in the preaching of Jesus and His disciples (Matthew 11:21-22; 12:41; Luke 5:32; Mark 6:12).

One of the last commandments Jesus gave before He returned to heaven was that repentance and forgiveness of sins must be preached to all nations (Luke 24:47; Acts 1:8). But the fully developed message of repentance and faith appears in the book of Acts, where it is emphasized from beginning to end. Peter preached *repentance for salvation from sin* on the Day of Pentecost and thousands repented (Acts 2:38). He continued with this same message soon afterward, and again many people repented of their sins and turned to God (Acts 3:19). In his later ministry through letters, he said of the Lord: "He is patient with you, not wanting anyone to perish, but everyone to come to repentance" (2 Peter 3:9).

Paul preached *repentance* to the city council in Athens (Acts 17:30). And in summarizing his ministry he said, "I have declared to both Jews and Greeks that they must turn to God in repentance and have faith in our Lord Jesus" (Acts 20:21). He adds this fact about the ignorance of repentance: "In the past God overlooked such ignorance, but now he commands all people everywhere to repent" (Acts 17:30).

13 In your notebook, list four New Testament persons who preached, and state the emphasis of each.

14 Circle the letter of the TRUE statements which concern the New Testament emphasis on repentance.

a The theme of repentance indicates God's call to people to acknowledge Him.

b John the Baptist's call to repentance was a continuation of the urgent plea of the Old Testament prophets for a return to righteousness.

c The message of repentance for the forgiveness of sins preached by Peter and Paul was limited to Jews alone.

d Repentance was a major theme of John the Baptist, Jesus and His disciples, and the early church.

Repentance is an oft-repeated theme in the Bible. For as long as there is need for salvation from sin, there is a need for repentance. This has been true since the fall of man, and it will be true until the time of grace and opportunity to repent has passed.

Who Should Repent

Objective 5. *Identify who should repent, and why.*

The call to repentance is universal. "God has overlooked the times when people did not know him, but now he commands *all of them everywhere to turn away from their evil ways*" (Acts 17:30, TEV). Every person is included in this call. All those who have never believed in Christ are invited to repent, receive God's forgiveness, and become a part of His family (John 3:15-17; Titus 2:11; Revelation 22:17).

Also, those who have already believed in Christ and become His followers are called to repentance. Sometimes Christians lose their zeal for Christ as their love for Him grows cold. Christians in the church at Ephesus were guilty of this (Revelation 2:5). They were urged to repent and renew their relationship with Christ. Others, such as those at Laodicea, became so spiritually indifferent that their very spiritual life was threatened (Revelation 3:15-17). True repentance is the only cure for the spiritually dead, indifferent, or unresponsive. Repentance is the only way back to God whenever there has been failure and sin. God's promise of forgiveness if we confess our sins (1 John 1:9) is directed primarily to Christians, although it can be applied to anyone who is ready to repent.

15 Choose the statements below which correctly state *who* should repent and the reasons *why* they should repent.

a) Every person who has not believed in Christ is invited to repent of his sins and follow Christ.
b) Christians who are overtaken by sin, lose their first love, or become spiritually unresponsive are called upon to repent, to maintain a clear conscience before God.
c) Christians, like non-Christians, must repent for salvation.

EXPERIENCE OF REPENTANCE

Objective 6. *Explain why repentance is necessary, how it is produced, and what are its results.*

Why Is It Necessary?

To the question, "Why is repentance necessary?" we may respond: "For all have sinned and fall short of the glory of God" (Romans 3:23). This includes all of us; no one is excluded (except the Lord Jesus Christ). You may recall from Lesson 1 that sin is failing to live according to the law of God or else breaking His law. The switch operator who fails to put down the safety gate and thus causes the express train to hit a car full of unsuspecting people who are killed is as guilty of causing death as a criminal who willfully shoots and kills a person. The switch operator is guilty of the *sin of omission*; for he knew what was required of him, but he failed to do it (James 4:17). The criminal who willfully shoots and kills another person is guilty of the *sin of commission*. He is guilty of breaking the law (1 John 3:4). Whether our sins are those of *omission* (failing to do what is commanded) or *commission* (doing what is forbidden), we may be sure that all wrongdoing is sin (1 John 5:17).

Having sinned, we stand guilty before God. The law demands payment of a penalty. And since sin pays its wages, death (Romans 6:23), in our sinful state we stand condemned and without help. But God offers pardon and eternal life for all who accept His forgiveness.

16 Explain why repentance is necessary. Use your notebook if you need more space.

....

....

How Is it Produced?

Paul says in Romans 2:4 (TEV), "Surely you know that God is kind, because he is trying to lead you to repent." God in mercy and love leads people to repentance (John 6:44), but He uses a number of ways to bring them to this experience. One way is ***through the ministry of the Word of God*** in general. When Jonah preached God's Word to the people of Nineveh, they believed it and gave up their wicked behavior and evil actions (Jonah 3:4, 8, 10).

In addition, ***the preaching of the cross produces repentance***. The message of God's love demonstrated at the cross moves people greatly. It appeals to those who are miserable and helpless in their sins—those in need of spiritual healing (Matthew 9:13). Such love, which provides a way for unworthy human beings to be forgiven, leads to repentance.

A fresh vision of God also brings repentance. When Job saw the majesty of God revealed, he despised himself and repented (Job 42:1-6). You see, then, that the goodness of God leads us to repentance through God's Word in general, through the preaching of the cross, and by means of a fresh vision of God. There are other means which He uses as well.

Have you ever heard it said that "the only time some people look up is when they are flat on their backs"? A loving Heavenly Father must often permit more drastic events to overtake us to get us to recognize our own need (Revelation 3:19). *Sometimes trouble, sickness, or tragedy help us to recognize our need of God.* Remember, it wasn't until the prodigal son recognized the awfulness of his problem that he "came to his senses," repented, and turned toward home (Luke 15:17-20).

Sometimes God uses *the example or witness of godly and dedicated* Christians to bring people to repentance. We may be sure that God will use whatever means are required in order to speak to the hearts of people.

17 Name some of the means God uses to bring people to repentance.

....

....

What Are Its Results?

The results of repentance are great, indeed. Repentance produces joy in the heart of the sinner, and at the same time it creates joy in heaven as the angels of God rejoice (Luke 15:10). Repentance opens the door that leads to faith and the forgiveness of sins. John says, "If we confess our sins, he is faithful and just and will forgive us our sins and purify us from all unrighteousness" (1 John 1:9).

In addition to the wonderful joy the sinner experiences when he repents, there are other beautiful benefits. When Job repented, God healed him and restored his children and his material blessings (Job 42:10-17). And when Jonah repented, God rescued him at the point of death (Jonah 2:1-10). Moreover, God promised that if His people would repent and turn away from their evil deeds, then He would hear them in heaven, forgive their sins, and make their land prosperous again (2 Chronicles 7:14).

Imagine that salvation is like a chain and then think of repentance, faith, and conversion as links in this chain. As each link in a chain is separate, so in the "chain of salvation." Each link is separate and yet it is linked to each of the other "links." As the process of repentance begins, it ignites a "chain reaction," in which faith, conversion, regeneration, justification, and adoption are joined to produce the miraculous experience of salvation.

CONVERSION

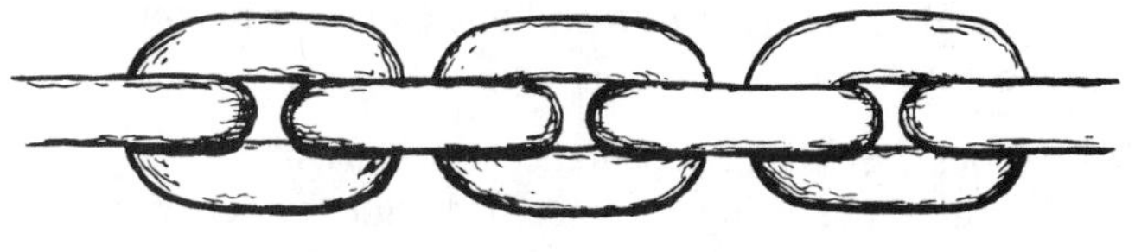

REPENTANCE FAITH FORGIVENESS

18 State some of the results of repentance.

....

....

self-test

Circle the letter of the correct answer in each of the following questions.

1 Repentance is important in the process of salvation because it
a) is the first step in a return to God.
b) demonstrates the worthiness of the one who repents.
c) expresses sorrow, which is the most important part of repentance.

2 Repentance is best defined as
a) the evident sorrow for sins.
b) recognizing sin, feeling sorry for what we have done, confessing it to God, and forsaking it completely.
c) the knowledge of shortcomings and the desire to do better.

3 The story of the rich man in hell, who cried out for pity, teaches us that
a) some people tend to recognize their sins at a late stage of life.
b) we ought to carefully review our lives from time to time to see if we are doing what we feel is right.
c) those who do not repent now will one day weep in sorrow. . .when it is too late.

4 The various aspects of repentance teach us that
a) every part of our being is concerned with the act of repentance.
b) basically, repentance is a simple step, and it costs us little or nothing.
c) repentance is a gift of God; therefore, it is an act in which people have no part.

5 While repentance has a prominent place throughout the Bible, we see that
a) repentance has a less prominent place in the New Testament because the emphasis now is on grace.
b) repentance outside the Gospels is not prominent and is therefore unimportant in the New Testament.
c) there is a full development of the teaching of repentance in the New Testament.

6 According to biblical teaching, who should repent? (Circle the best answer.)

a) Those who have never believed in Christ should repent.
b) Christians who fail God and become spiritually indifferent, and all sinners, are urged to repent.
c) Repentance is the requirement for the elect only.

7 Repentance, as we have learned in this lesson, is produced by the

a) goodness (kindness) of God alone. It is a gift and therefore man has no part in the act.
b) goodness of God. And the means He uses are the message of the Word in general, the preaching of the cross, a vision of God, or circumstances of difficulty, sickness, and tragedy.
c) good nature of people, who demonstrate their willingness to go God's way after they have carefully considered the consequences of their sins.

8 The Bible declares that repentance is necessary because

a) all people are guilty of sin.
b) it is a requirement for all people whether or not they are guilty of sin.
c) it is an evidence that people's intentions are right.

9 Circle the letter of the most complete answer. The results of repentance are that

a) the sinner is filled with joy, as are his family members and community.
b) heaven rejoices with the sinner who turns to God.
c) the world is filled with joy over the change brought about by the act.

10 Restitution is a biblical teaching. Its chief value lies in the fact that

a) it produces merit before God.
b) it gives this message to the world: the one making the restitution has changed.
c) it secures salvation for the one who performs it.

11 Identify the aspects of repentance by matching each aspect to its correct definition or application.

....**a** Celia feels sorry for the sins she has committed.
....**b** Henry realizes that his life is not pleasing to God.
....**c** Eric decides to quit his life of sin completely.
....**d** The prodigal son says, "I will arise and go to my father."
....**e** The prodigal son comes to his senses.
....**f** The prodigal sorrows over the awfulness of his problems.

1) Intellectual
2) Emotional
3) An act of the will

answers to study questions

10 Your answer may be worded slightly different from mine.

a The intellectual aspect of repentance deals with the recognition of our guilt and unworthiness before God.

b The emotional aspect concerns the sorrow and shame we *feel* because of our sin against God's grace and love.

c The aspect of will in repentance concerns the act of the will which results in forsaking our sins and turning to God.

1 c) recognizing one's sins, feeling sorry about them, turning from them, and giving them up completely.

11 **a** False.
b True.
c True.

2 **a** God *repented* because of people's wickedness. He was *sorry* that he had created them.

b God *repented* because Israel sinned and rejected Him. He "changed His mind."

c God *repented* because of Saul's disobedience. God said He was sorry that He had made Saul king.

12 Restitution is evidence of true repentance. It cannot save, but it does testify that we have undergone a change.

3 God has full and complete knowledge of all things.

13 John the Baptist preached repentance and emphasized the Messiah's coming. Jesus also preached repentance for the forgiveness of sins and that the kingdom was near. Peter preached repentance and emphasized saving faith. Paul based his ministry to Jews and Gentiles on the message of repentance (Acts 20:21).

4 b) response God made to man's failure.

14 **a** True.
b True.
c False.
d True.

5 b) regret for sins committed and a change of mind toward sin and God.

15 Answers a) and b) are correct. Answer c) is not correct, since Christians don't repent for salvation. They repent in order to maintain a clear conscience and fellowship with their Lord.

6 **a** Idols.
b Idolatry and superstition.
c Darkness and Satan.

16 All of us are guilty of sinning. We have failed to do God's will and we are guilty of breaking His laws. The penalty for unrepentant sinners is death, but for all who repent God offers pardon and salvation.

7 b) Alonzo runs with a very rough gang of street fighters . . .

17 God's goodness leads us to repentance. The means He uses are: His Word in general, the preaching of the cross, and a vision of God. Trouble, sickness, and tragedy may also bring us to repentance. The lives of Christians, as well as their witness, are means God uses to bring us to repentance.

8 b) A person recognizes that he is guilty of breaking God's laws . . .

18 Repentance causes joy in the repentant sinner and in heaven. It precedes faith and leads to forgiveness. It is the first link in the chain of salvation.

9 **a** 3) An act of the will.
b 1) Intellectual.
c 2) Emotional.

for your notes

LESSON 3

Man Trusts in God: Faith

One of the most important statements in all the Bible says simply, "And without faith it is impossible to please God" (Hebrews 11:6). Why is this short statement so important? I'm sure you will agree that a person's life is governed by what he believes. And for Christians it is governed by the Person in whom we believe. Faith in Jesus Christ and His offer of salvation is vitally important to each one of us and to every person in the world.

We cannot help but admire the steadfast courage of the Canaanite woman who would not be denied the healing of her daughter (Matthew 15:21-28). We also marvel at the humility of the centurion who felt unworthy to have Christ come into his house (Matthew 8:5-10). And we wonder at the persistence and earnestness of Bartimaeus who, in spite of the resistance of the crowds, shouted out to Jesus for mercy (Mark 10:46-52). Is it possible that a Canaanite woman, a Roman centurion, and a blind beggar had something in common—something that could truly impress the Master? Yes! The one thing which the Lord saw and rewarded in each of these cases was *faith*. Faith greatly impressed Jesus as He moved among people.

The basic element in the experience of conversion is *faith*. When a person truly repents, he must put his trust in the Lord Jesus. John tells us that "to all who received him, to those who believed in his name, he gave the right to become children of God" (John 1:12). In this lesson we consider the believing and receiving aspects of conversion: As a person turns from sin to God, he puts his whole trust in the Lord Jesus for pardon, and for the great change which is brought about in his heart by the Holy Spirit.

lesson outline

The Importance of Faith
The Nature of Faith
The Elements of Faith
The Experience of Faith

lesson objectives

When you finish this lesson you snould be able to:

- Explain the importance of saving faith in the work of salvation.
- Identify the elements in saving faith and explain the significance of each.
- Appreciate more fully the ministry of the Holy Spirit and the Word of God by which faith is created and maintained.

learning activities

1. Read Hebrews 11 carefully. As you read, think about those who believed simply and fully in the promises of God.
2. Read each one of the lesson objectives and note the major divisions of the lesson in the outline.
3. Work through the lesson development according to the procedure given in Lesson 1.

key words

abandon
alien
assent
citizen
compromise
conditional
conditioned
converted
dynamic
elements
endurance
intellect
intellectual
obstacle
passively
potential
resources
unconditional
vitality

lesson development

THE IMPORTANCE OF FAITH

Objective 1. *Explain the importance of faith in the Christian life.*

Every feature of our salvation is a supernatural work which God alone can do. Let's review these features:

1. Divine election in past ages.
2. The sacrifice of a Savior.
3. The provision of common and saving grace.
4. The drawing of the sinner by the Holy Spirit.
5. The immediate saving work of God in all its wonderful aspects.
6. The keeping work of the Father, the Son, and the Holy Spirit.
7. The delivering and empowering work of the Spirit.
8. The final perfecting and presenting of the saints in glory.

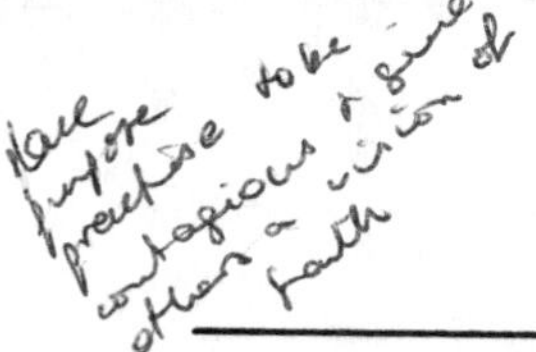

MAN TRUSTS IN GOD: FAITH

The only way we can receive God's marvelous provision of salvation is to accept it by faith. The eternal treasures which are provided for us by God's sovereign grace are available to us by our faith alone.

1 Read each of the sets of Scripture references below and then write after each what faith accomplishes.

a Ephesians 2:8; Romans 5:1 ....saving faith....

b Acts 26:18 compare with Acts 15:9 ....justification & sanctification....

c 1 Peter 1:5; 1 John 5:4; Romans 11:20 ..'kept' – guarded by faith, enabled to overcome the world

d James 5:15; Acts 14:9 ....healing....

e Galatians 3:2, 5, 14 ..promise of the Holy Spirit

f Romans 4:18-22; Mark 9:23 We overcome difficulty....

g Hebrews 11:6 ..belief in His existance pleases God

h Matthew 15:28 ..~~healing~~ encouragement....

i Mark 2:3-5 ..~~persistent faith~~ – put faith effort on behalf of

j Romans 14:23 ..unbelief is sin....

We see, then, that in addition to our salvation experience, every aspect of our Christian life depends on the exercise of faith. Our actions, to a large extent, are determined by what we believe. We believe that God knows everything we say, do, and think; therefore, we try to do those things which please him.

2 Explain in your own words the importance of faith in the Christian life.

..By grace through faith, all things are..
..possible. Faith is the condition for all things

Relationship of Faith and Repentance

Objective 2. *Recognize differences between repentance and faith in the process of conversion.*

In our last lesson we learned that the act of repentance begins a "chain reaction." But the *event of salvation* that is set in motion, which involves the aspects of both repentance and faith (and other aspects of salvation), is such that we should try to see these aspects as occurring at the same time. But for convenience in discussing each aspect, we have adopted the following order: repentance, faith, conversion, regeneration, justification, and adoption.

Turning from sin (repentance) and turning to God (faith) are the conditions for salvation. There is no merit to repentance and faith. God has already provided all that is necessary for salvation. But by *repentance* we remove the obstacle to receiving the gift of salvation, and by *faith* we accept the gift.

FAITH IS ACTION

Repentance concerns sin and the misery it causes, while *faith* dwells upon the mercy of God. *Faith* is the means by which we receive salvation (Romans 10:9-10). There can be no faith without true repentance, for only the one who is truly sorry for his sins feels the need of a Savior and salvation for his soul. On the other hand, there can be no godly repentance without faith in God's Word, for how else could one believe in the offer of salvation and the threat of eternal judgment?

3 In the following exercise note the difference between examples of faith and repentance in the process of conversion by marking **1** in front of those which identify repentance and **2** for those which identify faith.

. . . . **a** Recognizing sin and turning from it
. . . . **b** Turning toward God to receive His salvation
. . . . **c** Removing the obstacles between the sinner and the gift of salvation
. . . . **d** Receiving the gift of salvation
. . . . **e** Concerns the matter of sin and its consequences
. . . . **f** Concerns the mercy and love of God

1) Repentance
2) Faith

THE NATURE OF FAITH

Definition of Faith

Objective 3. *Recognize the basic biblical meaning of the word* faith.

We have seen that faith is a vitally important part of our Christian life. And we have noted that faith determines, to a large degree, our actions. But what is faith? Hebrews 11:1 gives us a description of one of the effects of faith, but does not define the term. For our purposes, faith will be defined as "the voluntary act and attitude of a person by which he places his complete confidence in a trusted object, allowing that object to govern his actions." In the spiritual realm the trusted object is God, and the voluntary act is brought about by hearing and believing the Word of God.

Faith is both belief and trust. In the Old Testament the term *believe* is used to translate the Hebrew word which means "to build up or support, to make firm or faithful, to trust." In the New Testament it is used to translate one Greek word which means "to have faith or trust, put trust in, commit," or another Greek word which means "to assent, rely, be persuaded, have confidence in." As we shall see later in detail, *to believe*, when used with God or Christ as its object, involves three things: 1) to be in agreement with the truth of what He says or reveals, 2) to receive and trust Him personally, and 3) to commit oneself to obey Him. The word *believe* is used quite frequently with the preposition *in* or *on*; for example, "Believe in the Lord Jesus, and you will be saved" (Acts 16:31), to emphasize the elements of trust and commitment. We must be careful not to limit *belief* to intellectual assent only. The truth about God is necessary, for the Scripture says that "anyone who comes to him must believe that he exists and that he rewards those who earnestly seek him" (Hebrews 11:6). However, belief about God is not enough: "You believe that there is one God. Good! Even the demons believe that—and shudder" (James 2:19). And while the demons believe, they remain demons.

Faith thus means to abandon all trust in our own resources and to cast ourselves completely on the mercy of God. As we are led toward conversion, the Holy Spirit helps us to believe in the truth of the Scriptures. In this way we gain confidence in the grace of God. This is faith.

As we become more familiar with the definitions and descriptions of faith, we must remember the following: "Faith is the flight of the penitent sinner to the mercy of God in Christ," which enables a person to say, "In saving faith, I forsake unbelief and self-confidence and take Christ. I rest my eternal destiny confidently in Him."

4 Select the completion which defines correctly the basic biblical meaning of the word *faith*. Faith may be defined as

a) that which we hope will come to pass as a result of our prayers and earnest desires.

b) the act by which we place our complete confidence in a trusted person, God, and allow Him to govern our actions.

c) the act of clinging with determination to a desired object or goal.

Kinds of Faith

Objective 4. *Identify the different kinds of faith.*

Faith can be described in a number of ways. While we usually think of faith in relation to spiritual experience, there is also a *nonreligious faith* with which we are familiar. For example, we believe in our electrical systems, and so we press switches and turn on the lights. We have faith in our traffic systems, so we drive at high rates of speed toward oncoming cars with nothing separating us but a thin white line on the road. We have faith in our banking systems so we deposit money in banks. And because we believe in airplanes and trust the skill of pilots, we fly. *Nonreligious faith* is evident in these and many other ways every day.

FAITH BRINGS RESULTS

Then there is *intellectual faith.* This faith believes something *about* Jesus but it does not believe *in* Him. Many people in our world believe there is a God, but this mental assent does not lead them to salvation. And some people believe that the Bible is the Word of God, but they never read it or commit themselves to follow its teachings. ***Intellectual faith*** lacks one vitally important feature: action. James 2:18 describes this kind of faith for us in vivid language: "But someone will say, 'You have faith; I have deeds.' Show me your faith without deeds, and I will show you my faith by what I do." *

The most important and complete kind of faith is *living faith.* It is contrasted with dead or *inactive faith. Living faith* is the result of our

* Our works show the genuineness of what we profess

saving faith and refers to the ongoing, obedient, commitment of our lives to Christ and His purposes. For *living faith,* we rely on the power of the indwelling Spirit for daily strength. Paul describes this kind of faith in Galatians 2:20, "I have been crucified with Christ and I no longer live, but Christ lives in me. The life I live in the body, I live by faith in the Son of God, who loved me and gave himself for me."

In contrast to *living faith*, dead or *inactive faith* produces no actions. Here again James speaks to the point: "As the body without the spirit is dead, so faith without deeds is dead" (James 2:26).

One of the qualities of *living faith* is good actions. As a healthy thriving plant grows, matures and produces fruit, so *living faith* is always accompanied by good actions. These good actions do not save a person, but they do give evidence of the vitality of his faith. One *does* good because by the grace of God he *is* good. Good actions, which are the fruit the Spirit produces, flow naturally out of *living faith,* because its source is God (Galatians 5:22).

5 In this exercise match the kinds of faith (right) with their characteristics (left).

....**a** Charles was once an active worker in his church and neighborhood, doing good wherever he could. Now he does what he pleases.	1) Intellectual faith 2) Nonreligious faith 3) Living faith 4) Inactive faith
....**b** Henry attends church, believes in its teachings and admits his belief *about* the truth of God as revealed in the Bible, but he has never made a personal commitment of his life to Christ.	
....**c** Jane believes in the electrical system, so she presses a switch and turns on the lights.	
....**d** Dolores accepted Christ five years ago, and expresses her trust in Him by service as she ministers to others at every opportunity.	

THE ELEMENTS OF FAITH

Objective 5. *Describe the elements of saving faith and explain the significance of each.*

There are three basic elements in saving faith: knowledge, assent, and trust. Saving faith is the voluntary act and attitude of a person by which he places his complete confidence in Christ, allowing Him to govern all actions. This *act* is brought about by hearing and believing the basic facts about the person and work of Christ which are in the Word of God. The facts cause us to commit our entire being to the Lord Jesus Christ. Like repentance, faith involves the intellect, the emotions, and the will.

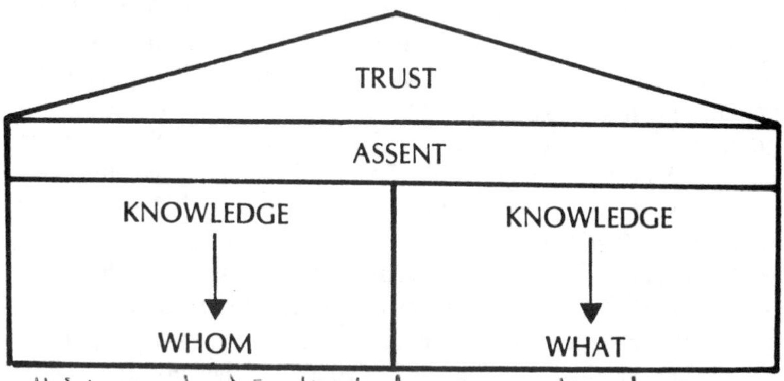

Knowledge. Suppose you were called upon to believe. You might well ask, "*Whom* must I believe?" Notice that the Bible doesn't say, "just believe"; it says, "Believe in the Lord Jesus" (Acts 16:31; also see Romans 10:9-10). Faith is also based upon the *knowledge* of God as revealed in nature and in the facts of Scripture. Faith develops through *knowledge* of the teachings of Scripture concerning man's sinful nature, the salvation provided in Christ, the conditions of salvation, and the many blessings promised to God's children. *Knowledge* of the Lord Jesus and the content of the Christian belief revealed in Scripture is a vitally important step to faith.

Assent. Assent involves an emotional commitment. It is one thing to *know* the scriptural and historical facts about Christ, but it is quite another thing to *believe* that they are true. We could believe (intellectually) the importance of the eternal issues involved in salvation and yet not receive these truths in our heart. Faith is the assent (agreement) of the heart to the rightness of what we know. The heart says *yes* to all that Christ is and offers to do for us. We must do more than *know* that these things are true; we must accept them for ourselves.

The example is given of a young man who commended a preacher on the sermon he had just preached. The preacher asked, "Are you a Christian?" The youth replied, "Yes." The preacher questioned further, "How long have you been a Christian?" The youth said, "Oh, sir, all of my life." The preacher pursued the issue, "Have you had a personal experience with Christ or demonstrated your faith in some way, then?" The youth smiled as he explained, "Sir, it was not I personally who was converted. Many years ago my great-great-grandparents were converted into the Christian faith. They brought the whole family into the faith. So all of us family members are Christians; we come from a long line of Christians." The preacher responded, "That's fine. But let's suppose that you see a young couple eating breakfast in your hotel. You ask the young man, 'How long have you been married?' He says, 'We are not married, but our great-great-grandparents were married. We come from a long line of married people.' Is that enough?" The youth saw the point and smiled. So our *knowledge* of Christ needs the *assent* of the heart to accept Him for ourselves.

Trust. If a person has knowledge of the gospel and assents to the truth of the gospel, but does not commit himself to the person of Jesus Christ, he does not have *saving faith.* Christian faith is more than accepting the revelation of God and His salvation as true. It is more than assenting to it as being necessary for oneself. *Trust* represents the act of the will, the decision by which we commit ourselves fully to Christ and to what we believe are His directing principles of life. It is certain that no one can be saved who does not of his own free will actively give himself to Christ.

6 Perhaps we can understand the elements of faith better by means of an illustration. Let's imagine that a person who has a disease goes to the doctor for an examination. Fill in the blank spaces with the appropriate element of faith (assent, knowledge, trust).

a The patient receives the report of his condition from the doctor.

This is ....

b The patient believes that the report is reasonable and is the truth.

This is ....

c The patient decides that he will apply the remedy for the disease and submit himself to the doctor for treatment. This is ....

7 Circle the letter of each TRUE statement which describes the elements of saving faith and the significance of each.

a Knowledge is the element of faith that calls upon the repentant sinner to believe, and thus be saved. The act of believing in itself has saving merit.

b Knowledge deals with the *whom* and *what*. Faith is based upon knowledge of Jesus Christ, the revelation of God in Scripture, and the teachings of Scripture as they apply to man's sin and salvation.

c Faith is the assent (agreement) of the heart to the truth of what we know.

d Assent deals only with the recognition of truth.

e The element of trust is the dependence one feels for another.

f Trust implies the act of the will by which one commits himself completely to Christ.

THE EXPERIENCE OF FAITH

We have considered the importance of faith in the Christian life, and we have discussed its nature and elements. But it is a fruitless exercise if we do not *experience* faith. I know a person who firmly believes in democracy, in basic human rights, the right of citizens to life, liberty, and the pursuit of happiness, and the right to participate in government. This person made outstanding marks in his studies of government, yet he is unable to exercise these rights because he has not become a legal citizen of the country in which he lives. In the same way, even though we may understand all about faith, if we do not apply it and accept what God has provided for us, we are like aliens from God. Let us keep this in mind as we consider the experience of faith.

Degrees of Faith

Objective 6. *Recognize examples of different degrees of faith.*

A *living relationship* with Jesus Christ will produce the desire to grow in faith. Observe the response of the twelve disciples to Jesus' example of loving forgiveness, "Increase our faith!" (Luke 17:5). The Twelve realized that to have divine love and compassion, they needed an enlarged spiritual capacity—greater faith to do what Jesus commanded. Faith grows and develops. For this reason we can speak of degrees of faith.

Notice that when writing to the church at Corinth, Paul expressed hope that the faith of the people would grow so that God might be able to do a much greater work among them (2 Corinthians 10:16). And in his first letter to the Thessalonians he prayed for an opportunity to minister to them again to supply what was lacking in their faith (1 Thessalonians 3:9-10). Their faith was then in its infancy, but it needed to grow and mature as they faced fierce and determined opposition. However, by the time Paul wrote his second letter to them, he was able to thank God because their faith was growing more and more (2 Thessalonians 1:3).

Often we are involved in situations that demand greater faith than we have. But as we walk with the Lord in obedience and love, our relationship will grow and our faith will increase. Consistent, earnest prayer and communion with Him bring greater faith and the answers to seemingly impossible situations (Mark 9:29). May our prayers have the intensity of the needy father who said, "I do believe; help me overcome my unbelief!" (Mark 9:24). Faith is living and dynamic—living faith grows.

8 Circle the letter of each TRUE statement below.

a Living faith like any living thing should experience growth toward maturity.

b Living faith implies that as one moves toward greater faith and maturity, he will never again experience weaknesses in his faith.

c Prayer is one source of growth for living faith.

d The disciples and people to whom Jesus ministered demonstrated some faith, but most recognized their need of greater faith.

9 Read Matthew 6:25-34, 8:23-27,14:22-32,16:5-12, and complete the following sentences with the correct word or words.

a The kind of faith demonstrated in each case was .little./.weak.faith

b (Matthew 6:31) *Little faith* will not protect us from worry........

c (Matthew 8:26) *Little faith* will not shield us from ..fear..........

d (Matthew 14:31) *Little faith* will not keep us from ..doubt........

e (Matthew 16:8) *Little faith* is not able to keep us from ....

..reasonings.,........ born.of. doubt

Little faith is a characteristic of spiritual infants, but God expects us to advance on to greater faith and spiritual maturity. ***Little faith***

keeps us spiritually ineffective and unable to carry on Christ's work. *Little faith* allows us to doubt.

In the introduction to the lesson, we saw examples of *great faith*. It is significant that on only two occasions did Jesus commend (praise) *great faith*. In the first case the Roman centurion believed that the authority of the word of Jesus would bring instant healing to his servant, even though he was some distance away (Matthew 8:5-13). In the second case, the Canaanite woman *kept* asking Jesus to heal her demon-possessed daughter *even though* He did not at first respond to her plea. She asked again, and once more she was denied. However, this time she sensed something in Jesus' tone which gave her hope. In her determination she said words that meant something like this: "Lord, I may not be one of your people, but I am one of God's creatures, and I believe your message. Out of your abundant mercy, grant me just a little portion." Recognizing that her faith would not give up, Jesus commended her *great faith* and healed her daughter.

10 Identify examples of *little faith* by placing a **1** in front of those examples that illustrate this degree of faith, and a **2** in front of those that illustrate *great faith*.

.... **a** One worries about the basic needs of life: food, clothing, and shelter.	1) Little faith
.... **b** A great storm threatens and one hopes that he will live through it.	2) Great faith
.... **c** Parents with children in school in a distant place hear they are in a serious danger. The parents commit this burden to the Lord in prayer, believing that God will protect their children.	

Another example of *great faith* is that demonstrated by Abraham. Even though he was old and his wife was not able to have children, he believed God's promise that he would have a son. In spite of the physical impossibility, Abraham persisted in believing God because he had *strong faith. Strong faith* enabled him to be "fully persuaded" that what God promised He would perform (Romans 4:18-21). Strong faith holds on until the answer comes.

The writer to the Hebrews describes great faith in another way in 10:22 where he says that we are to draw near to God "in full assurance of faith." This speaks of confidence we have as we draw near to God. *Fulness of faith* refers to the certain trust, the settled conviction, the supreme confidence we have in our wonderful Lord.

Every Christian experiences various degrees of faith in his life. Most of us have come to some circumstance that has for a moment shaken us, and we have responded with *little faith.* Whatever our past experiences have been, we can be sure that our faith will be tested. *Tested faith* is faith that proves its vitality. Testing is to faith what the fire is to steel: the heat of the fire strengthens the steel, and testing develops strength and endurance in Christians. As you read Hebrews 11, notice the activities of those who were tested and how they stood the test. Some lived on through many tests and in faith achieved great victories. Others who stood the test kept their faith, and in their martyr's death were promoted to a better life. Still others lived amid cruel mockings and whippings, bonds and imprisonment. They could have lived *normal lives*, but they refused to compromise with evil. These people lived for something better and more enduring than *things* of earth. Old Testament saints looked by faith to the coming of the Messiah. They died with undimmed vision! They now await the appearing of Jesus when, together, we shall be perfected in His presence—our salvation complete.

Peter says that the purpose of testing is to prove that our faith is genuine (1 Peter 1:6-7). And James notes that when faith succeeds in facing trials, it produces the ability to endure (James 1:3).

God permits us to be tested so that we can learn to trust Him completely in spite of our circumstances. As we learn to lean on Him for our needs, our love for Him grows and our faith increases also. Testing serves to make faith stronger and enduring through each experience of life. In this way it becomes precious.

11 Identify the degrees of faith by placing the appropriate number (right) with its description (left).

1) Little faith
2) Great faith

. . . . **a** One lives in a country which is troubled by many social problems. His job is threatened by labor problems, and his life is endangered by violence. He commits himself and his family to God, realizing that they are safe in God's hands whatever the outcome might be. In this assurance he continues to live as usual.

. . . . **b** One lives in a modern nation that is faced with war, economic crisis, and many social problems. He lives in fear of the outcome, thinking that at any moment a global war may begin. He is so filled with worry that he cannot sleep.

Source of faith

Objective 7. *Describe the source of faith in relation to God and the believer.*

Saving faith has both a human and a divine viewpoint. From the divine viewpoint, faith is the gift of God (Romans 12:3; 2 Peter 1:1). For example, in John's Gospel we read, "No one can come to me unless the Father who sent me draws him" (John 6:44). In the work of conversion, the gracious influence of the Holy Spirit is strongly implied, for He alone can move one's heart to repentance and toward God (Acts 3:19; Philippians 2:12-13). And in Hebrews we read that Jesus is "the author and perfecter of our faith" (Hebrews 12:2). Moreover, the Holy Spirit works in the body of Christ on special occasions as the "gift" of faith operates (1 Corinthians 12:9). And it is the Spirit who produces fruit in our lives, one of which is faith. Thus, from the divine viewpoint, faith is God-given.

GOD GIVES—WE RECEIVE

Nevertheless, we must not wait passively for God's gift of faith to come to us. The fact that people are commanded to believe implies their ability and obligation to do so. All people have the ability to place their confidence in some person or some thing. When belief is directed to the Word of God and confidence is placed in God and Christ, we have *saving faith.* It is produced by the Word of God (Romans 10:17; Acts 4:4). The Scriptures reveal our need, state the conditions, indicate the promises, and point out the blessings of salvation. It is our responsibility, then, to read and study the Word of God so that faith will begin and grow in our hearts.

12 Describe the source of faith in relation to God and the believer.

It is by the grace of God that we receive faith and it is our obligation to be bold & strengthen our faith through prayer & assistance of ~~the~~ His Holy Spirit.

Maintaining Faith

Objective 8. *List the means by which Christians can maintain faith.*

Earlier we discussed the importance of faith in the Christian life, and we have considered its source. However, faith cannot be taken for granted. It must be maintained. Trying to maintain life and growth in the Christian experience without nourishing one's faith is like trying to operate a car without fuel. The potential is there, but it is incapable of performing its intended function. Another comparison to maintaining faith is riding a bicycle: the rider must keep moving or he will fall. Let's see what the Bible says about this need to maintain faith.

In an inspired prophetic statement Habakkuk declared: "The righteous will live by faith" (Habakkuk 2:4). And in the New Testament this statement,"The righteous will live by faith," is repeated three times (Romans 1:17; Galatians 3:11; Hebrews 10:38). This truth indicates that spiritual life depends on living faith. The apostle Paul thus encourages the Colossians to continue in their faith, established and firm, not moved from the hope held out in the gospel, so that their salvation may be assured (Colossians 1:23). He exhorts the Corinthian believers to be on their guard and to stand firm in the faith (1 Corinthians 16:13) as they set themselves for the defense of the gospel. Moreover, he challenges Christians at Ephesus to take the shield of faith so that they "can extinguish all the flaming arrows of the evil one" (Ephesians 6:16). The need to have and maintain faith, therefore, is evident. Some ways that we can maintain faith are:

1. Prayer
2. Reading the Word
3. Relationships with others who demonstrate faith
4. Witnessing
5. Group worship

13 Read Ephesians 6:10-18, 1 Peter 5:8-10, and 2 Corinthians 10:4-5. Then answer the following questions in your notebook, listing ways that we can maintain faith.

a What is the Christian's spiritual armor (Ephesians 6:14-17)?
b All the pieces of armor are defensive except which one?
c The Christian warfare is not won by the armor and good intentions alone. Ephesians 6:18 says that we must have what additional help?
d Ephesians 6:10 and 1 Peter 5:10 indicate that our spiritual strength is increased by what?
e Verses 11-13 of Ephesians 6 name the enemy as what?

Thus, as a *natural* person requires food and nourishment to live in a healthy state, so in a *spiritual* person faith must be nurtured and exercised. Paul exhorts Timothy to "pursue faith" (1 Timothy 6:11-12), and later, he encourages him to "flee the evil desires of youth, and pursue . . . faith" (2 Timothy 2:22). As faith is maintained, it grows in vitality and usefulness, helping us to be conformed to the image of Christ. Nevertheless, the most significant factor to remember is that when we are in union with Christ, He intercedes for us so that our faith will not fail (Luke 22:32). As long as He is in control we continue to "grow in the grace and knowledge of our Lord and Savior Jesus Christ" (2 Peter 3:18).

Conditions and Effect of Faith

Objective 9. *List some of the significant conditions and effects of faith.*

"Everything is possible for him who believes" (Mark 9:23). When we place our faith in God, the possibilities open to us are unlimited. Faith is the key that unlocks the resources of heaven for us. Jesus said, "If you have faith . . . Nothing will be impossible for you" (Matthew 17:20). However, faith cannot be separated from the will of God. John qualifies this, "This is the assurance we have in approaching God: that if we ask anything *according to his will*, he hears us" (1 John 5:14). Here John states a condition for asking and receiving. Some promises in the Bible are unconditional; however, most promises are conditional, requiring an appropriate response in us if we are to receive the thing promised. We must remain in Christ, and His Word must remain in us (John 15:7); we must be obedient (1 Peter 1:14); and we must live by the Spirit (Galatians 5:16).

The effects of faith are unlimited. For faith draws from the unlimited resources of heaven for the many needs of people on earth. And faith graces their lives all the while, regardless of the circumstances, and imparts a peacefulness that passes all understanding.

14 List the effects of faith which are revealed in the following Scriptures.

a Acts 10:43 forgiveness of sins

b Galatians 3:14 baptism in the Holy Spirit

c Ephesians 3:17 the indwelling of Christ

d Romans 5:1 justification finding true peace with God.

e Philippians 3:9 righteousness from God

f John 1:12 the adoption to a child of God

g Galatians 4:6 sonship

h Acts 26:18 sanctification

i 1 Peter 1:5 under God's protection, preservation

j Mark 11:24 all our needs & desires by His will are met.

15 What conditions of faith were mentioned in this section of the lesson?

We must remain in Christ & His Word in us, being obedient & responsive to Gods will.

self-test

TRUE-FALSE. Write **T** in front of each statement that is true and **F** in front of those that are false.

T **1** One of the reasons why faith has such importance is that our actions are determined in part by whom or what we believe.

F **2** In saving faith, one places his trust in one sacred object and then lives in peace, knowing he has committed himself fully to a plan of salvation.

T **3** Saving faith is the voluntary act and attitude of a person by which he places his complete confidence in a trusted object, allowing that trusted object to govern his actions.

. . . . **4** Intellectual faith may be defined as the faith that is demonstrated in all the various aspects of daily life, such as belief in banks, electricity, and flying, to name a few.

. . . . **5** The continuous obedient commitment of one's life to God and His will is a characteristic of living faith.

. . . . **6** *What* and *whom* constitutes the knowledge element of faith.

. . . . **7** *Assent* involves the emotions and is the agreement of the heart to the rightness of what we know.

. . . . **8** *The act of decision* by which we commit ourselves to believe and live by what we consider to be the directing principles of life is connected primarily with the intellect.

. . . . **9** When we speak of degrees of faith we mean that when a person leaves one state of faith he moves to a larger degree of faith never again to experience a lesser degree of faith.

. . . . **10** The term *degrees of faith* indicates that faith is a living, growing thing that can and should mature in each of us.

. . . . **11** It is not possible for one to experience little and great faith in the same period of life.

. . . . **12** In the gospel record only two accounts are given in which Jesus commended *great faith.*

. . . . **13** Faith originates in God; man therefore, has no part in this operation.

. . . . **14** Living faith must be maintained by spiritual exercise: Bible reading, prayer, and the ministry of the Holy Spirit are examples of this spiritual exercise.

. . . . **15** If faith is living and healthy no scriptural limitations are placed on what we may ask and receive.

answers to study questions

8 **a** True.
b False.
c True.
d True.

1 **a** Faith saves us.
b We are made pure by faith.
c We are kept by faith and enabled to overcome the world.
d We are healed by faith.
e We receive the Holy Spirit by faith.
f We overcome difficulty through faith.
g Faith pleases God. Faith accepts without question the existence of God.
h Faith encourages us to keep on believing.
i Faith encourages us to put forth efforts in behalf of others.
j Negatively, lack of faith (unbelief) is sin.

9 **a** little faith.
b worry.
c fear or fright.
d doubt.
e reasonings born of doubt.

2 Your answer. I have noted that it affects every aspect of our life. It involves trusting God to supply all our needs (Philippians 4:19), spiritual and material.

10 **a** 1) Little faith.
b 1) Little faith.
c 2) Great faith.

3 **a** 1) Repentance.
b 2) Faith.
c 1) Repentance.
d 2) Faith.
e 1) Repentance.
f 2) Faith.

11 **a** 2) Great faith.
b 1) Little faith. Peter reminds us that we must "cast all our anxiety on him, for he cares for us" (1 Peter 5:7).

4 b) the act by which we place our complete confidence in a trusted person, God, and allow Him to govern our actions.

12 Faith is a gift of God. Faith is also generated by the activity of the Holy Spirit. Nevertheless, man is commanded to believe and this implies his ability to do so. Faith develops in a person's heart as he reads the Word of God.

5 **a** 4) Inactive faith.
b 1) Intellectual faith.
c 2) Nonreligious faith.
d 3) Living faith.

13 **a** The belt of truth, the breastplate of righteousness, shoes that represent preparation to go preach the good news, the shield of faith, the sword of the spirit which is the Word of God, and the helmet of salvation.
b The sword of the Spirit.
c Prayer, asking God's help is important.
d Union with the Lord and relying on His power.
e The Devil. (Not people, institutions, or prejudices. We wrestle against wicked spiritual forces that want to destroy our faith.)

6 **a** knowledge.
b assent.
c trust.

14 **a** Forgiveness of sins.
b Receive the Holy Spirit.
c Christ's indwelling.
d Justification.
e Righteousness.
f Sonship.
g Adoption.
h Sanctification.
i Preservation.
j Whatever we ask for.

7 **a** False.
b True.
c True.
d False.
e False.
f True.

15 Remain in Christ, have His Word in us, be obedient, live in the Spirit. (Other conditions were discussed earlier in the lesson.)

LESSON 4

Man Turns to God: Conversion

The story is told of a boy who ran away from home because he hated the responsibility his parents gave him. It was his duty to cut firewood and bring it from the woodpile into his house when needed. Gathering his clothes and few belongings together, he left home. But soon his money was gone, his clothes were dirty, and he was cold and aching from sleeping out in the open.

Finally he was so miserable that he decided to call home. He listened anxiously as his father answered the phone for some idea of his father's feeling. Very hesitantly he asked, "Father, will you forgive me? May I come home?" His father answered, "Son, we love you dearly and we have missed you so very much. Of course we want you to come home, but when you do, come by way of the woodpile."

A few days later the father returned to his home in the evening and found his son at the woodpile, dutifully cutting wood. But his attitude was different, for the boy was smiling as he applied himself to his job. It was easy to see that a great change had taken place. He was a changed person!

In this lesson we will consider the part that man has in his own *conversion*, which begins the experience of salvation. It is a dynamic experience that changes us into the image of Christ and causes us to respond with joy to His desires.

lesson outline

Nature of Conversion
Conversion in the Bible
Experience of Conversion

lesson objectives

When you finish this lesson you should be able to:

- Explain the relationship of repentance and faith to conversion.
- Identify the means of conversion.
- List at least five of the results of conversion.

learning activities

1. Read Acts 9:1-31; 16:1-40; 22:1-21; 26:4-18. These Scripture portions will give you a good overview of conversion examples.
2. Follow the lesson procedures as indicated in Lesson 1.
3. Take the self-test at the end of the lesson and check your answers.
4. Review Lessons 1-4, then answer the questions in Unit Student Report 1.

key words

apostasy
confrontation
conversion
decisive
enlightened
irresistibly
negative conversion
objective standard
persecutor
philosophy
transformation

lesson development

NATURE OF CONVERSION

In our discussion of the experience of salvation, we have spoken of *conversion*. Perhaps you have wondered how *conversion* differs from *salvation*. Let us consider the following example. We observe that a well-known drunkard no longer gambles, gets drunk, or goes to places of sin. He hates the things he once loved, and he loves the things he once hated. Those who know him say, "He's converted; he's a different man." They are simply describing what they see from the manward (outward) viewpoint. But from the Godward viewpoint we would say that God has pardoned him and made him a new creature. *Conversion* emphasizes the positive activity of *man* in the experience of salvation.

Definition of Conversion

Objective 1. *Identify the basic biblical meaning of* conversion *and list three basic steps to conversion.*

Conversion may be defined as the act by which we turn from sin to the Lord Jesus for forgiveness of sins. And, in addition, we are saved *from* our sins and delivered *from* the penalty of sin.

The word translated *conversion* means "to turn," to "make a complete turnabout." This turnabout involves more than a simple change of mind, attitude, or morals. It involves every part of a person's being: his desires, life-style, will, spirit, and outlook on life.

His change is a complete spiritual change. In the act of conversion he has, according to John 5:24, "crossed over from death to life."

The spiritual change brought about by conversion through Christ is not the same as other kinds of conversion. For example, I might be converted to a different view of politics, or religion, or morals without ever involving myself in the total commitment that is required of one who is dead to sin but alive to God (Romans 6:1-14). Paul explains this basic change of Christian conversion by noting that when "anyone is in Christ, he is a new creation; the old has gone, the new has come!" (2 Corinthians 5:17).

1 Identify the statement below which gives the basic biblical meaning of *conversion*. Conversion is

a) the act by which one changes his mind, or morals, or point of view.
b) essentially a change of feelings toward one's way of life.
c) the act by which one experiences a total change in his life as he turns from sin to God.

Consider the illustration given in the lesson introduction as you note three important steps in conversion. *First*, one must carefully consider the error of his ways. This is an important step of preparation, for until one recognizes the need to change he will feel no need for conversion. *Second*, there must be a decisive turning to God. This is the action step. *Third*, there must be obedience, for *conversion* means a *changed life*.

PREPARATION ACTION CHANGE

In our introductory illustration, we saw the preparation step, the careful consideration of his ways; the action step, the decisive turn homeward, and finally, we witnessed the complete change which was evident in the boy's life as he obediently took up his chores.

2 List three steps to conversion.

....

Relation to Repentance and Faith

Objective 2. *Recognize the relationship of faith and repentance to conversion.*

Conversion is closely related to repentance and faith. In fact, on occasion conversion is used to represent either or both, and thus represents all of the activities by which we turn from sin to God. You will recall that repentance turns us *from* sin and produces sorrow for it by pointing us to the cross. Repentance does not seek to excuse sin, rather it freely admits the sins committed and the attitudes held that are contrary to God's law. Faith is the positive activity by which we turn *to* God. We look to God who has provided the cross as a cure for the disease of sin which infects us. And we trust our life and future destiny to Him. When we *repent* and *believe*, we are converted.

3 Circle the letter of the completion which shows correctly the relationship of faith and repentance to conversion. Repentance and faith are

a) steps in the chain of conversion but are unrelated to conversion.
b) the same as conversion, for in these acts one turns from sin to God in total trust.
c) separated by a considerable time element from conversion.

Elements of Conversion

Objective 3. *Match the elements of conversion with their definitions.*

As we have noted previously, a person is a whole being. Generally speaking, then, what he does is a result of what he is wholly: intellect, emotions, and will. Each of these elements involved in repentance and faith is also involved in conversion. A person can't be converted unless he *knows* what he is doing. Neither can he be converted if he does not have *feelings* about what he is doing and is *inclined* toward conversion. And quite obviously, he can't be converted unless he *wills* it to occur.

4 Circle the letters of the TRUE statements.

a Repentance involves the "turning to God" aspect of conversion.
b Faith is the act by which a person turns to God and commits his life and destiny to Him.
c The act of conversion is basically an intellectual change.
d Conversion affects a person's whole being: intellect, emotions, and will.

5 Identify the elements of conversion by matching the proper element (right) with its description (left).

. . . . **a** Involves feelings and is the assent of the heart to the rightness of what we know	1) Intellect
. . . . **b** Is the knowledge factor, lets us know what to repent of and what we should believe	2) Emotions
. . . . **c** Involves the decision-making process, by which we commit ourselves to what we know and feel	3) Will

CONVERSION IN THE BIBLE

Conversion is a marvelous experience which we undergo as we begin our Christian life. Based upon our own individual experiences we might tell others *what* happened to us and *how* it happened. But the only measure for true conversion is the Word of God. It alone is the objective standard by which we judge whether conversion is genuine or not.

Use of the Word *Conversion*

Objective 4. *Distinguish between examples of conversion which involve spiritual change and those that do not.*

We have seen that the word *conversion* speaks of a complete turn-about or change in one's life. The most common words used in the Bible which refer to such a change have the same ideas in the original biblical languages. Sometimes the change referred to is purely physical (Acts 9:40). At other times, it indicates a change of emphasis (Acts 13:46). However, among the various uses of the word, there is a common use which speaks about spiritual change. In 1 Samuel 10:6 we see that when Saul was changed into a different person the conversion involved a definite spiritual change. (See also Mark 4:12; Psalm 51:13; and Luke 22:32.) In Acts 3:19, when Peter challenged the people to "repent, then, and turn to God, so that your sins may be wiped out," we again have the idea of spiritual change.

PAUL PERSECUTING CHRISTIANS PAUL HEALING SICK

There is also the idea of *turning away* from God. This is called *negative conversion* or *apostasy* (Jeremiah 2:27). Another example of a change from the good life to the bad life and its effects is seen in 2 Peter 2:22 where Peter compares apostasy to dogs who return to their vomit.

While we have used a number of examples of the way the word *conversion* is used in the Bible, it speaks primarily of a person turning to God and of God forgiving him.

6 Select examples of conversion which refer to spiritual change by writing **1** in front of those that involve spiritual change and **2** in front of those that do not involve spiritual change.

. . . . **a** Paul and Barnabas decide to *turn* in ministry from Jews to Gentiles in Antioch.	1) Spiritual change
. . . . **b** Jesus says to Peter, "And when you have turned back, strengthen your brothers" (Luke 22:32).	2) Nonspiritual change
. . . . **c** Jesus said, "Unless you change and become like little children, you will never enter the kingdom of heaven" (Matthew 18:3).	
. . . . **d** Isaiah says, "The abundance of the sea shall be converted unto you" (Isaiah 60:5).	

Examples of Conversion

Objective 5. *Compare and contrast notable biblical examples of conversion.*

Our conversion experience does not concern a religion. It does involve a *person*. We are not asked to acknowledge the Ten Commandments, a certain church creed, or the Sermon on the Mount in order to become Christians. But we are challenged to believe in a *Person* and accept Him as Lord of our lives, believing that He is risen and alive (Romans 10:9-10). At a certain young people's meeting a young lady asked the Christian speaker about the need for a personal experience with Christ. She said, "It is hard for me to accept this. If a person believes in Fascism, is he not a Fascist? If he believes in Communism, is he not a Communist? Well, I believe in Christianity, doesn't this make me a Christian?" The speaker replied, "Not necessarily." Then he added, "I notice you are wearing an engagement ring. Do you believe in marriage?" "Of course," she answered, "I'm planning to be married very soon." He answered, "What are your reasons for believing in marriage and wanting to be married?" She replied, "Marriage provides security for a woman, also a home and a family." The speaker turned to other young ladies and asked, "How many of you believe in marriage?" And with little exception all agreed that they did believe in marriage. The speaker continued, "Well, this *is* interesting. All of you ladies believe in the institution of marriage. And since I'm a licensed minister, I can perform marriages according to the laws of our government. This young lady here says that if one believes in Fascism, he is a Fascist. If he believes in Communism, he is a Communist. And if one believes in Christianity, he is a Christian. Since a number of you ladies have told me that you believe in marriage, permit me to pronounce you married."

The audience responded with laughter. The speaker then asked, "What is wrong with this reasoning?" Another young lady said, "Sir, you know marriage is not a philosophy like Communism or Fascism; it is a personal relationship." The speaker said, "This is precisely my point. Christianity is not just a philosophy, for in order to be a

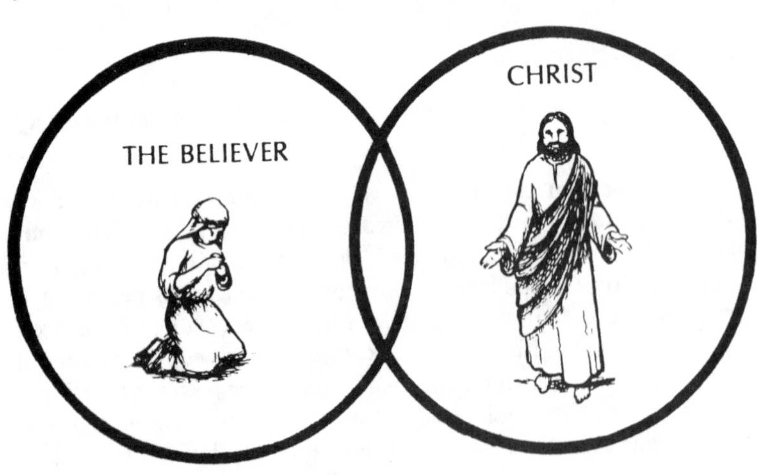

CHRISTIANITY IS A RELATIONSHIP

Christian one must have a personal relationship with the Lord Jesus who is a living person." Christian conversion, then, is uniquely different from all other conversions.

One very beautiful example of conversion in all its aspects is recorded in Acts 16:13-15. Of this occasion Lydia, a Gentile God-fearer, that is, one who worshiped the God of Israel without accepting all the ceremonial laws of the Jews, was attending a time of prayer. As Paul shared the good news of Jesus, she heard his message as the Lord opened her heart, and she *responded* gladly. She then gave evidence of her change by being baptized and by extending hospitality to Paul's group.

In this example we see some of the wonders of God's provision in bringing people to Himself. Though Lydia was an earnest seeker, she needed further knowledge of salvation, and God met this need. As she prayed, God brought her to a place of confrontation with the gospel. Thus, prayer is an important means of bringing about spiritual change. Her experience shows us that even though a person is sincere and apparently religious, he must have a decisive spiritual change if he is to be a truly converted Christian. Notice how the Word and the Holy Spirit work together in bringing about conversion also. And finally, observe that both the Holy Spirit and man's responsibility are involved in conversion.

7 Circle the letters of the TRUE statements.

a Conversion follows the same course with each person: he must go to church, hear a gospel message preached, and then join the church.

b Lydia's experience gives us proof that God loves the world, and that He is not willing that any should perish.

c Even though a person is sincere and seems to live a good life, he still needs to be converted.

d Conversion requires more than knowledge of one's sins and the desire to change; the knowledge and the assent must be followed by a personal experience of conversion.

The Philippian jailer is another example of Christian conversion (Acts 16:16-34). In this second case we learn that God uses various means to get a sinner's attention: sometimes by natural disasters such as an earthquake, a windstorm, or a personal crisis or serious problem in the home. These experiences which shock sinners so much help them to see their spiritual need and help them seek for a solution. Notice that the gospel is God's solution to the sinner's sense of need (v. 32). It is the instrument of conversion. Observe also, that conviction of sin ends in conversion only when the sinner's sense of guilt and sin is linked with belief in the Lord Jesus (v. 31). And, once again we see that true Christian conversion produces good deeds.

8 Read Acts 16:16-34. In this example all the elements of conversion are present. Following each element list the verse (or verses) and the proof that this element was in fact exercised.

a Intellect ....

....

b Emotions ....

....

c Will ....

....

A third example of conversion, that of Paul, gives still other principles of Christian conversion. Acts 9:1-31 reveals facts about Paul's conversion, some of which are quite different from our other examples. One important fact arises out of the miraculous events involved in Paul's conversion: sometimes unusual circumstances accompany a conversion experience, but usually they do not. It is wrong to assume that conversion requires an earthquake, a shining light from heaven, or some other attesting sign; for the miracle involved in conversion is the greatest miracle in all the world.

In Paul's experience we see that even though a person may be highly trained, have great natural abilities, and be very sincere in his religion, he may be totally without true spiritual life and in need of conversion. Paul's case shows that a person may have great zeal for God which is not based on knowledge (Romans 10:2); he is sincere but wrong. Since such a person is ignorant of the gospel and deeply committed to his religion and tradition, he reacts fiercely against the gospel. However, when this person understands the truth that Jesus is Lord, his enlightened knowledge lays a solid foundation for his conversion. And finally, Paul's conversion shows that God is not willing that people at any social, intellectual, or economic level should be lost. In the miracle of Paul we see that God's grace can change a persecutor into a preacher.

9 Write answers to the following questions based on the comparisons and contrasts you have noted in the biblical examples of conversion in this section.

a What elements are involved in each conversion experience?

Intellect, emotions & will ....

b On what basis does God deal with us?

..On the basis of the Word of God.........

c How do the experiences differ?

Does deals with us as individuals ....

d In what way are the experiences similar?

Every person comes to conviction, turns to God & believes in Him & confess Him as Lord, then is converted.

EXPERIENCE OF CONVERSION

Means of Conversion

Objective 6. *Select a statement which properly describes the means of conversion.*

It is important for us to understand what is involved in conversion. Some say that it is all done by God; others say it is all done by man. It is necessary for us to see the biblical balance. We will consider this issue in greater depth in Lesson 5, "God's Will in Salvation." There we will see the importance of man's free will in the experience of conversion; there we will also see God moving man toward Him. Balance is needed in our views which does not deny man's free will, nor limit God's sovereignty. Let us keep this in mind as we consider the means of conversion.

10 Read each of the following Scriptures and place those which show God calling on men to turn to Him in the left column and those which show God turning men to Himself in the right column. Proverbs 1:23; Psalm 85:4; Isaiah 31:6; 59:20; Jeremiah 31:18; Ezekiel 18:32; Hosea 12:6; Joel 2:12-13; Lamentations 5:21; Acts 26:20.

God calls men to turn to Him	God turns men to Himself
Proverbs 1:23	Psalm 85:4
Isaiah 31:6, 59:20	Jeremiah 31:18
Ezekiel 18:32	Lamentations 5:21
Hosea 12:6	
Joel 2:12-13	
Acts 26:20	

The Scriptures thus show the human and divine aspects of conversion. God always respects the will of man. When He created man and gave him personality, God made a creature that could either respond to His offer of salvation and turn wholly to Him, or reject and turn from Him. God begins the process that brings conversion through the Word and the Holy Spirit. But we must respond to the call of the Spirit through the Word and experience conversion. Remember: our willing response to God's call through the gospel does not involve merit. God respects our will and thus calls us to turn to Him.

When we turn to God, we simply allow Him to step across the threshold and take control of our lives (Revelation 3:20). We can picture this better, perhaps, by this example. When the Lord steps into our lives, He turns us on a new course. Before He steps in, we are like untrained pilots at the controls, and we are on a dangerous collision course. But when we turn to Him, we permit Him to take the controls. In this way we see that people turn to God, and God turns people in the way of truth and righteousness. It is completely correct to pray as the Psalmist did, "Turn us, O God . . . " (Psalm 85:4, KJV), and it is just as appropriate for God to appeal to us to turn. Notice that while the Lord stands at the door and knocks, we must open the door. God never forces His way into our lives.

The instrument God uses to bring about conversion is the preaching of the gospel. The Holy Spirit uses the Word to convict us of sin and to produce faith (Romans 10:17). We thus repent, believe in the Lord Jesus, and are converted. In this process God is glorified and we are redeemed. We have neither limited God's sovereignty nor our own free will.

The apostle Paul declared that his message was of Christ crucified (1 Corinthians 2:2). We know that he preached of the significance of Christ's death and resurrection (1 Corinthians 15:3-4). And his message included many references to the work of the Holy Spirit (see Romans 8, 1 Corinthians 12 and 14). But the emphasis of Paul's gospel message was the atoning death of Jesus Christ. And he proclaimed it not with a demonstration of his own speaking ability but in the power of the Holy Spirit. The results of this message reflected not the power of man but the power of God (1 Corinthians 2:1-5, 1 Thessalonians 1:5; 2:13).

11 Select the statement below which properly describes the *means of conversion*.

a) Conversion is the product of God's grace alone. It is brought about as the Holy Spirit draws a person to Christ; therefore, he need not believe nor respond to any message of the gospel, since he is irresistibly drawn to God.
b) Conversion is the result of man's assessment of his own situation. He realizes he needs to change, and the change comes about by his will alone.
c) God and man are both involved in the process of conversion. God brings man knowledge of his lost condition and convicts him of sin, but man must respond by repenting, believing, and turning wholly to God.

Purpose of Conversion

Objective 7. *Select correct statements concerning the purpose of God in conversion.*

The purpose of conversion may be viewed as two-fold: it is to turn away from our evil ways, sin, and eternal death (Ezekiel 33:11; Matthew 7:13), and it is also to turn us to the narrow way that leads to eternal life (Matthew 7:14). God's highest purpose is to bring us out of sin to Himself. In conversion we take the first step on the road to eternal life. We thus begin a new way of life.

Conversion enables us to live according to new principles of life based upon God's Word. We could say that our goal at this point is to make our outward life conform to the inward transformation that has taken place. Our *standing* in Christ as people of God becomes a powerful testimony to others because our *state* (our behavior in daily living) conforms to this. Notice the way Paul describes the ongoing process of growth in Christlikeness that begins at conversion: "And we, who with unveiled faces all reflect the Lord's glory, are being transformed into his likeness with ever-increasing glory" (2 Corinthians 3:18). Yes, in conversion we make a complete turnabout. Before we were earthbound; now that we have turned to God and are heaven-bound, we face upward so that we reflect His image to others. We thus become living letters bearing God's message to all people (2 Corinthians 3:2).

12 Write **1** in front of the statements below which state correctly the purpose of God in conversion and write **2** in front of those that do NOT correctly state this purpose.

1) God's purpose
2) Not God's Purpose

. . . . **a** Conversion is the process God uses to make a sinful person perfect instantly.

. . . . **b** Conversion turns one away from sin and to God.

. . . . **c** God's highest purpose is to bring people to Himself, and conversion is the first step in this process.

. . . . **d** The process of becoming like Jesus, begun at conversion, is a progressive work that goes on throughout our Christian life.

Results of Conversion

Objective 8. *List at least five results of conversion.*

Having received the Son of God as Lord and Savior, we learn something of the extent of this transaction: "God has given us eternal life, and this life is in his Son. He who has the Son has life" (1 John 5:11-12). One of the immediate results of conversion, then, is salvation from spiritual death (James 5:20). However, we are more than just *saved sinners*, as we shall see later. At the time of conversion we are considered part of God's family: "Dear friends, now we are children of God . . . " (1 John 3:2). Also, our sins are wiped out (Acts 3:19), not just covered over to be revealed later. In fact, the Psalmist says, "As far as the east is from the west, so far has he removed our transgressions from us" (Psalm 103:12). Isaiah reinforces this truth: "I, even I, am he who blots out your transgressions . . . and remembers your sins no more" (Isaiah 43:25).

As a part of God's family, we have new relationships. We join multitudes of others at the cross of Christ, and together as converted people we form a great fellowship. In fact, this is what we have been called unto (1 Corinthians 1:9). John says that the fellowship we have is "with the Father and with his Son, Jesus Christ" (1 John 1:3). The fellowship that Adam lost when he fell has been restored through the death of Christ. Moreover, as we walk in daily fellowship with Him, there are added benefits: "But if we walk in the light, as he is in the light, we have fellowship with one another, and the blood of Jesus, his Son, purifies us from every sin" (1 John 1:7). What a transaction! We exchange our place in the sinful world for an eternal palace in glory; we leave the poverty of the world for the riches of divine grace; we leave the broad road of destruction for the straight and narrow way, where the arms of our Heavenly Father await us. All this and heaven awaits us besides!

13 List at least five results of conversion.

....

....

....

self-test

MULTIPLE CHOICE. Circle the letter of the best answer.

1 Repentance and faith are related to conversion
a) in a very close way, for they are steps that prepare the sinner for conversion.
b) only in a very narrow sense, because they are completely different activities of man in things of the Spirit.
c) in that repentance deals with the intellect, faith with the emotions, and conversion with the will.

2 We have found that repentance, faith, and conversion are
a) exclusively the work of God. Man is passive in these acts.
b) acts that touch people at every point of their being: intellect, emotions, and will.
c) generally words that mean the same thing.

3 Conversion is brought about as a result of
a) man's response to the ministry of the Word and the activity of the Holy Spirit.
b) people's self-knowledge, which shows them that they don't measure up to a moral standard.
c) man's deep-seated seeking after a Savior whom he does not know and of whom he is ignorant.

4 Conversion speaks of a turning to God for forgiveness of sins. This turning is the
a) responsibility of people, since this is commanded by God.
b) activity which God brings about in people; therefore turning is a divine action which God works in people.
c) responsibility of man, *primarily*, for God commands it; nevertheless, people have prayed that God would turn them to Him, and God has done so.

5 The primary instrument God uses to bring about conversion is the
a) ministry of the Holy Spirit, which deals with each person on a different basis.
b) preaching of the gospel.
c) ministry of the body of Christ, the church.

6 MATCHING. Place a **1** in front of the following items which are results of conversion and a **2** in front of those that are not.

. . . . **a** We receive eternal life.

. . . . **b** We are saved from eternal death.

. . . . **c** We are made instantly righteous and perfect.

. . . . **d** Our sins are blotted out completely, never to be remembered against us again.

. . . . **e** We become involved in new relationships.

. . . . **f** Fellowship with other converted ones helps us grow and become strong.

. . . . **g** Our knowledge of spiritual things becomes full and complete.

. . . . **h** We have fellowship with the Sovereign of the universe and His Son, Jesus Christ.

1) Result of conversion
2) Not a result of conversion

Before you continue your study with Lesson 5, be sure to complete your unit student report for Unit 1 and return the answer sheet to your ICI instructor.

answers to study questions

7 **a** False. **c** True.
b True. **d** True.

1 c) the act by which one experiences total change . . .

8 **a** Verse 32. This verse indicates that the jailer and his household heard and understood the message.
b Verses 25-30. The miracle made a powerful impression on the jailer; hence his question, "Men, what must I do to be saved?" (Obviously he believed, for this led him from conviction all the way to making a decisive change.)
c Verse 33. We see here a deliberate act of the will in the jailer's ministry to them and in his submission to baptism.

2 Consideration of one's ways, a decisive turning to God, and obedience to Him.

9 **a** The total person—intellect, emotions, and will.
b These experiences show us that God deals with us on the basis of His Word.
c The experiences differ because God deals with us as individuals. Experiences differ slightly from person to person based on this fact.
d In every case the person must acknowledge his sins and turn from them, believe in Him, and confess Him as Lord. When he does this, he is converted.

3 b) the same as conversion, for in these acts one turns . . .

10 God calls men to turn to Him: Proverbs 1:23; Isaiah 31:6; 59:20; Ezekiel 18:32; Hosea 12:6; Joel 2:12-13; Acts 26:20. God turns men to Himself: Psalm 85:4; Jeremiah 31:18; Lamentations 5:21.

4 **a** False. **c** False.
b True. **d** True.

11 c) God and man are both involved in the process of conversion . . .

5 **a** 2) Emotions.
b 1) Intellect.
c 3) Will.

12 **a** 2) Not God's purpose.
b 1) God's purpose.
c 1) God's purpose.
d 1) God's purpose.

6 **a** 2) Nonspiritual change.
b 1) Spiritual change.
c 1) Spiritual change.
d 2) Nonspiritual change.

13 Your answer should include in any order five of the following: we receive eternal life, become part of God's family, have our sins wiped out, are saved from death, have fellowship with God and other Christians, purification from sin, and the joy of heaven.

Unit 2

WHAT GOD PROVIDES

LESSON 5

God's Will in Salvation

In our first unit of study, we examined the foundational elements of salvation and what God requires of man. There we observed that the salvation experience is like a chain reaction that is set in motion as man repents, believes, and is converted. Now we consider God's will in salvation and His provision of spiritual life, a new standing, and a new position for each one who responds to the gospel.

As we examine the will of God in salvation, we will realize anew that His eternal counsel and purpose in predestinating us to be conformed to the likeness of His Son is *past finding out*. To the honest, searching heart there will always be an element of wonder as he attempts to adjust God's sovereign will and purpose with man's free will. God's will is revealed in His great love for us, as well as in the rich mercy He displayed toward us by making us alive with Christ—even when we were dead in transgressions (Ephesians 2:4-5).

Grace is God's being for us when we were against Him. In pure grace He chose to create us with a capability of rejecting the love He extended to us. Then He revealed *unfathomable grace* when He gave for us, a rebellious race, the Son of His bosom. How could Christ come to identify Himself with guilty sinners, assume the responsibility for their sins, and give Himself on the cross as the ransom for their

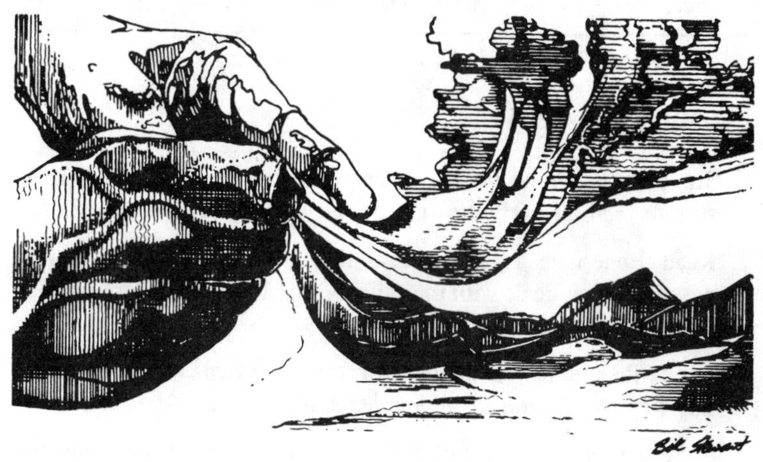

deliverance? The answer is that God so loved the world! Incomprehensible? Yes. And as we approach this lesson, we can do no better than worship where we cannot understand this infinite love, mercy, and grace.

lesson outline

Election
Views of Election
Election in the Bible
Foreordination (Predestination)

lesson objectives

When you finish this lesson you should be able to:

- Explain the significance of election in the work of salvation.
- Discuss the biblical evidence concerning who is elected, in whom they are elected, and what they are elected to.
- Appreciate the fact that understanding the principles of election and foreordination gives people assurance of salvation as they abide in Christ.

learning activities

1. Study the lesson according to the procedure given in Lesson 1. Be sure to read all Scriptures given, and answer all study questions.
2. Read Ephesians 1:3-14 several times. This is a key Scripture passage which deals with the will of God. Also, read 2 Timothy 1:9 and Romans 8:28-30.
3. Check the glossary at the back of this study guide for definitions of any key words you do not understand.
4. Take the self-test at the end of the lesson and check your answers carefully. Review any items you answer incorrectly.

key words

accountable	election	irresponsible
arbitrary	fatalism	motivating
destiny	fatalistic	predestined
deterministic	foreordain	sanctifies
dominant	foreordination	the elect
doomed		

lesson development

ELECTION

Objective 1. *Recognize the definition of* election *as it is presented in Ephesians 1:3-14.*

One of the major sections in this lesson concerns *election.* The other section treats the related teaching on *foreordination.* Taken together these two words tell us much about the purpose or will of God for the lives of men and women.

Clearly, anything that reaches into the past very far has a certain air of mystery about it. This is especially true when the subject deals with decisions of God in eternity. But, as we shall see, the subject of God's will for people who respond to Him is not surrounded by mystery. Rather, it speaks to us of comfort, security, fellowship, and eternal inheritance. As we consider the actions of our Heavenly Father described by the words *election* and *foreordination*, we will see the gracious provision He has made for those who accept His offer of salvation.

1 Read Ephesians 1:13-14 if you have not already done so. Based upon this Scripture and the preceding paragraph, we can say that the will of God, as expressed in the words *election* and *foreordination*, concerns the
a) eternal purpose He has for mankind in general.
b) divine purpose for those who respond favorably to His acts of love.
c) power exercised by God in doing what He wants in His universe.

Meaning of Election

In relation to salvation, *election* is the act of God's grace by which He *chose* in Christ Jesus for salvation all those whom He knew in advance (foreknew) would accept Him and continue in their faith in Him. Perhaps the following chart will help you to understand the concept of election more clearly:

MAN'S RESPONSIBILITY
1. God offered salvation to all people. 2. This salvation is made possible through the sacrifice of Christ. 3. Our salvation depends upon: a. Our acceptance of Christ's sacrifice. b. Our continued faith in following Christ.
GOD'S CHOICE
1. **Election** is an act of God's grace by which He chose for His own those who accepted His offer of salvation in Christ. 2. Because God has foreknowledge, He knew in advance who would accept His offer and continue in their faith.

MAN'S CHOICE = GOD'S CHOICE

In this general definition we see God's gracious provision: offering salvation to all people *in* Christ Jesus. Observe that there is also a *conditional* part for people: accepting salvation and maintaining it by faith in the finished work of the Lord Jesus Christ. Thus, in eternity past God *chose* (elected) to save people. Because they were not worthy of His grace, He chose them in the *merits* (or worthiness) of another, Jesus Christ. He chose them to be holy and without blame, to receive adoption as His children, to be to the praise of His glory, and to receive an eternal inheritance (Ephesians 1:3-14). You will recall from Lesson 1 that God has made provision for the salvation of all people. Our focus now, however, is on the benefits of this provision for people who accept His gracious offer.

2 The biblical teaching on election, as defined in Ephesians 1:3-14, shows us that

a) all men will respond favorably to God's purpose and be saved.
b) God acted in eternity, choosing those people in Christ whom He foreknew would respond favorably to His offer of salvation.
c) the purpose of God is that some people should be saved and experience His gracious provision while others are lost.

Biblical Examples of Election

Objective 2. *Distinguish between scriptural and nonscriptural teachings on election.*

To understand the meaning of *election* more fully, we will consider Hebrew and Greek words for it as used in the Bible. And we will consider Old and New Testament examples of *election* which will illustrate the idea.

In the Old Testament, the Hebrew word *bāhar* is used most often. It means "to choose" or "to select." It occurs 164 times, and in over 100 of these examples it is God who elects. These examples are very important, therefore, in demonstrating the activity of God in *election.*

3 Read the following Scriptures and state whom or what God chose.

a 1 Samuel 10:24 ..the King - Saul..............................

b 2 Chronicles 6:6 ..Jerusalem & David to be King

c 2 Chronicles 7:16 the house of Solomon...........

d Psalm 106:23 .Moses to Intercede for Israel.........

In the above question we see divine choices which concern *chosen* individuals, *chosen* objects, and a *chosen* place. The word *bāhar* most frequently refers to God's choice of Israel as His people. No essential quality in Israel can explain why she was chosen to be God's special people over other peoples (Deuteronomy 7:7). Israel's insignificance did, however, give opportunity for the demonstration first of God's grace, then of His power so that His name might be proclaimed in all the earth (Exodus 9:16). Of Israel's election we read simply: "I have chosen you and have not rejected you" (Isaiah 41:9).

ELECTION BRINGS RESPONSIBILITY

The *election* of Israel to be the people of God was a high and holy privilege. But this choice placed great responsibility on the people chosen. As a result, they were punished more severely than were the neighboring nations for willful pride or failure to obey the laws of God.

4 Consider Jeremiah 5:12; 7:4, 10; and Micah 3:11. What boast were the people of Israel making?

Nothing could harm them, no matter of disobedience.

Jeremiah 7:9-10 implies that the people believed strongly that their election was so secure that it relieved them of any responsibilities. But as we shall see, this was never God's intention for Israel. For along with the privilege there was the responsibility of responding to God's love in faith and obedience. And while Israel *as a nation* was elected, *individuals* were *accountable* for their own response to God's revealed will.

5 Read Ezekiel 18:1-32 and 33:7-20 and choose the *best* ending to the following statement. God's intention for those whom He elects (chooses), according to the above Scriptures is that they

a) simply acknowledge His control over their lives.
b) acknowledge His control of their lives by obediently and consistently following His direction.
c) do nothing, since *election* shows that God made a choice which He will honor regardless of the actions of the ones chosen.

Ezekiel learned that while God chose the nation of Israel, persons were individually responsible for living in obedience to God's laws (Ezekiel 18:4). Failure to live up to God's requirements could only lead to death (Ezekiel 18:13).

6 Examine Amos 3:1-2, Luke 12:48; and Romans 2:17-29. What principle do we see in these verses regarding God's dealing with man?

Those who are given a measure of election are responsible to produce that same measure of fruitfulness

These Scriptures which concern Israel's election teach us about the will and working of our gracious and holy Heavenly Father. They also reveal His holy character and His views toward sin. And they, as well as Romans 11:17-23, warn us so that we will not, like Israel, be cut off (separated) from God.

In the New Testament the Greek words for election occur about 50 times. These words are:

1. *Eklegomai*—"to choose"
2. *Ekloge*—"the act of choosing or choice"
3. *Eklektos*—"the chosen or selected one"

About half of these words teach us about the exercise of God's will in election. The principle of free choice is especially dominant. In the New Testament the verb form (called middle voice) indicates the direct personal interest of the one who does the choosing—in this case, God Himself. In election God never predetermines the future of man, nor is election to be separated from the responsible decision of man.

7 In the exercise below, place an **S** in front of the scriptural examples of teaching on election and an **N** in front of those that represent nonscriptural teaching on election.

. . . . **a** God's act of choosing is based upon the fitness or worthiness of the person chosen.

. . . . **b** The privilege of being chosen is beyond measure, and it requires responsible living on the part of those chosen.

. . . . **c** Biblical examples, in both Old and New Testaments, show that because God has elected people to be saved, they need not respond to God's grace . . . everything depends on Him alone.

. . . . **d** Since God has elected people to be saved, it is His responsibility to make them ready for heaven and keep them pure through His overpowering will.

. . . . **e** In Old Testament times Israel *as a nation* was elected, but *individuals* were accountable for their response to God's grace. In New Testament times the gospel is offered to all people, and each individual is responsible for what he does with God's offer of salvation.

VIEWS OF ELECTION

Objective 3. *Discriminate between statements consistent with two different views of election.*

Deterministic View

Some people see election a bit differently from what we believe is consistent with the total teaching of Scripture. They feel that God willed in eternity what the *destiny* of each individual would be. They believe that God *determined* that *some* should be saved and receive eternal life and *some* should be eternally lost. According to them, Christ died only for the elect. We might call this view the *Deterministic View.*

Deterministic View	Scripture Used to Support This View
1. The motivating cause of election is the sovereign will of God.	Ephesians 1:5
2. Election *guarantees* the salvation of those who are chosen in Christ. Election also means that those not chosen in Christ do not have the possibility of being saved.	Romans 8:28-30
3. It is from eternity.	Ephesians 1:4
4. It is unconditional. It *does not* depend on the faith of man or upon his good works. It rests completely with the good pleasure of God who is also the source of faith.	Acts 13:48 Romans 9:11 2 Timothy 1:9 1 Peter 1:2
5. It is irresistible. This means that God can and will exert such a strong influence on the human spirit as to make it willing.	Philippians 2:13

According to the ones who hold this view, salvation is entirely of God; man has absolutely nothing to do with it. If he repents, believes, and comes to Christ, it is because God's Spirit has drawn him. This is true, they say, because man is so corrupt and his will is so enslaved by sin that apart from God's help he cannot repent, believe, and choose rightly. Let us consider briefly some of the major characteristics of this view.

From this view comes the doctrine or teaching of *eternal security*, the belief that once one is in grace, he is always in grace—once saved always saved. For if God has determined in eternity that one should be saved, and he can first be saved and then kept only by God's grace, which is irresistible, then he may never be lost.

8 Circle the letters of all of the following statements that are held to be TRUE by those who hold the Deterministic View of election.

a God elects unconditionally. Man can do nothing to resist or cooperate with God's electing purpose.
b Election is based upon the love of God and the good works of man.
c Election is universal, that is, all people are elected to salvation.
d Those whom God chooses are made willing by His overpowering influence on their spirits.
e God determined in eternity the destiny of every human being. He created some to be saved and some to be eternally lost.

Free Will View

In contrast to the Deterministic View, there is another view of election held by many Christians. This is our view, which recognizes man's responsibility in salvation, and may be called the *Free Will View*. We believe the Bible teaches that it is God's will for *all* people to be saved. This is based upon the evidence that Christ died for all people (1 Timothy 2:6; 4:10; Hebrews 2:9; 1 John 2:2; 2 Corinthians 5:14), and offers His grace to everyone. While we agree that salvation is the work of God, totally free and independent of man's good works or merit (worthiness), yet man must meet certain conditions. The responsibility he has in election, having confident trust in what Christ offers, secures God's provision of salvation. This agrees with the statements of Jesus (John 3:15-18), namely, that *whoever believes* may have eternal life. Faith, that is, the act of believing in Christ as a condition for salvation, is not an act of merit; it is simply accepting the condition laid down by the Lord. We can either accept God's grace or reject it. The power of choice remains with us.

Since salvation is based upon our response to the offer God makes, we must by an act of our own free will determine whether we will accept or reject his offer. The main features of the Free Will View are:

Free Will View	Scripture Used to Support This View
1. Election is a sovereign act of God since He was under no obligation to elect anyone. All men stand condemned before Him because of sin; therefore, all people could have been justly *doomed*.	Ephesians 1:11 Romans 3:23
2. Election is an act of grace, because all those who were chosen were unworthy.	Ephesians 2:8-10
3. God elected on the basis of the merits of His Son.	Ephesians 1:3-4
4. He chose those He foreknew would believe.	Romans 8:29-30
5. God graciously grants all people sufficient power to make a choice in the matter of accepting Christ and His salvation. In His foreknowledge, God knows what each person will do with his power of choice; therefore, He elects to salvation those who choose to submit to Him.	Titus 2:11 1 Timothy 4:10

The Free Will View of election is that God elects "whosoever will" to be saved. The many Christians around the world who hold this view believe that the offer of salvation is broad enough to include everyone who wants to be saved. We believe that God, because of His knowledge, foresaw all those individuals who would accept the gospel and maintain their salvation. These He *predestined* (chose beforehand in eternity) to eternal life. The Free Will position is that *God foreknew the eternal destiny of these people* but *did not determine it.*

9 Circle the letter of the statements that are TRUE of the Free Will View of election.

a Election is based upon God's foreknowledge of man's response to the gospel.

b Election is conditional and rests upon the response of each individual to the offer of salvation.

c Faith in the Lord Jesus Christ is the basis upon which people are saved.

d Faith is not merit (worthiness); it is the obedient response of those who trust the word of God.

In summary, we hold the Free Will View as being the more biblical of the two. In the study of the doctrine of salvation, we believe that it is closer to the overall teaching of the Scriptures than the Deterministic View. We are influenced by the fact that election never appears in Scripture as a violation of human will. And never in the Bible is man treated as unaccountable. Accountability can only exist where there is free choice.

10 Read carefully the following Scripture and then respond to the statements below, basing your answers on this text: "For it is by grace you have been saved, through faith—and this not from yourselves, it is the gift of God—not by works, so that no one can boast" (Ephesians 2:8-9). Circle the letter of each TRUE statement.

a Salvation in the above text is totally the provision of God.

b God's offer of salvation is received through the exercise of faith.

c Salvation is a gift that is freely offered, but this offer must be believed and acted upon (received) if it is to become effective.

d The gift of God is irresistible, that is, it cannot be refused. People are not required to respond to God; He simply forces them to hear His announcement that they are the elect and receive His provision.

11 For the statements below use a **1** to identify those which reflect a Deterministic View of election and a **2** to identify those that reflect a Free Will View.

1) Deterministic View
2) Free Will View

. . . . **a** Election is unconditional and irresistible.

. . . . **b** Election requires man's response of trust in the salvation Christ offers.

. . . . **c** Salvation is available for all mankind but avails only for those who believe.

. . . . **d** In election God determined in eternity to create people. Some He designed to be saved and some to be lost—apart from anything they could believe or do.

. . . . **e** God graciously grants all people sufficient power to make a choice in the matter of accepting Christ and His salvation.

ELECTION IN THE BIBLE

Objective 4. *Identify on the basis of Scripture five aspects of election.*

Someumes we are inclined to turn to one or two "proof" sources to back our ideas or prejudices about a given subject. However, if we are to be fair in our efforts to understand a subject, we must gather all the available evidence, evaluate all related facts, and only then come to a conclusion. For example, one might conclude that on the basis of John 14:13-14 he might receive *anything* he asked for in Christ's name. However, as we consider the case more fully, we see that behind this same promise in John 15:16 there are the conditions of John 15:1-15. The additional light from this second source is significant in giving us the biblical basis for our understanding of the nature of effective prayer. With these facts in mind, let us consider further evidence in the Bible that deals with election.

12 Read the following passages in Deutermonomy 7:6-8; 10:12-15; and 14:1-2. Now complete each of the statements below based upon these scriptural references.

a These Scriptures teach us that God is ....
....

b God elected (chose) Israel because of ....
....

c The degree of God's love for Israel is shown in that He chose them from ....

d As a result of this election privilege Israel was called to ....
....

In the foregoing Scripture references, we saw God's sovereignty as He elected Israel. We also noticed that along with the privilege of being chosen, Israel received some very solemn responsibilities: to be obedient, live uprightly, and respond to God's grace in loving worship and praise. The punishment for disobedience was destruction (see Deuteronomy 7:10-11). Enjoyment of the provisions of election depended upon an obedient response from each individual (Deuteronomy 7:12-26; also chapter 8).

13 Read each of the following Scriptures and state who are the chosen ones.

a Acts 9:15 ....

b Romans 11:5 ....

c Romans 11:26 ....

d 1 Thessalonians 1:4 ....

14 Now read carefully, once again, Ephesians 1:3-4 and answer the following questions.

a Who did the choosing? ....

b With whom is the choice linked? ....

c When did the choosing take place? ....

d When is the choice realized? ....

e What is the purpose of the choice? ....

We should note well that while holiness is not the *basis* of our election, it is the *goal.* Paul says that God "saved us, not because of righteous things we had done, but because of His mercy" (Titus 3:5). When we are talking about the election of God's people, the emphasis is not so much election to salvation as election to holiness.

15 What do we learn from the following verses about election and our part in it?

a 1 Peter 1:1-2 ....

b 2 Peter 1:10 ....

16 Identify each aspect of election (left) by matching it with its proper definition, explanation, or completion (right).

.... **a** The one who does the electing	1) Before Creation
.... **b** The choice is realized	2) God
.... **c** The one with whom election is linked	3) Holy and blameless living
.... **d** The initial act of election	4) In our present lives—now
.... **e** The purpose of election	5) Christ

FOREORDINATION (PREDESTINATION)

Meaning of Foreordination

Objective 5. *Recognize statements which correctly define* foreordination *as it relates to the will and purpose of God in election.*

We come now to the second important word in our study of God's purpose for the salvation of people: *foreordination.* The words *fore-*

ordination and *predestination* mean the same thing. In the King James Version of the Bible, the words *predestinate* or *predestinated* are used only four times: see Romans 8:29, 30 and Ephesians 1:5, 11. The American Standard Version translates all four of these *foreordained.* The Today's English Version uses words that indicate "what God decided beforehand"; that is, in eternity. We use *foreordination* because some people think predestination refers to a kind of arbitrary, deterministic activity of God. Such a view or mind set encourages fatalism.

In Christianity we do not have a *fatalistic* view of God's election. We believe that God is sovereign, but we also believe that He has created people who can resist His will. The Bible demonstrates that people can resist the callings of the Holy Spirit to salvation—and be finally lost (Proverbs 29:1; Hebrews 3:7-19). It also indicates that whoever will may respond to God's offer and be saved (Revelation 22:17; John 3:36).

Foreordination comes from the Greek *proorizo*, which means "to decide upon beforehand." As applied to salvation this means that *in election* God has purposed to save those who accept His Son and the offer of salvation, and *in foreordination* He has determined to carry out this purpose. Thus, by foreordination we mean that God carries out His purpose to save those who accept this salvation. In other words, He has already made provision for all those He knew would accept Him.

17 Choose the TRUE statements below which define the word *foreordination* and its relationship to *election.*

a Foreordination means that God simply carries out in *time* the decisions and purposes which He made in eternity.

b In relation to salvation, foreordination refers to that which God has purposed for those who accept His redemption.

c Foreordination means that everything—every act, decision, attitude, response, motive, and circumstance—that concerns people was decided by God in eternity. People simply live out this prearranged program with no ability to affect it in any way.

Basis for Foreordination

Objective 6. *Select a statement giving the basis upon which God foreordains.*

Our goal in this lesson is to see the teaching concerning election and foreordination in the balanced way in which Scripture presents it. We shall see that the biblical view of election *is* balanced and harmonizes with the teachings of Scripture concerning the sovereignty of God and the responsibility of man.

18 Read Romans 8:29 and 1 Peter 1:2. These Scriptures demonstrate that election is based on ....Gods.....foreknowledge......

The simple meaning of the word *foreknow* is "to know beforehand." In Romans 8:28-30, Paul clearly shows that the divine order is foreknowledge, then foreordination (predestination). And Peter states that foreknowledge determines election (1 Peter 1:2). Thus God *foreknows*, then He *elects*, and finally He *carries out* His purpose (foreordination).

The question then arises: What did God know beforehand about those mentioned in Romans 8:29? There is no indication in this passage. However, in view of the total teaching of Scripture concerning man's real participation in salvation (through his faith), we

ANYONE MAY ENTER IN

take *foreknow* to mean *God's foreknowledge of man's faith.* Thus, God foreordains "whosoever will" to be saved. This plan is broad enough to include everybody who wants to be saved. This truth has been explained by the following illustration: Outside the door of salvation one reads the words, "Whosoever will may come"; however, when one enters the door and is saved, he reads the words, "Elect according to the foreknowledge of God."

Because of His foreknowledge, God knew in advance who would respond to His offer of salvation and continue to serve Christ. He foreordained them to an eternal inheritance. He *foreknew* their choice and eternal destiny, but He did not *decide* for them.

19 Choose the correct completion for this statement: God foreordains on the basis of
a) human merit, good works, and holy living.
b) His arbitrary decision to save some and to reject all others.
c) what He knows beforehand (His foreknowledge).

Foreordination in the Bible

Objective 7. *On the basis of scriptural evidence, identify that which is foreordained and that which is not.*

In the New Testament the word translated to *foreordain* or *predestinate* is used six times. In each instance it means "to determine" or "to decide beforehand." In the following verses let us consider *what* or *whom* God has foreordained. As we do, we will see more clearly the truth of foreordination.

20 Write *what* or *whom* God has foreordained in the verses that follow.

a Acts 4:27-28 the hardening of hearts against Jesus

b Romans 8:29-30 all of His Church

c 1 Corinthians 2:7 the mystery of His wisdom

d Ephesians 1:5 the adoption of Christianity by Jesus

e Ephesians 1:11-12 our inheritance & glorification

Consider the above verses again and observe what is *not* foreordained. The details of our lives are not fixed.

God's redemptive purpose in us as individuals is foreordained. And the basic purpose of foreordination is that we who accept God's salvation should have a living, holy relationship with Him as His children, being conformed to the image of Christ.

In the plan of salvation you will observe that God and man are closely associated. God extends grace, but man believes. God ordained that His people should do good works. People believe and their faith results in good works. They are not *saved* by good works, but good works are the evidence of their living relationship with Christ. God ordains good works, but people perform them. In the working out of salvation in our lives, God allows us to work with Him. His part is so great: He foreknew, He elected, He foreordained, He called, He glorified, He sanctifies, and so much more. Nevertheless, He permits us to work with Him.

To summarize our discussion of election and foreordination, let us remember the advice of Paul to the Ephesians:

> For it is by grace you have been saved, through faith—and this not from yourselves, it is the gift of God—not by works, so that no one can boast. For we are God's workmanship, created in Christ Jesus to do good works, which God prepared in advance for us to do (Ephesians 2:8-10).

21 We know that all things are known by God, but all things are not determined by Him. Identify the elements which Scripture indicates are determined by God by placing a **1** in front of those statements and a **2** in front of those things that are NOT determined by God.

1) Determined by God
2) Not determined by God

. . . . **a** The plotting against Christ by His enemies

. . . . **b** Your life decisions—for example, what job you will perform, whom you marry, where you will live

. . . . **c** Christian to be conformed to Christ's image

. . . . d A divinely ordered wisdom accomplished though Jesus

. . . . e Some to be saved and some to be lost (based on God's act, not on man's response)

. . . . f Those who believe the gospel and receive Christ to be adopted as Christ's sons

. . . . g Christians to live for the praise of His glory

. . . . h Where you will worship, how you will respond to spiritual things, whether you will be generous or stingy in regard to God's work

---

self-test

After you have reviewed this lesson take the self-test. Then check your answers with those given at the back of this study guide. Review any items you answer incorrectly.

MULTIPLE CHOICE. Select the one best answer to each question.

1 In terms of salvation, election is important because it
a) determines whether one can be saved.
b) describes the process by which the believer becomes ever more like his Lord.
c) demonstrates the powerful rule of God which overpowers the will of people.

2 Believers, who were chosen by God before the creation of the world, were chosen in
a) their own merits on the basis of their good works.
b) an arbitrary way by God, who purposed the salvation of some and the rejection of all others.
c) Christ Jesus.

3 On the basis of the overall scriptural facts, we can say that those who are elected are
a) those who respond to God's offer of salvation.
b) the select few whom God chooses to save.
c) those who prove their desire to be saved by their good works.

4 Foreordination, which means "to decide beforehand," is based upon
a) human merit.
b) God's foreknowledge.
c) unchangeable divine laws.

5 Which one of the following scriptural references is NOT closely linked with the will of God in salvation?
a) Ephesians 1:3-14
b) 1 Peter 1:1-2
c) John 14:1-3

6 Since Scripture clearly states that foreordination is based upon God's foreknowledge, we conclude that what God foresees in those who respond to His offer of salvation is
a) faith.
b) individual merit.
c) nothing outside Himself, since He decides who will or will not be saved.

7 God foresees all things in His creation. And as concerns his offer of salvation to all people, He foreordains
a) that those who accept will be saved, and those who refuse will be lost.
b) that those who accept shall be conformed to Christ's image for the praise of His glory.
c) both of the above, a) and b).

8 Foreordination concerns the response of people to God's offer of salvation. On the basis of His knowledge of what they will do with this offer, He foreordains their future. God, however,
a) does not fix either people's salvation or destruction. This decision depends on the exercise of their free will.
b) must demonstrate His sovereignty by making a choice whether each person will be saved or lost.

9 If we know that "whosoever will" may be saved, our responsibility to the world is to
a) try to decide which ones are the elect and then witness to them.
b) proclaim the gospel message by every means possible to all creatures.
c) realize that God will see that all the elect will hear the gospel and respond. We needn't be concerned about it.

10 The knowledge that, as we abide in Christ—our source of salvation—we can never be lost, should give us
a) great pride in our decision to follow Christ.
b) contentment, for now we realize that it is His responsibility to keep us from falling.
c) a deep sense of appreciation for God's grace, and a sense of security and confidence as we respond to the Holy Spirit's effort to help us become more like Christ.

answers to study questions

11 **a** 1) Deterministic View.
b 2) Free Will View.
c 2) Free Will View.
d 1) Deterministic View.
e 2) Free Will View.

1 b) a divine purpose for those who respond favorably to His acts of love.

12 **a** a God of mercy, love, and faithfulness. He is a God of glory and majesty too.
b His great love.
c among all nations.
d obedience and holy living.

2 b) God acted in eternity, choosing those people in Christ whom He foreknew would respond favorably to His purpose.

13 **a** Paul.
b A remnant.
c All Israel.
d The Christian community.

3 **a** Saul.
b Jersualem and David.
c The temple.
d Moses.

14 **a** God.
b Christ.
c Before the world was made.
d In our lives right now—see verse 3 "He has blessed us . . . "
e That we should be holy and without fault.

4 They said that because they were the elect of God, they would not be punished in spite of their disobedience to Him.

15 **a** Election is based upon foreknowledge.
b We are called upon to respond positively to God's grace. And once we have experienced His saving grace, we must maintain our relationship with God.

5 b) acknowledge His control of their lives. . .

16 **a** 2) God.
b 4) In our present lives—now.
c 5) Christ.
d 1) Before Creation.
e 3) Holy and blameless living.

6 The greater one's knowledge of God, the greater is his sin in disregarding it—and the greater the punishment. Also, election does not free one from judgment if he sins. Maintaining one's place before God is more than outward identification; it requires an inward, spiritual response.

17 **a** True.
b True.
c False.

7 **a** Nonscriptural.
b Scriptural.
c Nonscriptural.
d Nonscriptural.
e Scriptural.

18 foreknowledge.

8 **a** True.
b False.
c False.
d True.
e True.

19 c) what he knows beforehand (His foreknowledge).

9 **a** True.
b True.
c True.
d True.

20 **a** The plotting (of Herod, Pontius Pilate, Gentiles and Jews) was foreordained to carry forward the redemptive work of Christ.
b Christians are foreordained to be conformed to Christ's image.
c A divinely ordered wisdom was foreordained which was accomplished through Jesus Christ.
d Christian believers are foreordained to be God's children.
e Christians are foreordained to live for the praise of His glory.

10 **a** True.
b True.
c True.
d False.

21 **a** 1) Determined by God.
b 2) Not determined by God.
c 1) Determined by God.
d 1) Determined by God.
e 2) Not determined by God.
f 1) Determined by God.
g 1) Determined by God.
h 2) Not determined by God.

LESSON 6

God Makes a New Creation: Regeneration

Rani Chowdhury felt such hunger and need in her heart! *It must be that I do not have the right religion*, she thought. So she changed from Hinduism to another system of religion. That wasn't it, either, so she went shopping for a religion as a woman might look for bargains in the bazaar. Nothing brought her peace. Then she heard of the Christian religion. *I will repent of my sins,* she said, *I will have this baptism I have heard of, and that will wash away my sins.* But even though she was baptized and tried very hard to live a good life, she knew that something was still lacking. She realized that she had changed one religious system for another. She was like a person in a soiled garment going from one room to another. She was still in the soiled garment. Changing rooms had not made her clean. The problem was that she had never experienced the new birth. She had accepted Christianity, but not the *Christ* of Christianity.

Because she was sincerely seeking truth, the Holy Spirit opened her understanding. She saw herself now, not simply as a person who needed a religion, but as a lost sinner who needed a Savior. She responded to the Spirit's call, put her trust in Jesus, committed her life completely to Him, and owned Him as her Savior and Lord. In that hour she knew Christ personally. She was *born again*; not only converted, but *regenerated.* She received a new nature, and her life was truly changed.

In this lesson we consider this aspect of salvation, regeneration: the divine act which imparts *spiritual life* to the repentant sinner as he is joined in personal union with Christ.

lesson outline

Definition of Regeneration
Need for Regeneration
Experience of Regeneration

lesson objectives

When you finish this lesson you should be able to:

- Explain regeneration as it is presented in the Bible.
- Cite Scriptures which show that the need for regeneration is universal.
- Discuss the experience of regeneration.

learning activities

1. Read John 3 through carefully several times; note especially the development of Jesus' teaching on the new birth, verses 1-21.
2. Look up the meanings of any key words you do not understand.
3. Work through the lesson development as usual. As you do the study questions, be sure to write your own responses before looking ahead to the answers we have given. Take the self-test when you have finished and check your answers.

key words

consuming
corruption
crisis
destined
implantation
motivation
passive
quicken
re-creation
sacraments
symbolize
unregenerate

lesson development

DEFINITION OF REGENERATION

In Unit 1 we considered the response of people to the gospel call in repentance, faith, and conversion. These elements are the active response from each sinner. Now we consider the activity of God in salvation, and we shall see that people are at this point primarily passive. For it is God alone who can ignite the spark of spiritual life in the hearts of those who are spiritually dead because of their disobedience (Ephesians 2:5).

Man's highest destiny is to live with God forever; but human nature in its present condition does not possess the capacities for living in a heavenly kingdom. For this reason heavenly life must come down from above to transform human nature for membership in that kingdom.

Characteristics of Regeneration

Objective 1. *Identify statements which give the characteristics of biblical regeneration.*

Regeneration is the act of God which imparts spiritual life to the repentant sinner as he receives the Lord Jesus Christ (Titus 3:5). It is a supernatural act which takes place the instant the sinner receives Christ. Not only does the repentant one receive divine life, but he also receives a new nature (2 Peter 1:4). Thus he becomes a new creation (2 Corinthians 5:17).

Notice that in regeneration it is the Holy Spirit who *quickens* those who are spiritually dead (John 6:63; Romans 8:1-10; Ephesians 2:1). John Wesley said that regeneration is "that great change which God works in the soul when He brings it into life; when He raises it from the death of sin to the life of righteousness." In this act, then, God quickens spiritually dead people by the Holy Spirit and plants spiritual life in them. These people experience spiritual renewal, restoration, and re-creation. They have been regenerated by the Holy Spirit.

1 Circle the letter of each TRUE statement.

a The experience of regeneration is primarily natural and gradual.

b Regeneration is the work of the Holy Spirit in the soul of the one who receives Christ.

c Spiritual rebirth is a divine activity and it occurs when one receives Christ.

d Regeneration brings about a new nature in the one who receives Christ; he becomes a new creation.

Biblical Terms for Regeneration

Objective 2. *Give a definition of* regeneration *based on Scripture references.*

In Lesson 1 we discussed the fall of Adam and the sin which he passed on to the human race. We learned that all people bear the marks of the Fall, among which is a corrupted nature. Because of the Fall, people lost their communion with God. But through the work of Christ on Calvary, the results of the Fall were modified. As people repent, believe on the Lord Jesus, receive Him as their Savior, and are converted, their spiritual life or communion with God is restored. Regeneration is thus the restoration of spiritual life. It is the instant supernatural change brought about by the Holy Spirit in the life of one who has repented and believed.

The most common term used to define regeneration is that of being "born again" or "born from above." And while the word *regeneration* appears in the King James Version only in Matthew 19:28 and Titus 3:5, the experience which it speaks about, being reborn or born of God, is quite common in Scripture. Apart from birth there can be no life. Natural life begins when one enters the world through birth, and one must enter the spiritual realm in the same way.

Jesus said to Nicodemus, "A person is born physically of human parents, but he is born spiritually of the Spirit. Do not be surprised because I tell you that you must all be born again" (John 3:6-7, TEV). Our parents gave us natural birth; but God gives us spiritual birth. And spiritual birth makes God our Father (John 1:13; 1 John 3:9). Paul speaks of the regeneration experience as one of re-creation, "When anyone is joined to Christ, he is a new being; the old is gone, the new has come" (2 Corinthians 5:17).

The old unregenerate nature is like a seed on the surface of the earth. As long as it remains thus, it will never begin to grow, blossom, and bear fruit. It has the potential for life, but it needs something else so that it can live and produce. It needs to be *quickened.* And as we have noted above, regeneration is the act of God by which spiritually dead people are quickened by the Holy Spirit so that the germ of divine life implanted in them can begin to grow, blossom, and bear fruit.

2 Look up each of the following Scriptures and note first on the left the specific words used to describe regeneration. Then on the right give the specific reason (if any), for being regenerated. The first one has been done for you.

WORDS USED TO DESCRIBE REGENERATION	REASON FOR BEING REGENERATED
a John 1:13 Born of God	Will of God
b John 3:3 Born again	See His Kingdom
c John 3:5 Born of water & spirit	enter His Kingdom
d John 3:7 Born again	
e John 3:8 Born of the Spirit	the will of the Spirit
f 1 Peter 1:3 living hope ⟷	begotten us again
g 1 Peter 1:23 Born again	
h 1 John 2:29 Born of Christ	to do right
i 1 John 3:9 Born of God	to avoid sin
j 1 John 4:7 Born of God	to know love
k 1 John 5:1 Born of God	to love brethren
l 1 John 5:18 Born of God	Rejecting Sin

In the exercise above, the column ***Reasons for Being Regenerated*** suggests some important principles concerning regeneration. Let's list them here:

1. From eternity God willed (desired) our regeneration (Ephesians 1:4).
2. The new birth enables us to live with hope, love, and purity.
3. Our new life will take us into eternity, into God's kingdom.

3 Other words are also used in Scripture to describe regeneration. Look up the following references and write the description of regeneration given in each. The first one has been done for you.

a John 5:24 Crossed over from death to life

b 2 Corinthians 5:17 Old things pass away. All becomes new

c Galatians 6:15 Not by circumcision but a new creation

d Ephesians 2:10 Renovates our nature to do good works

e Ephesians 4:24 new man created in righteousness & holiness

f Titus 3:5 renewing of the Holy Spirit

4 Based on these Scriptures, regeneration may be defined as the experience of being spiritually reborn, of becoming a new creation in Christ by the power of the Holy Spirit

Nature of Regeneration

Objective 3. *Identify words which describe the nature of regeneration.*

A Passive Experience

As we have mentioned previously, in regeneration people are relatively passive. People's responsibility in regeneration may be compared to the relationship which exists between a doctor and a patient. The doctor cannot proceed with an operation until he has the consent of the patient. However, once this is given, the doctor assumes complete control. Nevertheless, no patient is ever *completely passive*, because the doctor does not begin to act until the patient is in agreement. In salvation we face the same situation. God does not act until we are in agreement. What a source of joy it is that we can trust our souls with all their sicknesses, hurts, and sorrows to the Great Physician.

A Sudden Experience

The experience in which new life is divinely imparted to the souls of people takes place *suddenly.* Birth is always a crisis, and spiritual birth is no exception to the rule. Each of us can point to a specific day as his birthday. We came into the world suddenly, at a certain moment. And in the same way the new birth is a crisis experience. It may take a while for us to get to the point of crisis, but when it happens, it happens suddenly. Consider it in this way: Someone offers you a gift; there is a moment of time when you don't yet have the gift; the next moment you receive it. The gift was offered and taken suddenly. Spiritual life is like this. One moment you don't have it, the next moment you receive it. The new birth is a definite and decisive experience. New life from above is received *suddenly.*

GOD'S PART

REPENTANCE

REGENERATION

A Mysterious Experience

New spiritual life also appears *mysteriously.* Jesus did not attempt to explain the *how* of the new birth, but He did explain the *why*: "Flesh gives birth to flesh, but the Spirit gives birth to spirit" (John 3:6). The physical and the spiritual belong to two different realms, and one cannot produce the other: the human nature can reproduce the human nature, but only the Holy Spirit can produce the spiritual nature.

Christianity is not merely a system of ethics or a moral code; it is the giving of new life: the life of God is implanted in the heart of man by the operation of the Holy Spirit. In His sovereign way the Holy Spirit suddenly and mysteriously moves upon man's inner nature and brings life and light where once there was darkness, death, and barrenness. In this mysterious operation of the Spirit a new creature is born. And it is only when people have been born of the Spirit that they receive a new nature. This new nature makes people suitable for heaven, and that is why Jesus stated the unchangeable principle, "You must be born again!" (John 3:7). For if a person is to enter heaven, he must have a new nature suitable for heaven.

A Developing Experience

Finally, though new spiritual life comes suddenly, it develops progressively. As we shall see in detail later, all who receive Christ are separated unto God. With this separation unto Him comes the responsibility to live daily for Him. Each new believer is called to maintain his dedication to God and develop into the likeness of His Son (Romans 8:29).

5 Identify words which describe the nature of regeneration by placing the number of each word (right) in front of its proper description (left).

. . . . **a** Describes the quality of new spiritual life which develops into the image of Christ.
. . . . **b** People give their assent, and then the Great Physician implants new spiritual life.
. . . . **c** Birth by the Spirit is like the wind: we see the effect but not the cause.
. . . . **d** New birth is a crisis experience.

1) Passive
2) Sudden
3) Mysterious
4) Developing

Wrong Ideas About Regeneration

Objective 4. *Explain what is wrong about erroneous ideas concerning regeneration.*

There are some very common wrong ideas concerning regeneration. And while I cannot deal with these in great depth, I want you to be aware of them. Then as you read and study in days to come, you will be able to explore these matters more fully.

The most commonly wrong idea is that people experience regeneration when they are baptized. Those who hold this view believe that all the effects of the Fall are removed by water baptism, and one's sins after baptism are dealt with through the sacraments of the church, such as communion (the Lord's Supper). These people believe that baptism is the means of salvation. Let us examine the Scriptures for evidence of the purpose and place of baptism in the life of the one who receives Christ.

You will remember that John the Baptist came preaching and baptizing. His message was, "Repent, for the kingdom of heaven is near" (Matthew 3:2), and his hearers confessed their sins and were baptized by him (see Matthew 3:6; Mark 1:4-5; Luke 3:3, 7-8). Jesus also began His ministry gaining and baptizing believers, "although in fact it was not Jesus who baptized, but his disciples" (see John 4:1-2). And just before He returned to heaven, Jesus commanded His disciples to "go and make disciples of all nations," after which they were to baptize them (Matthew 28:19). The apostles obediently followed their Lord's command and baptized believers as an essential part of their ministry. On the Day of Pentecost, Peter declared "Repent and be baptized" (Acts 2:38). It is clear that baptism was instituted by the Lord, and preached by the early church. It is also clear that new believers were baptized *following* repentance of sins and belief in the Lord Jesus Christ.

In John 3:5 Jesus uses water as a symbol of the cleansing one receives through His atoning work. In the Old Testament, water symbolized the washing processes that took place in the temple ritual. The orthodox Jew would interpret water in a religious context as that which cleanses. Thus when Jesus spoke to Nicodemus, He was saying he could enter the Kingdom only if he were cleansed from sin and given new life by the Holy Spirit. In Titus 3:5, when Paul says that God "saved us through the washing of rebirth and renewal by the Holy Spirit," he refers to the cleansing from sin that takes place in us. For at the moment of regeneration "the old has gone," cleansed by a supernatural act, and "the new has come" (2 Corinthians 5:17). At this point the new believer is commanded to follow his regeneration experience with water baptism.

BAPTISM:
AN OUTWARD
SYMBOL OF AN
INWARD CHANGE

Baptism is an outward witness to the world of the change of nature within. It symbolizes the death and burial of the sinful nature and the birth of the new nature (Romans 6:3-5). Peter says, moreover, that baptism is a symbol of obedience (1 Peter 3:21). In this verse he also declares that baptism has no value in washing away bodily dirt; and we might add that baptism has no value in washing away and removing sin and the effects of the Fall. (See Hebrews 9:22, 26-28.) Thus, while baptism is the scriptural duty of every believer, it simply testifies to the reality of regeneration. And it is a public expression of one's faith in Christ.

6 Circle the letter in front of each TRUE statement.

a Regeneration is the act by which one receives new spiritual life, while baptism is the symbolical act by which one gives outward expression of the inward work of regeneration.

b. The order which we see in John the Baptist and Jesus' ministry was repent (turn away from your sins) and then be baptized.

c. The experiences of the Philippian jailer (Acts 16:30-34) and those at the house of Cornelius (Acts 10:44-48; 11:17) show us that after having active faith in the Lord and their lives changed, then people qualify for baptism.

Another common but wrong idea is that regeneration makes a person perfect. I'm reminded of a saying that was coined to answer such an error: "Christians aren't perfect, they are just forgiven." Let us compare the new birth to natural birth. While a baby has within him the possibility for maturity, he is still a baby. In the spiritual realm a new believer is a spiritual baby. He has the possibility for maturity, but he is just an infant. Regeneration does not produce a fully developed spiritual person; nevertheless, it does begin a spiritual relationship between Christ and the believer. "No one who lives in him keeps on sinning" (1 John 3:6). Instead, he begins the journey and progresses toward Christian maturity.

Some mistakenly believe that regeneration comes by living a good life, a life that is characterized by performing good works. They reason that since they are good, God will be fair and grant them salvation. However, the Bible says that all have sinned and need a Savior (1 John 1:10). Whoever has the Son of God has eternal life and whoever does not have the Son of God does not have spiritual life (1 John 5:11-12). God would never have provided so costly a sacrifice to save people if they had not been completely and hopelessly lost (John 3:16-18). It is only as we believe in Him and commit ourselves to Him that we can be changed and be made ready for heaven. Good works are the fruit of a changed life; they are not the root, the source of it.

Some other people wrongly believe that education will cure the problems of the world and regenerate people. In recent times people have had an almost limitless belief in themselves and their achievements. But in spite of the vast increase of knowledge, people's problems remain. Wars in this century continue and increase in extent, and the death of millions of innocent people testifies to the inability of education to change corrupt human nature, the source of people's problems. Education can enlighten the mind and expand one's outlook on life by correcting false ideas and practices, but it cannot apply a cure to the corrupt nature of people. Knowledge that is not consecrated to God merely fills a person with pride (1 Corinthians 8:1). It has no power to bring about the instant change in the nature of the one who seeks to be born again. Only the Holy Spirit can do this. If education brought regeneration only a few of the world's people could experience the new birth, but education is not the means of regeneration. God has made regeneration available to all people.

Still other people mistakenly believe that church membership equals regeneration. This appears to be reasonable, but church membership simply identifies us with an institution. It does not deal with the basic problems of spiritual deadness and corrupt natures. It is a good thing to be enrolled in a church, but it is necessary to be born again first in order to be a member of the body of Christ.

And finally, still other people feel that by participating in ceremonial cleansing, rituals, observances, and prayers they will be regenerated and made acceptable to God. Yet the ones who do these things may know nothing of freedom from sin and a changed life. A person may perform all the duties that his religion requires and yet be spiritually dead.

7 Why is each one of the following ideas about regeneration wrong?

a Regeneration takes place when people are baptized.

Baptism is an outward testimony not an inward change

b Regeneration makes a person perfect.

Everyone is imperfect until the day Christ returns in the sky

c Regeneration is the result of leading a good life.

good works are the fruit of rebirth not the source or root that causes it.

d People are regenerated as they become more educated and enlightened.

Then, only few would be offered rebirth

e Church membership equals regeneration.

Anyone can become a church member but until they are saved then they cannot know Christ.

f Regeneration is brought about by observing religious rituals, ceremonies, and prayers.

This still leaves the person not personally knowing Christ.

NEED FOR REGENERATION

Objective 5. *Select a statement which explains why regeneration is necessary.*

Regeneration is necessary for two basic reasons: because of the nature of man and the nature of God. Jesus pointed out that the deepest and most universal need of all people is a complete change of their whole nature and character. People have been affected—damaged—by sin as a result of the Fall, and this damage is reflected in their behavior and their various relationships. They sin because they are sinners, and their actions reflect what they are: "For all have sinned and fall short of the glory of God" (Romans 3:23); "There is no one righteous, not even one" (Romans 3:10); "Therefore, just as sin entered the world through one man, and death through sin, and in this way death came to all men, because all sinned" (Romans 5:12).

Have you ever wondered why people act as they do? Why do they sin? They sin because of what they are! If you are in Adam, you will do what he did. If you are in Christ, you will do what He does. I am a Duncan, because I was born into the Duncan family. I look like my father. I walk as he did. I don't consciously do this because I want to imitate him, but because I am his son and bear the Duncan traits. I was born into the family. In the same way, we bear the traits of our fallen human family.

Our human nature is to sin, and until we receive a new nature we will continue to sin. Our old nature will reveal itself. It cannot be otherwise. In our spiritually dead condition our actions are characterized by anger, passion, hateful feelings, insults, and obscene talk—the deeds of the old self or nature (Colossians 3:8-9). In this condition we cannot have fellowship with God, for there is nothing in us to make us worthy. We are slaves to sin (Romans 7:14), and the ability to do good is not in us, even though the desire to do good may be in us (v. 18). Spiritually dead people follow the world's evil way. And they obey the enemy of God, Satan, the spirit who now controls the people who disobey God. They live according to natural desires, doing what suits the wishes of their own bodies and minds. They are destined for God's anger (Ephesians 2:1-3).

8 Circle the letters of the TRUE statements.

a People need to be regenerated because they are spiritually dead, and in this condition they are unfit to have fellowship with God.

b People commit sin because of their bad environment and the bad influence of their families, and not because of personal sin.

c Sin is the result of the corrupt sinful nature that we inherited from Adam.

Sin has completely corrupted people in spirit, soul, and body. In addition to being *spiritually* dead, people's *intellects* were also affected by the Fall. In spite of the achievements of modern society, people are dead to the things of God (1 Corinthians 2:14), and the most intelligent people who have not been regenerated "are darkened in their understanding and separated from the life of God because of the ignorance that is in them due to the hardening of their hearts" (Ephesians 4:18). But even in their fallen condition, people are the crown of God's creation. They still bear the image of God, and although they lack understanding of God, their intelligence in other areas is remarkable. In the Fall they did not lose the ability to know, to understand. However, lacking the spiritual dimension, they have incomplete knowledge. They have the facts, but they don't know how to interpret these facts. Therefore, they develop their own philosophy of life, which generally does not include God. Or, their concept of God is seriously in error and does not represent correctly the nature of God nor the way He should be worshiped.

9 Read Romans 1:18-32 and answer the following questions.

a How do people know about God?

b What can people learn about God from the natural world?

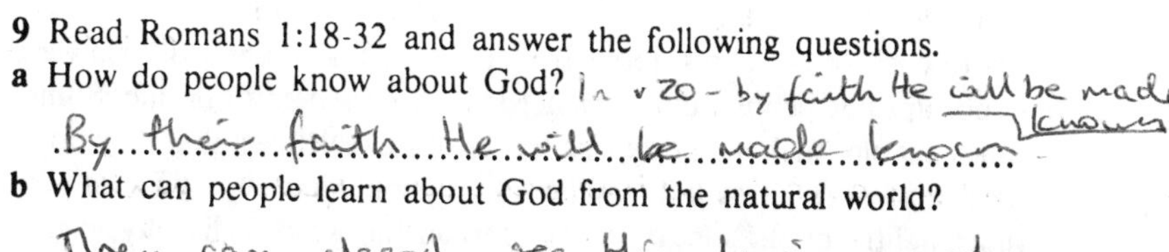

c What leads to people's downfall?

Rejection of Gods Truth which is known deep within / desires etc

d What statement is repeated three times?

God gave them up

Our discussion of the need for regeneration may seem to indicate that only very wicked people need to be born again. But the Scriptures declare that *all people* are guilty before God and need to be made spiritually alive.

10 Look up the following Scriptures and identify in each case who it was that was seeking salvation and was in need of regeneration.

a Luke 18:18-25

a rich young ruler

b John 3:1-21

Nicodemus

c Acts 10:1-48

relatives & close friends of Cornelius

d Acts 8:26-40

An Ethiopian eunuch

e Acts 16:13-15

Lydia of Thyratira

In each of the cases above we have seen that the individuals were good, upright people, but they needed to receive spiritual life. Sometimes people, such as the Jewish leader of Luke 18, feel that they don't need a Savior. There is a saying about people like this: "Those who think lightly of the disease will linger on the way to the physician." Most religions outside of Christianity believe that people are struggling up a mountainside by many different paths, but that all paths lead to the same place. In their teaching we almost hear the serpent's hiss, "You will be like God" (Genesis 3:5). They seem to feel that they are saved by their own efforts, that they will eventually become gods through their own striving.

But in Christianity we see the true picture. People are all in the desert of sin, seeking and thirsting for reality. The answer to their spiritual problems requires that they come to the oasis, to the source of life. Some see mirages or illusions and refuse to come to Christ, the oasis. Here the claim is not that Christ is one way among many; He is the only way. For in Jesus Christ, God comes down to people and reaches them in the depths of their corruption. He quickens them into spiritual life, raising them to a new life.

The new birth means a new nature and the ability to live a life that is pleasing to God. And only the new birth can produce the holy nature in people that makes fellowship with God possible. Holiness is an absolute requirement for people to be accepted with Him (Hebrews 12:14). Thus regeneration changes the nature of people, and then their new divine life is acceptable to a holy God.

CHRIST IS OUR OASIS

11 Circle the letter which indicates the best completion for this sentence. Regeneration is necessary because of the

a) holiness of God which demands a complete change in the nature of people.
b) need of God for fellowship with people.
c) need of people to exercise their intellects as they seek the knowledge that saves.

EXPERIENCE OF REGENERATION

We have noted that while regeneration is a mysterious experience, it is nevertheless real. "The wind blows wherever it pleases. You hear its sound, but you cannot tell where it comes from or where it is going. So it is with everyone born of the Spirit" (John 3:8). We can see the results of regeneration even if we cannot fully explain all of the operation. But we can experience it! Our wonder at the marvel of the new birth experience bids us worship where we cannot fully comprehend.

Means of Regeneration

Objective 6. *Identify true statements concerning the means of regeneration.*

There are two aspects to the work of regeneration; the human and the divine. As we have seen, God alone regenerates. We are born of the Spirit. He alone imparts new life; nevertheless, unregenerate people have a responsibility in the matter: to respond to God's invitation.

12 Read the Scripture references given here and state how regeneration is produced in each case.

a John 3:6 The Holy Spirit produces spiritual birth.

b 1 Corinthians 15:45 By the resurrected Christ we are given life

c Titus 3:5 The Holy Spirit cleanses & renews us

d James 1:17-18 By Gods Word of Truth

e 1 Peter 1:23 God's Word

In these Scriptures we see that all three Persons of the Trinity are involved in regeneration. In addition, we note the importance of the Word in regeneration. Let us now consider the means God uses to bring about regeneration.

John explains the importance of believing God's written Word for regeneration: "I write these things to you who believe in the name of the Son of God so that you may know that you have eternal life" (1 John 5:13). In believing the Word, one believes the testimony concerning Jesus and therefore trusts not only the Word but also the Lord Jesus whom the Word reveals (1 John 5:9-10). "And this is the testimony: God has given us eternal life, and this life is in his Son. He who has the Son has life; he who does not have the Son of God does not have life" (1 John 5:11-12).

Believing God's testimony in His Word means more than simple intellectual agreement to what is written. As we saw in an earlier lesson, the kind of believing that truly regenerates must involve the total being: intellect, emotions, and will. Paul says:

> If you confess with your mouth, 'Jesus is Lord,' and believe in your heart that God raised him from the dead, you will be saved. For it is with your heart that you believe and are justified, and it is with your mouth that you confess and are saved (Romans 10:9-10).

The preaching of the Word of truth is the means God uses to bring about the regeneration of people (James 1:18; 1 Corinthians 4:15). Thus His Word becomes an agent in the work of regeneration, "For you have been born again . . . through the living and enduring word of God" (1 Peter 1:23). The preaching of the Word, then, is the means God uses to bring people to salvation.

A person is *born again* by receiving Jesus Christ. This involves an *act of the will.* Christ does not forcibly enter the door; "Here I am! I stand at the door and knock. If anyone hears my voice and opens the door, I will go in and eat with him, and he with me" (Revelation 3:20). Receiving Jesus Christ involves an act of *faith*, "Yet to all who received him, to those who believed in his name, he gave the right to become children of God" (John 1:12). And of course the *act of the will* and the *assent of the heart* are based upon the *knowledge of God's offer of salvation*, involving the total person in the experience of regeneration.

We see that regeneration comes immediately from God. The new birth is of God, for regenerated ones are "children born not of natural descent, nor of human decision or a husband's will, but born of God" (John 1:13). This new birth is also known as being born of the Spirit (John 3:6). And it is referred to as "washing of rebirth and renewal by the Holy Spirit" (Titus 3:5). And through the Spirit, Christ enters the door of the heart (Revelation 3:20). The Trinity is thus involved in producing regeneration.

13 Circle the letter in front of TRUE statements.

a Regeneration is the result of living a good life and of producing good works.

b The preaching of the Word of God brings about regeneration.

c Education, which has raised the world from darkness into modern civilization, brings regeneration.

d Membership in a church is one of the important means of regeneration.

e Observance of religious ceremonies, rituals, and saying prayers makes possible the regeneration of people.

f Regeneration comes directly from God, is called "birth by the Spirit," and occurs as one opens his heart's door to Christ.

Evidences of Regeneration

Objective 7. *Identify evidences of regeneration.*

When a person is born again, he becomes aware of new life within. He has a new desire for living, and he has real purpose in living. He has a new set of values and his whole outlook on life changes (2 Corinthians 5:17). God's Spirit joins with our spirit to declare that

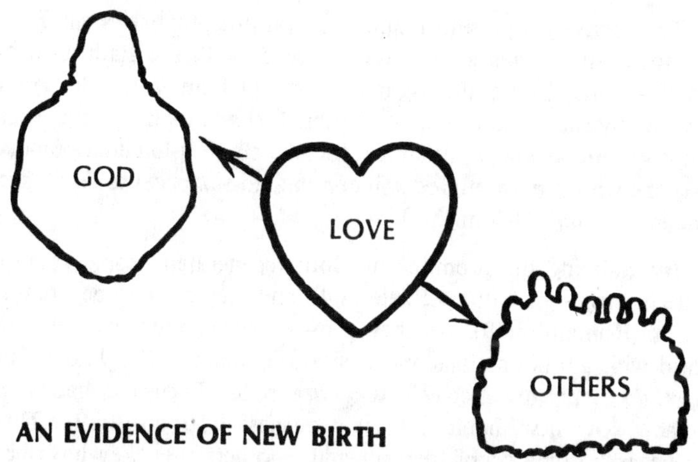

we are His children (Romans 8:16; Galatians 4:6). The newborn person becomes aware of the prompting and leading of the Holy Spirit within, which is additional proof of his experience (Romans 8:14).

The regenerated person has a consuming love for God. The center of his interest is now God and no longer self. God's love has been poured out into his heart by the Holy Spirit (Romans 5:5); and he responds by loving (1 John 4:19). One who is truly born again loves not only the God who has given him new life, but also his fellowman (1 John 4:21; 5:2). This love for one another is one of the great evidences that the old nature has died and the new one reigns: "We know that we have passed from death to life, because we love our brothers" (1 John 3:14).

14 Circle the letter which indicates the best ending for this sentence. The inward evidences of the new birth are

a) a consciousness of one's own self-sufficiency, the desire for greater self-understanding, and a new philosophy of life.
b) the awareness that one is bound to a new set of rules and regulations, that disobeying these rules will lead to certain punishment and eternal death.
c) an awareness of new life, a consciousness of belonging to God's family and of His leading, keeping power.

The born-again person is delivered from the practice of sin. But if he should sin he has someone who pleads with the Father on his behalf—Jesus Christ the righteous one (1 John 2:1). His sin is cleansed by the blood of Christ (1 John 1:7) and he finds forgiveness and restoration; however, he must forsake sin as a habitual practice: "No one who is born of God will continue to sin, because God's seed remains in him" (1 John 3:9).

By claiming the promises of God, regenerated people come to share in the divine nature (2 Peter 1:4), and they grow to be like their Savior (Romans 8:29). As they grow in spirit, they overcome the world with all its passions and desires (Galatians 5:24; 1 John 5:4). They *do* right now because they *are* right. Their old habits are replaced by new habits of righteousness (1 John 2:29). These evidences become proof to them and to others that they have been truly born again.

15 Identify evidences of regeneration by writing **1** in front of each description which is an evidence of regeneration and a **2** in front of those which are not.

1) Evidence
2) Not evidence

. . . . **a** Awareness of new life, new desires and new values

. . . . **b** Consciousness of the Spirit's presence in our lives making our experience real

. . . . **c** The leading, prompting, and convicting of the Holy Spirit

. . . . **d** Awareness of one's sins, guilt, inability to cope with sin and to live above it

. . . . **e** Love of God and of fellow people

. . . . **f** Awareness that if one sins, God provides forgiveness and restoration

. . . . **g** Growth in the knowledge of spiritual things and in the likeness of Christ, as one overcomes the world with all its sinful desires

. . . . **h** Becoming a judge of others and their evidence of Christianity

Fulfillment of Regeneration

Objective 8. *Describe the fulfillment of regeneration.*

Regeneration begins spiritual life in us. The new birth experience, as we have seen, initiates a potential for development, which has as its goal Christlikeness (1 John 3:2). We have been chosen, set apart, to become like Jesus (Romans 8:29). Development of spiritual life will continue as long as each one of us lives and will not be completed until we are glorified. As we look forward to His glorious appearing, we maintain our lives in purity (1 John 3:3). Becoming like Jesus thus involves change as we endeavor to pattern our life after His (1 Peter 2:21). Even now as we dedicate ourselves to Him and His cause, we "are being transformed into his likeness with ever-increasing glory, which comes from the Lord" (2 Corinthians 3:18).

16 What happens after we experience regeneration?

We never cease experiencing until Christ comes back.

---

self-test

SHORT ANSWER. Complete the following sentences with the correct word or words.

1 The most common term used to define *regeneration* is being born again

2 The Bible teaches us that the new birth is the means by which people are regenerated, recreated, renewed, brought back into fellowship with God.

3 In regeneration the sinner becomes a new creation in ..spirit....

....

4 According to John 3:16, who can be regenerated?

...Anyone...who...believes...in...Him...............

5 Two of the evidences of regeneration are ...love...for...God &
fellowmen, & their old habits replaced..
by new ones of righteousness

MULTIPLE CHOICE. There is only one correct answer for each question. Circle the letter of the correct answer.

6 One of the commonly wrong ideas of regeneration is that
a) it is the same as conversion.
b) a person is regenerated by baptism.
c) regeneration is purely a change of mind.

7 Regeneration is a necessity because of the
a) guilt feelings of people.
b) requirements of society.
c) holy nature of God.

8 The new birth is necessary, also, because of the
a) corrupt nature of people.
b) requirements of the Law.
c) customs of mankind.

9 The experience of regeneration is one in which
a) the sinner moves in sincerity up the side of the mountain, and by his own efforts he reaches the top with all other sincere people who have worked out their own salvation.
b) each sinner who is lost in the desert of sin comes to Christ, the oasis, and commits his life unto Him, fully trusting Him to grant spiritual life and a new nature.
c) the sinful person attempts to be changed by education, and he confidently believes that any faults he may have will be cured by more knowledge and his good intentions.

10 Which of the following statements is an accurate analysis of the experience of regeneration?

a) The work of regeneration is a complex operation in which God and people share equally in producing new character in the lives of individuals who truly seek after God.

b) Regeneration is essentially the establishment of new goals, ideals, and efforts by the person who seeks to reform his pattern of life.

c) The work of regeneration occurs in a mysterious and sudden way, spiritually changing the one who repents, turns his back on sin, believes in Christ, and commits himself completely to God.

answers to study questions

9 a In verse 20 we learn that one way God reveals Himself is in Creation.

b They can clearly see His eternal power and His divine nature.

c They know God but they do not give Him the honor that belongs to Him, nor do they thank Him.

d God has given them over to their filthy desires, shameful passions, and corrupted minds.

1 a False.

b True.

c True.

d True.

10 a A certain ruler who had faithfully kept all the Jewish religious requirements.

b Nicodemus was a Jewish leader of the Pharisees; in fact, he was a great teacher.

c Cornelius was a captain in the Roman army. He was a religious man.

d The Ethiopian eunuch was an important official in the queen's court.

e Lydia was a woman who worshiped God.

2 WORDS USED	REASONS FOR
a Born of God.	Will of God.
b Born again.	To see the Kingdom of God.
c Born of water and the Spirit.	To enter the Kingdom.
d Born again.	No reason given.
e Born of the Spirit.	The will of the Spirit.
f Begotten us again.	To have a living hope.
g Being born again.	No reason given.
h Born of Him (God).	To do right.
i Born of God.	To avoid sin.
j Born of God.	To love the brethren.
k Begotten of Him (God).	To love the brethren.
l Born of God.	To avoid sin.

11 a) holiness of God which demands a complete change . . .

3 **a** Crossed over from death to life.
b One is a new being.
c A new creature.
d Created in Christ Jesus.
e The new self.
f The Holy Spirit saved us and gave us new life by cleansing us.

12 **a** The Holy Spirit produces spiritual birth.
b The "last Adam" (Christ) is the life-giving Spirit.
c The Holy Spirit gives us new birth.
d God gave us birth through the word of truth.
e Through the living and eternal Word of God we have been born again.

4 reborn, new creature, Holy Spirit.

13 **a** False.
b True.
c False.
d False.
e False.
f True.

5 **a** 4) Developing.
b 1) Passive.
c 3) Mysterious.
d 2) Sudden.

14 c) an awareness of new life, a consciousness . . .

6 **a** True.
b True.
c True.

15 **a** 1) Evidence.
b 1) Evidence.
c 1) Evidence.
d 2) Not evidence.
e 1) Evidence.
f 1) Evidence.
g 1) Evidence.
h 2) Not evidence.

7 **a** Baptism is only a symbol or witness of the change that has already taken place.
b Spiritual maturity is a gradual process which begins when a person is born again and continues as he becomes more and more like Jesus.
c Each of us has sinned and we need a Savior. If we receive Him as Lord of our life, we have eternal life; if not, we are lost.
d Education cannot deal with our corrupt, sinful nature, the source of our problems.
e Church membership does not deal with the sin problem and our spiritual deadness.
f None of these deals with a person's spiritual deadness and his corrupt nature.

16 We progress in the process of being changed into our Lord's likeness as we keep our eyes fixed on Him. One day as He appears we shall be "like Him" for we shall see Him as He really is (1 John 3:2).

8 **a** True.
b False.
c True.

LESSON 7

God Declares Man Not Guilty: Justification

Pedro was an active boy who gave his teacher much trouble in his school classroom. He scribbled on some of the clean pages of his workbook, making it difficult for her to correct his work. Then the time came for "Open House," when the teacher displayed all of the students' work for their parents to see. On the evening of "Open House," Pedro went with his parents on a tour of the school. When they came to his classroom, he was almost afraid to go in. His parents went ahead, and he listened anxiously as the teacher talked to them. Finally, when he could stand it no longer, he went into the room and looked at the displays.

What a mess he had made of his workbook! He had horrible feelings of guilt and shame. But when he looked at his book, he found that it contained only good pages. All the messy ones had been removed. As his parents moved away, he asked the teacher, a godly Christian, what had happened. She answered, "Because I love you and want to help you, I cut the bad pages out. I want to think of you as if you had never made a mistake or done wrong."

The boy was greatly moved by this teacher's loving spirit. Her act of love completely changed his life. This story gives us a beautiful picture of God's love in forgiving people and treating them as if they had never sinned. It is this aspect of salvation—justification—which we will study in this lesson.

lesson outline

Nature and Meaning of Justification
Source of Justification
Experience of Justification

lesson objectives

When you finish this lesson you should be able to:

- Explain how in justification the righteousness of God is maintained even as the sinner is declared not guilty.
- Discuss the source of justification in both its positive and negative aspects.
- Defend this statement: People are justified by faith alone.
- Appreciate the grace of God which justifies the sinner and imputes the righteousness of Christ to him.

learning activities

1. Read Romans 3, 4, and 5 and Galatians 3. These chapters will give you helpful background information for this lesson.
2. Learn the meanings of any key words that are new to you.

key words

appropriate
appropriation
cancellation
conviction
credit
fate
impute
imputing
justification
meritorious
offenders
pilgrimages
rites
ritual
unreconciled
uprightness
verdict

lesson development

NATURE AND MEANING OF JUSTIFICATION

We continue our examination of the activity of God in salvation with the study of justification. This demonstration of the grace and mercy of God has to do with our standing before Him. In the chain of the salvation experience, regeneration and justification must be studied together. This is so because they take place at the same time. When God by His Spirit regenerates a person, He also justifies him, declaring him righteous and free from the penalty for his sins. Moreoever, He treats him as if he had never sinned. This is a superb picture of love and grace that should cause each of us to respond in loving devotion to God.

Its Nature

Objective 1. *Select a statement which correctly describes the nature of justification.*

Job's question, "But how can a mortal be righteous before God?" (Job 9:2), and the Philippian jailer's question, "Men, what must I do to be saved?" (Acts 16:30) raise one of life's greatest questions: How can a person who is a sinner get right with God and be assured of His approval? We find the answer to this question in the New Testament, particularly in the Epistle to the Romans, which presents the plan of salvation in a very complete way. The theme of Romans is found in chapter 1, verses 16 and 17. It may be summed up as follows: The *gospel* is God's power for people's salvation because it explains how sinners can be changed in position and condition so that they will be right with God.

The Scriptures also teach that God's righteousness does two things: it judges and it saves (1 John 1:9; Romans 3:24-26). His righteousness demands judgment for sin. And yet He provides a way for guilty sinners to be declared "Not guilty!" and no longer subject to judgment. This provision is made by the work of propitiation which we studied in Lesson 1.

1 Do you remember what the word *propitiation* means? If you don't remember, turn to Lesson 1 and review briefly. Then fill in the blank spaces with the appropriate words to complete the definition.

Propitiation meets the need that arises from the ....anger.... of God. *To propitiate* means to ..appease..... *Propitiation* refers to the work of Christ...Jesus.., the sinner's atoning substitute, by which his sins are ..appeased..............., the divine anger is ....covered...................... and the punishment due to sin is not placed on the ....sinner..................................

2 Read Romans 3:21-26 and state what is the main idea of this passage.

By Christ's sacrifice, God is righteous

& so too then are the faithful righteous

3 In 1 John 1:9 we read: "If we confess our sins, he is faithful and just and will forgive us our sins and purify us from all unrighteousness." How is this verse related to our discussion of God's righteousness and the problem of people's sin?

If we confess, He forgives us & wipes us clean thus justifying us

These Scriptures in Romans and 1 John teach that God does not set aside His own moral standard of uprightness when He justifies people. His righteousness is maintained. For a long time it appeared that God was overlooking sin (Romans 3:25). But the work of Christ on Calvary showed that He was not overlooking sin. In patience He had simply withheld His righteous judgment, for He knew from eternity what His love had provided. Then, at the right time, Christ came to demonstrate that through the cross God's righteousness is maintained even as the guilty sinner is declared "Not guilty!" For in Christ the repentant sinner receives the righteousness of Christ and because of this he is declared to be righteous (Romans 3:26).

4 Select the statement below which correctly describes the nature of justification.

a) Justification refers to judgment and speaks of the act by which God *declares* that those who are in Christ are righteous.
b) By nature justification is the act by which God *makes* one righteous.
c) Justification refers to the judgment of sinners as they stand before the throne of God.

Its Meaning

Objective 2. *Identify the meaning of justification in the experience of salvation.*

The primary meaning of the word *justification* refers to a *declaration* of righteousness. It is an objective work that takes place outside of us. It does not deal with our spiritual state (whether it is one of maturity or immaturity); rather, it deals with our *standing* before God. Justification means, then, that because Christ is righteous, God declares us to be righteous when by faith we experience salvation through the atoning work of Christ on the cross. Because of Christ, we can stand before God as righteous.

In the Old Testament a person who was justified was said to be "lined up" with God's law. In the New Testament, however, the righteousness of Jesus Christ is credited to us.

5 There is an important difference between justification in the Old and New Testaments. Read first Exodus 23:7; Deuteronomy 25:1; and

Proverbs 17:15. Now read Romans 4:1-8 and 5:1-11 and state the difference. Write the answer in your notebook.

Remember that because of sin man lost his true relationship to God. And as a result, he suffered from guilt, condemnation, and separation (Genesis 3:1-24). Justification restores man to his true relationship to God. In Romans 8 we see what this restoration includes:

1. It provides for the removal of guilt by crediting mankind with Christ's righteousness: "Who will bring any charge against those whom God has chosen? It is God who justifies!" (8:33).
2. It provides for the removal of condemnation because of the forgiveness of sins: "Who is he that condemns?" (8:34).
3. It provides for the removal of separation: "Who shall separate us from the love of Christ?" (8:35).

We see, then, that in justification God's attitude toward the sinner is reversed, because of the sinner's relationship to Christ. But justification includes *more* than pardon for sins, removal of condemnation, and restoration to God: it also places guilty offenders in the position of righteous people! The following comparison illustrates this important concept. A ruler pardons a certain criminal. He even restores the criminal's rights as a citizen which were lost in his conviction. However, he cannot return the criminal to his former position in society as one who has not broken the law. As a result, the criminal is a *marked* person. This person's greatest need is to be restored to favor and fellowship with society as if he had never been convicted of a crime. For only in this way can he be accepted in his society.

By contrast, when God justifies a sinner, He blots out the sinner's past with its sins and offenses. Moreover, He treats the person *just as if he had never sinned*, and, in addition, He declares him righteous in His sight. We must notice, however, that justification is more than just a *declaration*; it is also a position that the justified person receives on the basis of Christ's sacrifice. Christ's righteousness is actually applied or credited to the redeemed person, and he is considered as righteous. What a glorious thought! Only in this way can a just God justify the ungodly. Since Christ has become righteousness for the sinner (1 Corinthians 1:30), he, the redeemed sinner, is placed in the position of a righteous person. And this has been made possible because Jesus took the offenses of the sinner upon Himself at Calvary, and these sins were transferred to Him (2 Corinthians 5:21). Someone has said "Justification is first subtraction—the cancellation of sins; second, it is addition—the imputing of righteousness."

6 Complete the sentences by matching each phrase (left) with the words that relate to it (right).

. . . . **a** The law demands	1) we are restored to favor and fellowship with God.
. . . . **b** The wages of sin	2) faith alone.
. . . . **c** The sacrifice of Christ	3) paid the penalty and satisfied the Law's demands.
. . . . **d** The one who believes on Christ	4) receives forgiveness of sins.
. . . . **e** Justification is an act	5) of God's free grace by which He pardons sin and declares the repentant sinner is righteous on the basis of Christ's righteousness.
. . . . **f** Justification is received by	6) that a penalty be paid for its violation.
. . . . **g** On the basis of justification	7) demand death for the offender.

Read Paul's short letter to Philemon in the New Testament. As you read through this letter, see if you can locate an illustration of justification.

Did you notice that in verse 18 Paul says that if Onesimus owes Philemon anything, Philemon should charge it to Paul's account. Onesimus would then be set free from any obligation to Philemon. Paul's right and warm relationship with his friend Philemon would be credited to Onesimus.

7 Circle the letters of the TRUE statements.
a Justification is a subjective work which takes place in us and deals with our state of spiritual maturity.
b Justification is an objective work which takes place outside of us and refers to a declaration of righteousness.
c In justification people's guilt is removed by crediting them with the righteousness of Christ.
d When God pardons sinners, He blots out their past and treats them just as if they had never sinned.

Its Relation to the Law

Objective 3. *Recognize differences in the purposes of justification and the Law.*

Paul says that no one is put right in God's sight (justified) by doing what the Law requires (Romans 3:20). This is no reflection on the Law, for it is holy, right, and good (Romans 7:12). It means that the Law was not given for the purpose of making people righteous, but to provide a standard of righteousness. The Law was given to Moses by God so that the nation of Israel would have a clear understanding of right and wrong (Exodus 20). The Old Testament records the history of the Jewish nation and its repeated disobedience to the Law.

Let's consider three reasons why the Law cannot justify a person. First, the Law cannot justify us because *it has no power to change* weak and sinful human nature. The Law can detect sin and diagnose our sinful condition, but it cannot provide a solution which will remove the cause of sin. The Law is like a ruler which will ***measure*** the length of some material, but will not ***increase*** its length: "Through the law we become conscious of sin" (Romans 3:20). Like a mirror, the Law can reveal our corruption and wickedness, but it cannot cleanse us from our uncleanness. We can look intently into a mirror all day, but no amount of looking will cleanse a dirty face. The Law shows us what God's standard of righteousness is. It also shows us our inabilities and shortcomings and how we fail to line up with God's law. But it cannot change us. Just as the priest and the Levite left to his fate the man attacked by robbers, the Law leaves us hopeless and helpless (Luke 10:30-37). It has no power to recover us from our awful fate. Only Christ, the Good Samaritan, can do this!

Second, the Law cannot justify because *it cannot be changed.* It measures out just punishment to the one who breaks the Law, but it knows no mercy. To be justified by the Law, a person would have to keep the Law without ever making a single mistake (Galatians 3:10; James 2:10). And our corrupt human nature cannot do such a thing.

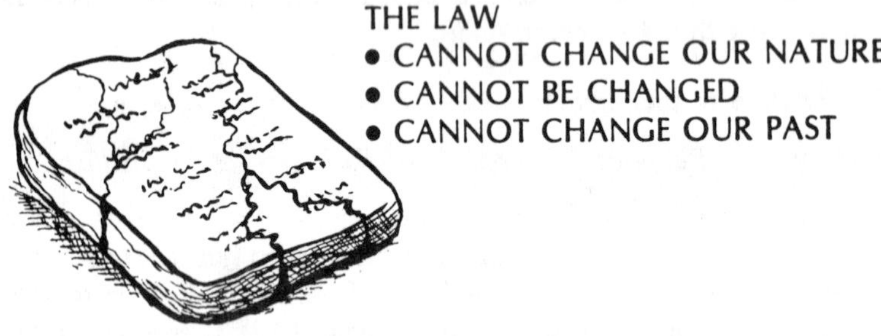

Third, *the Law cannot change the past* or cleanse the inner corruption of Adam's descendants. A person might suddenly decide to begin keeping the Law perfectly. His life from this point on might be acceptable to God, but the record of his past would not be. It is the whole life that must be straightened out before God. Only the blood of Jesus can wash away his sins of the past *and* create a new nature within him.

For these reasons, Paul says that the Law can never justify anyone (Galatians 2:21). It should be plain to us that the Law was not given to *relieve* sin but to *reveal* it.

8 Choose the correct completion. The Law cannot justify anyone because it
a) cannot deal with a person's sinful nature, which is the root of the problem.
b) is unable to show a person his weakness and need.
c) deals primarily with a person's past and does not address itself to matters of moral behavior.

The Law was thus necessary to provide a standard of righteousness. It was given to reveal people's sin, their sinful nature, and their helplessness, so that they could be guided to grace. Although the Law cannot bring a person to salvation, it can bring him to the Savior: "So the law was put in charge to lead us to Christ that we might be justified by faith" (Galatians 3:24).

The relationship between keeping the Law and justification may be compared to a trip in an airplane. An airplane is a means to an end. A person has no intention of making his home on the airplane; rather, his objective is to reach his destination. And when he reaches his destination, he leaves the airplane. The Law was given to take Israel to a specific destination, and that destination was belief and trust in God's saving grace. But when the Redeemer came, the people of Israel were so spiritually blind that they acted like a person who refuses to get off the airplane when he reaches his destination. Many of the Jews refused to leave their seats on the old covenant "airplane" (the Law) in spite of the fact that the New Testament declares that "Christ is the end of the law" (Romans 10:4).

In Galatians 3:24-25 Paul explains the relationship between keeping the Law and justification. He illustrates the relationship by using the figure of a tutor who teaches, trains, and disciplines his pupil until that child reaches the legal age of inheriting. So the Law was the means God used to show His people their hopeless state, the standard of God's righteousness, and their inability to fulfill the Law's requirements. But now, since Calvary, God has revealed that people can be put right with Him by faith in Christ, for He has met the standard of righteousness. He has paid the penalty for sin and His righteousness has been credited to us. Christ has now fulfilled the Law and we are justified freely on the basis of His grace and righteousness (Romans 3:24).

9 Match each description (left) with the concept it defines (right).

.... **a** Makes us right in God's sight	1) The Law
.... **b** Reveals to us God's standard for righteousness	2) Justification
.... **c** Cleanses us from past sins and changes our nature	
.... **d** Has no power to change our human nature	
.... **e** Provides a solution to remove the cause of sin	
.... **f** Makes us conscious of sin	
.... **g** Does not include mercy	

Its Contrast With Regeneration

Objective 4. *Contrast the characteristics of justification and regeneration.*

You will notice that some characteristics of justification and regeneration take place *in us*. Others take place *outside us*. For example, justification takes place outside us before the throne of God, where He declares us righteous. Justification is God's decision concerning our standing. It is that which Christ does *for* us. Justification changes our relationship to God.

As we noted earlier, justification and regeneration take place at the same time. They are simply different aspects of one work. However, regeneration is God's work done *within* us. It deals with our state and the changing of our nature. Both regeneration and justification are instantaneous works.

10 Which of the following are characteristic of justification, regeneration, or of both? Write the identifying number in front of each characteristic in the left column.

1) Justification
2) Regeneration
3) Both

..1.. **a** A work outside us

..2.. **b** A work inside us

..3.. **c** An instantaneous work

..1.. **d** An effect produced on our standing before God

..3.. **e** An effect produced on our inner condition

11 When we say that justification is an objective work we mean that

it takes place outside of us

12 In what order do justification and regeneration occur?

at the same time as both aspects of 1 work

SOURCE OF JUSTIFICATION

Objective 5. *Choose statements which describe the biblical source of justification.*

Deep within the human nature there is the idea that a person must do something to become worthy of salvation. In the early church some Jewish Christian teachers claimed that sinners were saved by faith *plus* the observance of the Law. And since that time this mistaken idea has grown in some areas of the Christian church. It has taken the form of self-punishment, the making of sacred pilgrimages, the performance of religious rites, and the payment of money to receive pardon for sins. In heathen religions, too, people seek to please their gods by the works of their hands. The reason they give for these efforts to become worthy is as follows: "God is not gracious and people are not righteous; therefore, people must become righteous so that God will be gracious."

Martin Luther was troubled with this mistaken idea; therefore, he tried by self-denial to work out his own salvation. His cry, ***Oh, Luther, when will you become pious enough so that you will find God gracious?*** represents the heart cry of millions. Then, at last, he found the truth which is the basis of the gospel. God *is* gracious and therefore *He wills* to make people righteous. Justification, therefore, does not come by the works of the Law or by any other human works: "He saved us, not because of righteous things we had done, but because of his mercy" (Titus 3:5).

Scriptures not only say that we are not justified by works but also they condemn the attempt to be justified in this way. This is the clear teaching of the apostle Paul in his letter to the Galatians.

13 Read the following Scriptures in Galatians and after each write the condemnation which results from attempting to be justified by works of the Law. The first one has been done for you.

a 1:8-9 He who preaches another gospel is condemned to hell.

b 2:21 If a person is saved by works then the cross is redundant

c 3:1-3 Condemned as fools if not reaching salvation by faith.

d 3:10 The law makes demands that no-one can keep, condemned.

e 5:4 Grace is never seen by keeping the Law.

Clearly Paul teaches against justification by works, but some will ask, Doesn't James teach that justification comes by works and not by faith alone? To help resolve this question, read carefully James 2:18-26.

Notice that James does not condemn *saving* faith. It is an inactive and purely intellectual faith that he speaks against. James declares that inactive faith cannot justify; therefore, he insists on active faith—that is, a faith which issues forth in works. Paul insists that good works do not justify us (Titus 3:5). He asserts that it is saving faith, apart from works, which justifies (Romans 3:21-22). Someone has said, "We are not saved by faith and works; rather, *we are saved by faith that works.*"

Perhaps we can understand better the difference of approach between James and Paul if we consider what each one was contending with. Paul was clearly fighting against the notion that a person was justified by faith *plus* keeping the Law. James, on the other hand, was fighting against those who claimed that since believers are justified by grace alone, they are not obligated to keep requirements of the Law or to pay the penalties for breaking it. Those who held this view contended that the Christian is free from all moral law and can utterly disregard it, a view which encouraged loose morals and low living.

Thus, James and Paul do not contradict each other; rather, they are like two soldiers who are fighting back to back against an enemy who is attacking on two sides. Paul fights against those who depend on the Law for salvation, while James is fighting those who think salvation permits them to ignore the Law.

14 Read the following Scriptures and answer each question.

a Genesis 15:1-6 and 16:15-16. How old was Abraham when God promised him a son and his trust in the Lord caused him to be accepted by God?

86 ....

b Genesis 17:1. How old was Abraham when the promise was renewed?

99 ....

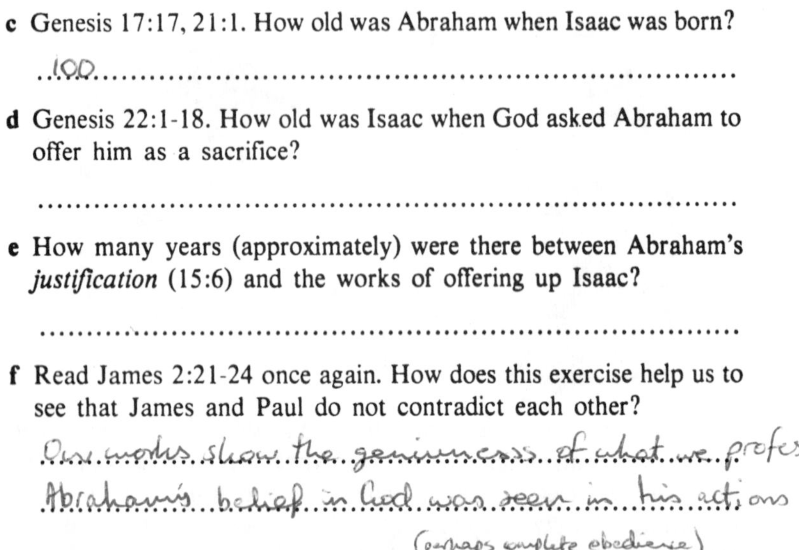

c Genesis 17:17, 21:1. How old was Abraham when Isaac was born?

....

d Genesis 22:1-18. How old was Isaac when God asked Abraham to offer him as a sacrifice?

....

e How many years (approximately) were there between Abraham's *justification* (15:6) and the works of offering up Isaac?

....

f Read James 2:21-24 once again. How does this exercise help us to see that James and Paul do not contradict each other?

....

....

Paul commends the kind of faith which trusts God alone, while James condemns inactive faith which is merely intellectual assent. Paul rejects works without faith, while James commends actions which show that faith is real. The justification which Paul preaches refers to the beginning of the Christian life. James, on the other hand, speaks of justification as referring to that life of obedience and holiness which is the outward evidence that a person has been saved.

Scripture teaches clearly that the source of justification is the free grace of God. Scripture also teaches that the basis of our justification is the atoning work of Christ, for we "are justified *freely* by his grace through the redemption that came by Christ Jesus" (Romans 3:24). God's grace and the cross of Christ are the source and basis for our justification.

The word *freely* in Romans 3:24 has the extended meaning of "without reason or cause." This shows that the grace of God is given not as a result of anything we have done to deserve it, but as a gift, an undeserved favor which cannot be paid for or earned. Good works or commendable Christian service are not payment for God's grace.

They are, however, a practical and normal expression of our devotion and love to God.

You should be aware of misunderstanding that exists concerning grace. Perhaps the following illustration will help you to understand more clearly the meaning of grace. A certain man and a judge were good friends. One day, the man was charged with a crime and was brought to trial in the court where his friend was the presiding judge. After hearing the evidence the judge sternly handed down the verdict: "Guilty as charged. The fine is $400.00." The man was shaken because his friend had not bent the law in order to clear him of the charge, and instead had given him a heavy penalty. However, as the judge walked out of the courtroom, he handed his own personal check to the clerk as full payment for the penalty. In order to keep the integrity of the law, the judge pronounced the verdict. Yet, in mercy he provided a way for his friend's penalty to be paid.

Grace does not mean that God is so loving that He overlooks sin and avoids righteous judgment. As the holy and just ruler of the universe, God cannot treat sin lightly, for this would detract from His holiness and justice. But God's grace is revealed in the fact that He Himself, through the atonement of Christ, paid the full penalty of sin; therefore, He can justly pardon the sinner. His pardon of sin rests upon strict justice: "He is faithful and just" (1 John 1:9). God's grace is demonstrated in His provision of the atonement by which He justifies the ungodly but repentant and at the same time upholds His holy, unchangeable law.

15 Circle the letter in front of each TRUE statement which describes the biblical source of justification.

a Since works are evidence of living faith, they are the basis of justification.
b Justification has as its source the grace of God.
c The atonement of Christ provides payment for the penalty of God's broken law, and because of this God can justly pardon the ungodly.
d When a person believes on Christ, his merit in believing forms the basis for justification.

EXPERIENCE OF JUSTIFICATION

Illustrations of Justification

Objective 6. *Discuss the two biblical illustrations of justification given by Paul in Romans 4.*

In Romans 4 the apostle Paul discusses the experience of two men who are outstanding examples of justification. Read this chapter quickly and then notice especially verses 6-8.

> David says the same thing when he speaks of the blessedness of the man to whom God credits righteousness apart from works: 'Blessed are they whose transgressions are forgiven, whose sins are covered. Blessed is the man whose sin the Lord will never count against him' (Romans 4:6-8).

Notice that in this illustration we do not see faith *without* works, but rather faith *apart from works*. In this setting (vs. 1-9) works do not come first, but faith alone. "However, to the man who does not work but trusts God who justifies the wicked, his faith is credited as righteousness" (Romans 4:5).

This kind of faith, however, has accompanying works as evidence of its vitality. Paul describes the *root* of justification, which is faith apart from works. And, as we have seen, James writes of the *fruit* of faith, which is good works. The fruit bears witness to the kind of root which produces it. In this analogy we must remember faith is the root which produces good works; good works, which are fruit, ***do not*** produce the root which is faith.

In this masterful treatment of justification, Paul uses Abraham as a second example to illustrate justification by faith *apart from ritual.* Paul points out that Abraham was justified by faith (Genesis 15:6) before he was circumcised (Genesis 17:10-14). In addition, he shows that Abraham was not justified by keeping the Law: "It was not through law that Abraham and his offspring received the promise that he would be heir of the world, but through the righteousness that comes by faith" (Romans 4:13).

From these illustrations we see what God's pattern for justification is: we are to come as we are and receive what He offers.

16 How do the two biblical illustrations used by Paul in Romans 4 show that faith is the root and works are the fruit of justification? Use your notebook for this response.
(Roms 4:13 - by faith; Romans 4:6 - faith apart from works)

Extent of Justification

Objective 7. *Select a statement which correctly explains the extent of justification.*

In Lesson 1 we evaluated the Scriptures which dealt with the extent of the atonement and concluded that it was unlimited. But when we speak of the extent of justification, we find that there is a difference. Justification is limited to those who receive Christ. Each person must *appropriate* the work of Christ (Revelation 3:20). We can, however, say that the *provision* of justification is unlimited, but the *appropriation* of it is limited to those who will take advantage of that provision.

WE MUST APPROPRIATE THE GIFT

There was once a young man who was convicted of a serious crime and condemned to die. His mother pleaded with the governor of the state to intervene and grant her son a pardon. After considering the case carefully, the governor responded by granting a pardon. The warden of the prison received the pardon and quickly went to the cellblock to inform the young man. However, the rebellious prisoner refused to see anyone, including the warden, even though the warden tried repeatedly. And so the young man was scheduled for execution. On the way to the death chamber he was informed that the warden had tried to see him to offer the governor's pardon. Only then, when it was too late, did he realize the awfulness of his situation; he would die even though he might have been free had he accepted the pardon. So in justification all who will appropriate or accept the offer by believing in what Christ has done for them may be freely justified.

17 Which one of the statements below correctly explains the extent of justification?

a) The extent of justification applies to the degree of justification; that is, some are more justified than others.

b) Justification, like the atonement, is universal in extent without any conditions as to its acceptance or appropriation.

c) God has provided justification for all, but only those who appropriate it by receiving Christ are justified.

The Means of Justification

Objective 8. *Explain the statement: Faith is the means of justification.*

As we have seen, neither the Law nor good works justify a person; therefore, what people need is the righteousness of God. The righteousness of God is a gift that is freely offered (Romans 3:24). But this gift must be accepted. To the questions—How is the gift of righteousness accepted? and What is the means of justification?—we respond with a sound, biblical answer:

1. "A man is justified by faith apart from observing the law" (Romans 3:28).
2. "Righteousness from God comes through faith in Jesus Christ to all who believe" (Romans 3:22).

3. "Therefore... we have been justified through faith" (Romans 5:1).
4. "Noah... became heir of the righteousness that comes by faith" (Hebrews 11:7).
5. "... that I may gain Christ and be completely united with him... I now have... the righteousness that comes from God and is by faith" (Philippians 3:8-9, TEV).

Faith, then, is the hand that reaches out to take what God offers. It is not the *basis* for justification but it is the *condition*. Someone has noted that there is no more merit in this kind of faith than there is in a beggar who holds out his hand for a gift. Faith is never presented as the price of justification, but faith is the means of appropriating it.

Since the means of justification is faith, several errors may be cleared away. First, the pride of self-righteousness and self-effort is removed since fallen people are incapable of either goodness or justice. Titus 3:5 says that "he saved us, not because of righteous things we had done, but because of his mercy." Second, the fear that we are too weak and too sinful to see our salvation experience through to successful completion is also removed. Faith is both important and powerful for it unites a person to Christ. In union with Christ a person has the motive and the power to live a life of righteousness: "For all of you who were baptized into Christ have been clothed with Christ" (Galatians 3:27). "Those who belong to Christ Jesus have crucified their sinful nature with its passions and desires" (Galatians 5:24). Paul expresses his gratitude for the vitality of the faith of believers at Philippi: "Being confident of this, that he who began a good work in you will carry it on to completion until the day of Christ Jesus" (Philippians 1:6).

18 Circle the letter of each TRUE statement.

a We receive justification by grace through faith—faith provided by Christ's sacrificial work.

b Faith is the basis, not the condition, for justification.

c The fact that we are justified freely by faith removes all cause for human boasting and trust in human righteousness.

d Faith links a person to Christ in such a way that he is clothed with the life of Christ.

Faith, which is the means of justification, is awakened in a person by the influence of the Holy Spirit, usually as the Word of God is proclaimed. The Scriptures tell us that "Faith comes from hearing the message, and the message is heard through the word of Christ" (Romans 10:17). Faith lays hold of God's promise and appropriates salvation. It leads a person to rest on Jesus as his Savior and the acceptable sacrifice for his sins. This trust in the Lord Jesus gives peace to his conscience as well as the hope of eternal life. Since faith is living and spiritual, it fills a person with gratitude towards Christ, and it overflows with good works.

19 When we say that faith is the means of justification we mean that

Having faith in Christ's atoning work, we are justified by grace & the cross

20 How do we get faith?

By ~~believing~~, reading & hearing Gods Word

The Results of Justification

Objective 9. *List the results of justification as revealed in Scripture.*

The results of justification are many. One of the many results is that, with the problem of sin settled, a person enters the company of the blessed and partakes of immediate benefits: "Blessed is he whose transgressions are forgiven, whose sins are covered" (Psalm 32:1). We shall see that there are many other wonderful benefits as well.

21 Read each of the following Scriptures and list the results that are linked with justification. Use your notebook for your answers.

a Acts 13:39 A person is set free from curse of keep and the Law of Moses

b Romans 5:1 Peace

c Romans 5:9 Saved from the wrath of God

d Romans 5:10-11 Reconciliation with God through Christ

e Romans 8:30 Glorification

f Romans 8:33-34 free from accusation & condemnation

g Titus 3:7 heirs of eternal life

Salvation, God's greatest gift, makes us new creatures in Christ. Paul declares in 2 Corinthians 5:18-21 that:

> All this is from God, who reconciled us to himself through Christ and gave us the ministry of reconciliation: that God was reconciling the world to himself in Christ, not counting men's sins against them. And he has committed to us the message of reconciliation. We are therefore Christ's ambassadors, as though God were making his appeal through us. We implore you on Christ's behalf: Be reconciled to God. God made him who had no sin to be sin for us, so that in him we might become the righteousness of God.

self-test

MULTIPLE CHOICE. Choose the one best answer for each question.

1 In justification the righteousness of God is upheld even as the sinner is declared "not guilty" because
a) God overlooks the sins of people on the basis of His great love.
b) in love God provided a just way through the cross for the sins of people to be transferred to Christ and also for Christ's righteousness to be transferred to them.
c) God provided an alternate way for people to be justified by permitting them to pay the penalty for their sins by doing good works which atone for sin.

2 In justification a sinner is
a) actually not righteous even though God declares him righteous.
b) said to be righteous if he performs good works.
c) declared righteous because Christ's righteousness is credited to him.

3 Justification not only brings pardon for sins but also
a) restores a person to fellowship and places him in a position of righteousness with God.
b) peace with God and freedom from condemnation.
c) brings the benefits of both a) and b).

4 The clear teaching of Scripture is that a person is justified by
a) faith alone apart from works or the keeping of the Law.
b) keeping the Law perfectly, and faith in Christ.
c) sincerity of belief, good intentions, and abundant good works.

5 Justification rests on the
a) love of God alone.
b) grace of God and the cross of Christ.
c) desire of people to be put right with God.

6 In our last lesson we saw that while faith is the source of justification it is
a) not any more effective than good works.
b) no more of our merit than is the beggar's act of reaching out to receive a gift.
c) limited by the worthiness of the person who believes on Christ.

7 As guilty sinners stand condemned before a holy God, they need
a) perfect justice.
b) an abundance of good works accredited to their accounts.
c) mercy.

8 Many sincere non-Christian people, according to your lesson, believe that the source of justification is the
a) righteousness of people which results from good deeds.
b) mercy and grace of God apart from works.
c) arbitrary will of God which justifies only elect people.

9 The meaning of justification, simply put, is
a) "Just because I've never sinned."
b) "Just because He overlooks sin."
c) "Just as if I'd never sinned."

10 The extent of justification
a) is unlimited, like the extent of the atonement.
b) is limited to those who appropriate it by accepting God's provision.
c) is limited to those who hear the gospel.

answers to study questions

11 It takes place outside of us when we are declared righteous before the throne of God.

1 anger, appease (or satisfy), Christ, covered, appeased (or satisfied), sinner.

12 They occur at the same time.

2 Christ's sacrifice shows that God is righteous and at the same time declares that people who put their faith in Christ are righteous.

13 **b** If a person is saved by works then Christ died for nothing.
c It is foolish to attempt to be justified by works of the Law.
d Those who attempt to be justified by keeping the Law live under a curse.
e The person who thinks he can be put right with God simply by obeying the Law has cut himself off from Christ.

3 God is just and right when He forgives our sins.

14 **a** We can't say specifically, but he may not have been older than 86.
b He was 99.
c He was 100.
d We can't say for sure, but he could have been approximately 15. He was old enough to carry wood up the mountain (v. 6). Abraham would have then been 115.
e We don't know exactly, but it could have been as much as 30 years.
f James knew quite well the chronology of Abraham's life. He knew that Abraham was justified from the beginning (Genesis 15:6) and he commended the living works which showed that faith was real. Abraham was justified because he ***believed God,*** and his belief in God was seen in his actions.

4 a) Justification refers to judgment and speaks of the act...

15 **a** False.
b True.
c True.
d False.

5 In the Old Testament only the innocent person is declared "not guilty"; whereas in the New Testament it is helpless and wicked sinners who are declared to be righteous.

16 Your answer. I've noted that in his illustrations, Paul shows that David speaks of justification *apart from works*. He speaks of the blessedness the guilty one has in receiving the verdict of "not guilty" on the basis of faith alone. Abraham represents the beauty of justification by faith *apart from ritual*, for he was credited with righteousness before God by his faith. This happened before he performed the rite of circumcision. These illustrations show that faith is the *root* and works the *fruit* of justification.

6 **a** 6) that a penalty be paid for its violation.
b 7) demand death for the offender.
c 3) paid the penalty and satisfied the Law's demands.
d 4) receives forgiveness of sins.
e 5) of God's free grace by which He pardons sin and declares the repentant sinner is righteous on the basis of Christ's righteousness.
f 2) faith alone.
g 1) we are restored to favor and fellowship with God.

17 c) God has provided justification for all...

7 **a** False.
b True.
c True.
d True.

18 **a** True.
b False.
c True.
d True.

8 a) cannot deal with a person's sinful nature...

19 we must have active faith in order to be justified.

9 **a** 2) Justification.
b 1) The Law.
c 2) Justification.
d 1) The Law.
e 2) Justification.
f 1) The Law.
g 1) The Law.

20 We get faith through reading and hearing the Word of God.

10 **a** 1) Justification.
b 2) Regeneration.
c 3) Both.
d 1) Justification.
e 2) Regeneration.

21 **a** A person is set free from all the sins from which the Law could not free him.
b We have peace with God.
c We are saved from God's anger.
d We who were formerly enemies of God have been reconciled to God.
e Because we have been justified, we have the assurance of glorification.
f We are free from accusation and condemnation.
g We become heirs, having the hope of eternal life.

LESSON 8

God Takes Man Into His Family: Adoption

Louis was sadly neglected by his drunken parents. He lived a life of misery, fear, and hardship. Gradually he became hardened in his attitudes toward people and bitter in his outlook on life. The government welfare agency placed him in a number of foster homes, but because of his hardened condition no one kept him very long. Many families who knew his pathetic story *could have* taken him in, but they *would not*. Finally, Mr. and Mrs. Burnett decided to adopt the boy, and all the legal arrangements were made to complete the adoption. However, at this point the family who *would have* adopted him *could not* because Mr. Burnett died suddenly.

At last another family took Louis and eventually adopted him. He responded to their love and concern for him and grew up to be a well-adjusted adult, later entering the ministry. Today, his life is a source of blessing and comfort for others. But it all began when he was adopted into a family whose compassion, love, resources, and name gave him a place of acceptance in society.

God has done the same thing for us. For in addition to forgiving our sins and giving us life through the new birth, He has placed us in His family as sons and daughters with all the rights and privileges that accompany sonship. The wonder of this act of adoption is that, knowing our awful, sinful, lost, rebellious condition, He *would* expend heaven's resources for us. None of us can ever doubt that He *could*

redeem us; the wonder will always be that He *would.* He is our Heavenly Father, and we are His children! Is He not, therefore, worthy of our unending praise and devotion?

lesson outline

Nature of Adoption
Time of Adoption
Experience of Adoption

lesson objectives

When you finish this lesson you should be able to:

- Discuss the biblical teaching concerning adoption into the family of God.
- Describe the relationship between regeneration, justification, and adoption.
- Explain the means and benefits of adoption.
- Appreciate God's great love and goodness in adopting us into His family.

learning activities

1. Read Romans 8, Galatians 4, and Ephesians 1. If you can, please read these chapters first for overview and then again for detailed understanding. Notice especially the Scriptures which deal with adoption.
2. Work through the lesson development according to your usual procedure. When you have completed the lesson, take the self-test and check your answers.
3. Carefully review Unit 2 (Lessons 5-8), then complete the unit student report for Unit 2 and send it to your ICI instructor.

key words

acquits	Graeco-Roman	liberation
disembodied	heir	paternal
down payment	inheritance	patriarchal period
earnest	internally	renovation
externally	judicial	verify
forfeit	liable	

lesson development

NATURE OF ADOPTION

Adoption, like regeneration and justification, is a work of God in the person who turns to Christ. It deals with a person's ***position*** in the family of God and concerns his ***privileges*** as one of God's sons. As we have seen, God's purpose for the one who turns to Him is more than just freeing him from slavery. His aim is to make sons and daughters. Paul declares: "He chose us in him before the creation of the world. . . In love he predestined us to be adopted as his sons through Jesus Christ" (Ephesians 1:4-5).

GOD TAKES MAN INTO HIS FAMILY: ADOPTION

Meaning of Adoption

Objective 1. *Identify the explanation of the word* adoption *as it is used in the New Testament.*

The word translated *adoption* literally means "to place a son." It refers to a place and condition given to one who has no natural claim to it. Most of us are familiar with the act of adoption, in which one (usually an orphan child) is taken into a new family where he is treated as a natural son, and given all the rights and privileges which belong to this relationship. However, the apostle Paul deals with the idea of adoption in a spiritual sense. He uses the term *adoption* to indicate the act of God's grace by which the one who receives Christ becomes a son of God. This believer's relation to God as His *child* is made possible by the new birth (John 1:12, 13). However, his adoption is the act of God by which he has been placed in the rank or position with God of an adult son (Galatians 4:1-7). He thus has all the privileges of being a son and is regarded as a true son.

Now that we have introduced the concept of adoption, let us review briefly. You undoubtedly remember that in regeneration a person receives *a new life* and *a new nature.* In justification he receives *a new standing.* And in adoption he receives *a new position.*

1 To review a bit further, match the doctrines (right) with the appropriate completion or definition (left).

.... **a** Deals with a person's standing before God
.... **b** Speaks of the change in a person's nature
.... **c** Refers to a person's being in God's family
.... **d** Gives the rights of sonship
.... **e** Credits Christ's righteousness to the believer and transfers his guilt to Christ
.... **f** Introduces a person into spiritual life by means of the new birth

1) Regeneration
2) Justification
3) Adoption

The Greek word translated *adoption* does not appear in the Greek translation of the Old Testament, but examples of adoption are given. These Old Testament examples show that certain customs were common in patriarchal times. According to these customs, a childless husband and wife could adopt an adult son who would serve them in life and bury them at death. For this service the adopted son would receive an inheritance unless the parents had a natural-born son at a later time. If this happened, the natural-born son would become the heir and the adopted son would forfeit (give up or lose) his rights. This custom may help to explain the relationship of Abraham and Eliezer (Genesis 15:2-4). In addition, if a wife were unable to bear children, she might provide a slave to produce children for her husband (See Genesis 16:2). Should the slave maiden bear children, law forbade the wife to send her away. This helps to explain Abraham's concern over Sarah's conduct (Genesis 21:11-12).

2 Read the Old Testament Scriptures below and tell in each case who was adopted.

a Exodus 2:10: Moses

b 1 Kings 11:20: Genubath

c Esther 2:7, 15: Esther

In the Old Testament the concept of sonship is more important than the concept of adoption. Likewise, being a son by divine regeneration receives primary emphasis, but the concept of adoption is not excluded.

3 Read Exodus 4:22-23; Deuteronomy 14:1-2, 32:18-20; Jeremiah 31:9; Hosea 1:10; 11:1; Malachi 1:6; 3:17 and answer the following questions.

a In these Scriptures, who are the *sons of God*?

Israels people, Gods chosen

b Which Scriptures refer to sonship by birth?

Ex. 4:22-23, Deut. 32:18-20, Jer., Hosea,

c Which Scriptures imply adoption as sons?

Ex 4:22-23. Mal. 1:6, 3:17, ...

We see the idea of adoption was not foreign to the people of God in Old Testament times. However, the Old Testament practices of adoption don't seem to have direct bearing on the New Testament teaching. Instead, it is the Graeco-Roman custom of adoption that appears to have formed the background for the apostle Paul's use of the term, for it contrasted the freedom of a son in the household with the bondage of a slave.

Adoption was a very common practice in the Graeco-Roman world. If a husband and wife had no children, the husband could adopt a son who would become his heir. The adopted one might have living parents, but this did not interfere with adoption. For often families were willing to give up their children in order to give them better opportunities in life. Once a child was adopted, however, the natural parents had no further control over him, while the adopted father had complete authority over his adopted son. He regulated his son's relationships, controlled whatever the son might own or earn, and had the right to discipline him. However, he was also liable for anything his son might do, and he was required to provide for the needs of his son.

Being a part of an extended family gave an adopted child the training he needed to be successful in his future life. He learned to respect elders and to assume responsibility. And through loving correction, he learned valuable lessons in discipline that prepared him for the tests and demands of life. As he matured, he also acquired the social graces that prepared him for adulthood. All in all, the new family relationship gave great advantages to the adopted son or daughter.

Paul's teaching on regeneration, justification, and adoption reflects this idea of adoption. He describes the process by which God takes a person out of his former state, introduces him into His family by the new birth, forgives him for the actions of his former life, and places him in His family as an adult son. The adopted son is thus made a part of the family of God, with its privileges and responsibilities. As a result, all his time, possessions, and strength should be subjected to God's control. Adoption, then, is the act of God's grace by which He places as sons and daughters in His family the ones who receive Jesus Christ and confers on them all the rights and duties of sonship.

4 Circle the letter of each TRUE statement.

a The apostle Paul reflects the usage of the Old Testament custom of adoption in his teaching on adoption.

b In the Graeco-Roman world the practice of adoption was fairly common.

c An adopting parent in the Graeco-Roman system had absolute control over the adopted son, and also had to provide for the needs of the son.

d We become part of God's family when we assent to the doctrine of adoption.

e We are placed as adult sons in the family of God by the act of adoption when we experience the new birth.

Adoption is an important teaching of the New Testament, even though it is mentioned in relatively few Scriptures. Since it is so closely related to regeneration, some people may feel that its discussion is less important. Nevertheless, adoption is an important teaching of Paul, and it is one of the most beautiful and touching teachings in the New Testament.

5 Read each Scripture below which refers to adoption. Note in its immediate setting what adoption is contrasted with in each passage. The first one has been done for you.

a Romans 8:15-16: *With being a slave to fear*..........

b Romans 8:20-23: being subjected to futility......

c Romans 9:4-12: ..children of the flesh..................

d Galatians 4:3-7: ..living under the laws - in bondage

e Ephesians 1:5-7: ..with our former life of sin.

Notice how in Romans 9:4 Paul refers to Israel's relation to God as one of *adoption.* From the order in which he places adoption in this Scripture we see that all the blessings flowed from Israel's special relationship with the Lord. The specific reference here is to the nation of Israel. But in view of the New Testament teaching that the church is the true Israel, it is fitting for us to see similar principles of operation in each. In a sense, then, our special relationship with God is the basis on which we receive all the blessings He bestows. What good thing will He refuse His children? (See Psalm 84:11.) Paul responds, "He who did not spare his own Son, but gave him up for us all—how will he not also, along with him, graciously give us all things?" (Romans 8:32). And while we may not always know what is best for us, God works only for good with those who love Him—those whom He has adopted (Romans 8:28). However, we must always remember that the blessings we receive are not ours because we deserve or earn them.

6 Read Luke 17:7-10. In your notebook write what should be our attitude concerning our work for the Lord.

Gods rewards are of grace, not of merit.

As His adopted sons, we are to recognize that all our efforts are unworthy of the great love He has demonstrated in bringing us into His family and placing us as His sons. Moreover, the benefits of the relation continue as our Heavenly Father ministers to our needs.

Mr. and Mrs. Potter adopted a young man from another country. They gave him the first name *Dan* and of course Dan assumed the family name in the process of adoption. Dan blended into the family life completely and he was treated with all the rights and privileges of the Potter children. The Potters became legally responsible for Dan. They made it possible for him to receive a good secondary education and to attend college also. As an *adopted son*, Dan was well-fed and clothed, and on special occasions, such as his birthday and Christmas, he was remembered just like all of the other family members. In short, he was loaded with all of the family benefits because of his adoptive relationship. This is but a poor illustration of the kind of love that our Heavenly Father demonstrates in saving us, making us heirs of His promises, and daily loading us with benefits.

7 Circle the letter of the correct explanation of the word *adoption* as it is used in the New Testament context.

a) Adoption is the legal act by which a person becomes a child of God.
b) Those who become children of God through the new birth are placed in the position of adult sons by adoption.
c) Adoption refers to the act of a person who decides to adopt a new way of life by going God's way.

TIME OF ADOPTION

Objective 2. *Explain the significance of the three phases of adoption.*

Adoption occurs in three phases. First, we see that there is a *past* phase. In Ephesians 1:4-6 Paul says, "Before the creation of the world... he predestined us to be adopted as his sons through Jesus Christ, in accordance with his pleasure and will—to the praise of his glorious grace, which he has freely given us in the One he loves.

8 Reread Ephesians 1:4-6 and answer the following questions.

a Who is the adopting one? ....

b Who are the adopted ones? ....

c Who made it possible? ....

d What is the source of adoption? ....

e What is the purpose of adoption? ....

Notice that God is the prime mover in adoption. It proceeds from His love according to His will, returns to Him in an adopted family, and ends in the praise of His glorious grace. Notice at the end of verse 4, and in verse 5, that God's decision in eternity to adopt us as His sons is based on His love. His love alone prompted the eternal decision to adopt us. And since adoption results from the free exercise of God's grace, all human merit is ruled out.

We see in this Scripture that while adoption brings tremendous privileges, it also involves responsibilities: "For he chose us in him before the creation of the world to be holy and blameless in his sight" (Ephesians 1:4). If we claim God as our Heavenly Father, then we must live so that He will not be ashamed to call us sons. The experience of adoption involves more than simply securing a ticket to heaven. It requires us to allow the Holy Spirit to demonstrate that we are obedient sons and daughters as we reflect the glory of God (2 Corinthians 4:6). What impression would you have of a person who always wore white, clean clothing but who never took a bath? The person's inconsistency wouldn't make sense, would it? How much more inconsistent it is for a person to claim the righteousness of Christ and yet live in a manner unworthy of his Christian sonship.

9 The significance of the *past phase* of adoption is that
a) the age of a teaching increases its value.
b) it shows us that the redemptive plan of God (which includes adoption) is eternal.
c) we are able to see how the plan began in the Old Testament.

Then there is a *present* phase: "Dear friends, now we are children of God" (1 John 3:2). Notice also that Paul uses the present tense in Galatians 4:6: "You *are* sons." The fact of our present sonship should do several things to us. First, it should free us from any doubt about the future. We do not have to wait until we stand in God's presence to know whether we are His children. We know *now* on the authority of His Word *and* by the testimony of the Holy Spirit that we *are* God's children (Romans 8:16).

Second, it should impress us with the necessity of living in this world consistent with our status as sons of God. John says that those who look forward to Christ's appearing keep themselves pure, just as Christ is pure (1 John 3:3), while Paul urges us to "say 'No' to ungodliness and worldly passions, and to live self-controlled, upright and godly lives in this present age" (Titus 2:12). Godly living is therefore appropriate for the children of God.

Examine carefully Romans 8:14-17 and Galatians 4:4-7. These Scriptures speak of adoption as present experience. They show us that adoption delivers us from slavery, enables us to address God as *Father*, and makes us heirs of God. Once indeed we were slaves to sin,

Satan, and self. We were haunted by fear, especially the fear of death (Hebrews 2:14-15), for we knew that judgment awaited us. But Christ Jesus came to redeem us from the bondage of sin, giving His life to pay the redemption price and to set us free to be the sons of God. Therefore, we need not live in fear any longer: neither fear of death nor fear of God.

10 Read Hebrews 12:28. In what sense are we to fear God?

With a reverance ....

....

But we are not to be *afraid* of God. Fear of this kind is not pleasing to Him, for it arises from guilt and has to do with punishment. Rather, as our lives become one with Christ's, His love is made perfect in us (1 John 4:16-19). We are able to "approach the throne of grace with confidence, so that we may receive mercy and find grace to help us in our time of need" (Hebrews 4:16).

Adoption permits us to call out directly to God, "Abba, Father" (Romans 8:15; Galatians 4:6). This expression has a tone of familiarity and endearment that arises out of our love, respect, and appreciation for our Heavenly Father. As we pray thus, we experience His gentle assurance that we are His children and that He loves us. The Holy Spirit guides us in appropriate worship to the Father. And He enables us to come courageously and lovingly to the Father in accordance with His will (Romans 8:15-17, 26-27).

Another present benefit of adoption is that *we are heirs of God.* And while we have not yet received our full inheritance, we are heirs just the same. Paul declares that God himself has set us apart and has placed his mark of ownership upon us, and has given us the Holy Spirit in our hearts *as the guarantee* of all that he has in store for us (2 Corinthians 1:21-22; 5:5). The Holy Spirit in our life is the seal that we belong to God. Paul also claims that the experience of the Holy Spirit is a foretaste of the blessedness of heaven; and it is the down payment, the guarantee, that some day the redeemed will inherit completely the blessedness of God.

11 Circle the letters of the TRUE statements.

a One of the blessings of the present phase of adoption is the knowledge that we are God's children.

b Knowledge of our adoption causes us to relax as we need not be concerned about our present behavior.

c To fear God means to reverence and honor Him.

d Our reverence is the seal that we belong to God.

e God has given us the Holy Spirit as a guarantee that our full inheritance yet awaits us.

Adoption also has a *future* phase. It is not at the present complete. Nevertheless, we live in anticipation of the glory that will be ours at the coming of Christ. Then we shall fully realize the benefits of sonship.

12 Read Romans 8:23. What does adoption refer to in this Scripture?

The future phase when our inheritance is complete

In Romans 8:18-23 Paul paints a magnificent picture. He speaks with a prophet's vision. He sees all creation waiting for the glory that shall be. At the present he points out that creation is in decay. It is longing for sin's power to be broken, for decay and death to be banished, and for liberation from the effects of the curse. We Christians, like nature, long for release from the present world with its physical limitations, pain, and death. Even now our physical being is gradually decaying (2 Corinthians 4:16). Through the experience of

the Holy Spirit, however, we have received an *earnest* or *down payment* of the future glory. But we yearn for the *full realization* of what adoption into the family of God means.

The final phase of adoption will be the adoption of our bodies. Paul did not think of a person in the state of glory as a disembodied spirit (2 Corinthians 5:1-5). A person in this present world is a body *and* a spirit; and in glory the total person will be saved. However, the glorified body will no longer be subject to decay and the impulses of sin. It will be a glorious spiritual body fit for the life of a spiritual person: "The Lord Jesus Christ... will transform our lowly bodies so that they will be like his glorious body" (Philippians 3:20-21). See also 1 Corinthians 15:35-54. When our adoption is at last completed, then our bodies will have undergone a marvelous transformation. Because of this *future phase* of adoption, let us, with Paul, rejoice that life in Christ is an eager anticipation of a liberation, a renovation, and a re-creation worked out by the glory and power of God. Speaking of the future change we shall undergo, Paul declares that "it is God who has made us for this very purpose and has given us the Spirit as a deposit, guaranteeing what is to come" (2 Corinthians 5:5).

In adoption, God's grace flows like a river out of eternity into time and back into eternity again. And His grace, like a strong current, engulfs us and carries us along toward the goal of future blessedness and glory and immortality.

13 Explain the significance of the three phases of adoption. Use your notebook for this response.

EXPERIENCE OF ADOPTION

Means of Adoption

Objective 3. *Select a statement which identifies the means of adoption.*

You might ask, How is adoption brought about? And to this question I respond, Adoption is brought about by God through the agency of the Holy Spirit as people respond to the truth of the gospel.

A person's part in adoption is *to believe* in Jesus Christ and *to receive* Him. As we have seen previously, however, this belief involves the total person: intellect, emotions, and will. It involves *knowing* the truth of the gospel (John 8:32) and *giving heart assent* to it (Romans 10:10). And to receive Jesus and to make a complete commitment of one's life to Him requires a definite *act of the will.* The faith we demonstrate in believing and receiving does not produce adoption; it does, however, set the stage for it (Galatians 3:26). John adds that "to all who received him, to those who believed in his name, he gave the right to become children of God" (John 1:12).

God's part in adoption is, of course, primary. A person's response to His offer of salvation gives Him the opportunity to begin His transforming work. In an instant He forgives sin, imparts a new nature, gives a new standing before Himself, and accords a new status in His family. As the Holy Spirit makes our sonship real, we are able to respond to God, "Abba, Father" (Romans 8:15) with a sense of amazement and wonder. For our adopted status, our new sonship, is not the result of any merit in us. It is God's love and grace alone that bring us into His family where there are no distinctions, "There is neither Jew nor Greek, slave nor free, male nor female, for you are all one in Christ Jesus" (Galatians 3:28). And all, through the Spirit of Christ in their hearts, cry out together, "Abba, Father!" (Galatians 4:6).

14 Select the statement below which correctly identifies the means of adoption.

a) The means of adoption is primarily the result of a person's efforts and desires.
b) The irresistible grace of God is the means of adoption by which all whom God elects are made His sons apart from any decision on their part.
c) The means of adoption is God's love and grace with which He receives us when we respond to the gospel and receive Christ.

Distinctiveness of Adoption

Objective 4. *Identify similarities and differences among characteristics of adoption, regeneration, and justification.*

We have viewed salvation as a single work of God. And we have used the illustration of a chain reaction to describe how the various aspects relate to other aspects of the work. Each of the doctrines of salvation has special meaning as well as meaning in relation to the others. Let us review briefly some of the similarities and differences that exist among regeneration, justification, and adoption.

We see that adoption and justification involve the administration of divine justice; therefore, they are considered ***judicial acts***. Both of them give status: justification gives the guilty sinner the status of ***acquitted***, while adoption gives him the status of ***adult son*** (about which we shall comment further). And both involve a relationship to God. However, the character of the relationship is different. Justification is a relationship between a righteous Judge and a "guilty" sinner; whereas adoption is a relationship between the Father and a son. Justification is basically legal; whereas adoption is basically paternal. Justification proceeds from righteousness; whereas adoption proceeds from love.

RIGHTEOUS JUDGE	LOVING FATHER
SINNER RECEIVES PARDON	SON RECEIVES POSITION
JUSTIFICATION	ADOPTION

Regeneration and adoption are concerned with our being in the family of God. Regeneration is the experience that introduces us into the family of God; adoption follows and gives us the status of adult sons.

The unique position we occupy at the moment of regeneration is this: being born of God, and therefore His legitimate offspring, we are advanced in relationship and responsibility to the status of ***adult sons***. However, all the experiences of childhood and adolescence, which are normal in human life, are excluded in spiritual sonship. And as a result, we are instantly free from tutors or governors and are responsible to live the many-faceted spiritual life of ***adult sons*** in the Father's household. In the spiritual realm there is no period of irresponsible childhood. The Scriptures recognize no distinction in conduct between beginners in the Christian life and believers who are mature. What God says to the mature and established believer, He says to all other believers—even to those who are newly born again. Lest we stumble at these responsibilities because of Paul's reference to Corinthians as "mere infants in Christ" (1 Corinthians 3:1), we must recognize that Corinthian Christians were babes because of carnality, not because of the length of time they had been Christians. As adult sons, therefore, we are immediate heirs of God and joint heirs with Jesus Christ. And this privileged status enables us to inherit immediate blessings and benefits, as we shall see.

15 Identify similarities and differences between characteristics of adoption, justification, and regeneration by circling the answers of statements which are TRUE.

a Justification and adoption are considered judicial acts because they involve the administration of divine justice.

b Justification gives the status of ***righteous*** to one who believes in Christ, while adoption gives him the status of ***adult son***.

c The relationship involved in justification is that of a father to a son; whereas in adoption the relationship is that of a righteous judge to a guilty sinner.

d Both adoption and regeneration concern the believer's being in the family of God.

e Adoption introduces us into the family of God and regeneration gives us the status of adult sons.

f Whereas regeneration is an instantaneous act, adoption requires a time of probation, that is, of testing, to see whether the adopted one is deserving of the benefits of sonship.

Blessings of Adoption

Objective 5. *Recognize statements which describe the blessings of adoption.*

Adoption produces certain benefits that we have chosen to call *blessings*. One of the greatest is the witness of God's Spirit with our spirit which shows that our sonship is real and assures us of the Father's love and concern for us (Romans 8:15). But there are many other important benefits also.

16 Read the following Scriptures and list the effects of adoption.

a Matthew 7:9-11 good things / gifts ....

b Psalm 23:1 Our needs met - I shall not want.

c Psalm 144:1-2 victory ....

d John 14:26 Holy Spirit is to help us in all.

e Hebrews 12:7 chastening - corrective discipline.

f Hebrews 4:14-16 grace & mercy from Christ in time of need.

g Romans 8:17 We are not alone ....

Notice that all of the preceding results of adoption are present experiences. Note, too, that the emphasis is on what God does. Some additional provisions that result from adoption are:

1. Our Father supplies our needs out of His boundless supply (Philippians 4:19).
2. He delivers us from legal bondage (Galatians 4:4-5).
3. He delivers us from fear (Romans 8:15; 2 Timothy 1:7).
4. He brings us into fellowship with Himself (1 John 1:3).

These blessings and countless others are directed to meeting believers' basic needs.

In adopting us God intends to bring glory to His name. In adoption He magnifies His grace and love. In fact, all that God does in saving us will ultimately bring glory to His name. And perhaps His glory is nowhere more evident than in the many blessings which flow out of adoption.

17 Circle the letter of the statement which does NOT describe the blessings of adoption.

a) We receive all of the Father's understanding, care, and compassion, as well as the necessities of natural and spiritual life.
b) We receive protection, instruction, and correction which arises out of His loving concern for us. And we receive assurance of sonship also.
c) We have confidence and boldness as we enter into God's presence, and we become heirs of God and joint heirs with Christ.
d) We are assured that once we are adopted, we are guaranteed eternal life regardless of our manner of life after adoption.

Evidences of Adoption

Objective 6. *Give examples of internal and external evidences of our adoption.*

Adoption is basically an objective work; that is, it takes place outside of us. We depend primarily on the Word of God to verify the fact of our sonship. It is, then, the chief external evidence of our adoptive status. Nevertheless, adoption becomes apparent to us by the things we experience internally and demonstrate externally.

18 Consider each of the following Scriptures and list the evidences of adoption that are referred to.

a Romans 8:4; Galatians 5:18: ....

b Galatians 4:5-6: ....

c Ephesians 3:12: ....

d 1 John 2:9-11; 5:1: ....

e 1 John 5:1-3: ....

While none of us is perfect in demonstrating these evidences, we will grow progressively in Christlikeness as we walk in the Spirit and are led by Him (Romans 8:15-16). This progressive change in us will be an obvious demonstration that we are His children.

Knowing that you are a part of the family of God should make you eternally grateful and joyful. This knowledge should also cause you to make a firm commitment: that by the grace of God, you will never do anything to bring dishonor or shame to the family of God. May you ever seek to bear the name with dignity and pride, never forgetting that you are part of a vast royal priesthood of believers whose purpose is to show forth the praises of Him who has called you out of darkness into His wonderful light (1 Peter 2:9).

19 Give an example of something which confirms internally to us our adoption by God. Use your notebook for this answer.

20 Give an example of an external evidence that we are children of God. Use your notebook for this response also.

The doctrine of adoption calls to mind the case of John and Joan Murphy, a childless couple. The Murphys had been married over ten years when they were asked if they were interested in adopting a baby who was to be born to a young lady who could not take care of it. They were assured that the baby was coming from a distinguished family. The Murphys accepted the offer and rejoiced, believing that this was an answer to their prayers. They eagerly shared the good news with their friends. When little Beth was born, she appeared to be perfect, a beautiful bundle of joy. However, within a few hours the doctor who had delivered the baby telephoned the Murphys and told them frankly that little Beth had a cleft palate—a deformity in the roof of the mouth. He said, "Do you still want her?" John answered without hesitation, "Yes! We've told everyone that little Beth is an answer to prayer—a gift from God. And even though this deformity has appeared, we love her just the same." However, just before the Murphys went to claim the baby, opposition arose about the legality of the adoption, since the Murphys lived in a state other than the one in which little Beth was born. The Murphys' minister, who had helped arrange the adoption, went to the Attorney General, the state's highest legal authority, for advice. From the Attorney General he learned that if the Murphys would immediately take the baby to their home, there would be no legal barrier to the adoption. Thus, the Murphys rushed to the hospital and took little Beth to be their child. Within a few months Beth underwent surgery to correct the cleft palate. The operation was successful and little Beth was perfectly normal.

In this story we see an illustration of the love of God who adopted us when we were lost, hopeless, unfit, and condemned to die. We were tainted by a carnal nature—less than the perfect specimens God desired. But he loved us and drew us to Himself. And even as He was bringing us to Himself, the archenemy of our souls sought to block the transaction and keep us in bondage. But God through Christ removed the obstacles to our adoption by His death on the cross. And we have now been brought into His family: cleansed, healed, clothed in His righteousness, and made immediate beneficiaries of His blessings. For this transaction which liberated us and brought us into His family we may rejoice throughout eternity.

self-test

1 The biblical teaching on adoption shows that it is an act of God's grace by which we are

a) assured of adopted status as God's sons in the future when we see Jesus face to face.
b) placed as sons in God's family, receiving all the rights and privileges of sonship.
c) declared to be the sons of God, although we must await the benefits of sonship until we reach "maturity."

2 When we become sons of God by receiving Jesus Christ, God treats us as

a) servants who are still under the bondage of servitude.
b) young children still under "tutors and governors."
c) those who have received the adoption of adult sons—as heirs who can draw on the rights of inheritance.

3 The part of people in adoption is to
a) strive to become worthy of sonship in the family of God.
b) believe in the Lord Jesus and receive Him.
c) desire adoption with all the benefits this status provides.

4 From the divine side of adoption, God's part is seen in that He
a) accepts us as *minor children* who must come to spiritual maturity *before* adoption is complete.
b) declares us adopted and invites us to act as if our sonship is real.
c) receives us, adopts us as His own, and gives us the Holy Spirit who seals our sonship.

5 When we speak of the time of adoption, we understand that adoption
a) has eternally been part of God's redemptive plan.
b) refers exclusively to the act of adoption which makes one a child of God at regeneration.
c) speaks primarily of the future when even the physical body will be changed.

6 Which of these is NOT a benefit of adoption?
a) Deliverance from the bondage of legalism
b) Provision of correction
c) Inheritance of God's provisions
d) Status as legal bondservants

7 Adoption into the family of God as taught by the apostle Paul was influenced most by
a) Old Testament precedent and practice.
b) the Graeco-Roman custom of adoption.
c) Middle Eastern and Oriental customs.

8 Adoption, which was conceived in eternity,
a) is fully consummated in time.
b) is begun in time and will be completed in eternity future.
c) will only be revealed and completed in eternity future.

9 The final phase of adoption concerns the adoption of our
a) spirits, by which our salvation is determined.
b) souls, by which we become complete spiritual beings.
c) bodies, making us completely fit for the life of spiritual persons in His presence.

10 Matching. Match the description (left) with the correct doctrine (right).

.2. . **a** Is a change of rank and position, deals with a person's privileges as a son of God	1) Regeneration
.1. . **b** Is a change of a person's nature	2) Justification
.3. . **c** Is a change of a person's standing before God	3) Adoption

> Before you continue your study with Lesson 9, be sure to complete your unit student report for Unit 2 and return the answer sheet to your ICI instructor.

answers to study questions

11 **a** True.
b False.
c True.
d False.
e True.

1 **a** 2) Justification.
b 1) Regeneration.
c 3) Adoption.
d 3) Adoption.
e 2) Justification
f 1) Regeneration.

12 It refers to the final redemption of our bodies.

2 a Moses was adopted by Pharaoh's daughter.
b Genubath was adopted by Queen Tahpenes.
c Esther was adopted by her cousin Mordecai.

13 Adoption flows out of the decision of God in eternity past, becomes a reality in the believer's present experience, and is fully realized in eternity in the future.

3 a The people of Israel.
b Exodus 4:22-23; Deuteronomy 32:18-20; Jeremiah 31:9; Malachi 1:6.
c Deuteronomy 14:1-2; Hosea 1:10; 11:1; Malachi 3:17.

14 c) The means of adoption is God's love and grace . . .

4 a False.
b True.
c True.
d False. (We become part of God's family by means of the new birth experience.)
e True.

15 a True.
b True.
c False. (Actually the reverse of these statements is true.)
d True.
e False. (Actually, the reverse of these is true.)
f False.

5 b With the groaning of creation and our own expectation of the future fulfillment.
c Adopted ones are contrasted with those who are not God's adopted people.
d With bondage under the Law.
e With our former life of sin.

16 a We receive good gifts from the Father.
b We receive the necessities of life.
c We receive protection.
d We receive instruction.

e We receive correction which arises out of His loving concern for us.
f We have confidence and boldness as we come into the presence of God.
g We become heirs of God with Christ. (See also 1 Peter 1:3-5.)

6 When we have done everything we have been commanded to do, we have no cause for pride or self-satisfaction. At this point we are *only ordinary servants*; we have *only* done our duty.

17 d) We are assured that once we are adopted . . .

7 b) Those who become children of God through the new birth are placed in the position of adult sons by adoption.

18 **a** We are led by the Spirit.
b We have a sense of belonging to the Father.
c We have confidence as we approach our Heavenly Father.
d We have love for all the people of God.
e We obey God.

8 **a** God.
b We are.
c Jesus Christ.
d The good pleasure of God's will.
e That we might praise Him for His glorious grace.

19 Your answer. Perhaps you mentioned the peace, assurance, and joy we experience when we accept Christ and live for Him.

9 b) it shows us that the redemptive plan of God . . .

20 Your answer. The fruit of the Spirit in our lives (Galatians 5:22-23) is outward evidence of our adoption into God's family.

10 We are to stand in awe (reverence) of Him. He is the sovereign of the universe, and He is our Creator.

Unit 3

WHAT GOD COMPLETES

LESSON 9

The Perfecting of Man's Nature: Sanctification

Most people like to hear stories which involve a struggle between a hero (the good man in the story) and a villain (the bad man). The good man always does what is right, and the bad man always does what is wrong. When the hero is winning, we are happy. If the villain appears to be winning, we start cheering for the hero to take control. This kind of story ends with the hero winning in the struggle against the villain.

We are all born with a sinful, wicked nature. This sinful nature is the "villain" or "bad man" in our lives. It is that part of us which causes us to do wrong. When we accept Christ as our Savior we receive a new spiritual nature. We could call this nature the "hero" or "good man" in our lives. When we allow the old, sinful nature to control us, our new nature becomes weak and the old nature becomes strong. But if we allow the Holy Spirit to control us, He strengthens our new nature and we are able to overcome the temptations of the old nature. Like the villain in the story, the old nature is never completely overcome in this life, but it becomes weaker and weaker until it no longer has control over us. And as our new nature becomes stronger, we become more and more like our Savior, Jesus Christ.

The process by which we become more and more like Christ is called *sanctification*. It becomes possible through the new birth, or conversion experience. It develops as we yield to the Spirit and allow our new nature to control our lives. In this lesson we will see how the process takes place, and what we can do to allow this new nature to be the "hero" which helps us to win in the struggle against sin and become like Christ.

lesson outline

Nature of Sanctification
Receivers of Sanctification
Experience of Sanctification

lesson objectives

When you finish this lesson you should be able to:

- State the purpose of sanctification.
- Differentiate between positional and progressive sanctification.
- Discuss the process of sanctification in the life of a believer.
- Appreciate the ministry of the Holy Spirit in the life of the believer which has as its goal the development of spiritual maturity and Christlikeness.

learning activities

1. Read Romans 6, 7, and 8, and Colossians 3:1-10 in preparation for the lesson development.
2. Check the glossary at the end of the study guide for definitions of words you do not understand.

key words

ethical
majestic
moral
positional
profane
progressive
restrain
secular
subjection
upright

lesson development

NATURE OF SANCTIFICATION

Objective 1. *Recognize an example of sanctification.*

We believers are involved in three "deaths." First, we are the victims of condemnation because of our death *in* sin (Ephesians 2:1; Colossians 2:13). Sin has corrupted us and brought us to the condition of spiritual death or separation from God. Second, we are involved in death *for* sin in justification. Since Christ endured for us upon the cross the sentence for our sin, we are counted as having endured it in Him. What He did *for* us is considered as having been done *by* us (2 Corinthians 5:14; Galatians 2:20). As a result we are considered legally free from the penalty of sin if we believe in and accept what He did for us. And finally, we must experience death *to* sin (Romans 6:11). What is true *for* us must be made real *in* us. Death to the *penalty* of sin must be followed by death to the *power* of sin. This "death" is brought about by the power of the Holy Spirit who dwells within us (Romans 8:13).

Sanctification involves putting off the *old self* and putting on the *new* (Ephesians 4:22, 24). The old self is the corrupt nature which every one of us has when he is born into this world. The new self is the new nature that is born in a person at regeneration. When Paul speaks of getting rid of this old self, he does not mean that the old self is destroyed; rather, he means that it is replaced by the new self. And when he speaks of *putting on* the new self, he means that the born-again person should begin to exercise the graces of the new self: ". . . compassion, kindness, humility, gentleness and patience." Moreover, he charges born-again persons: "Bear with each other and forgive whatever grievances you may have against one another. Forgive as the Lord forgave you" (Colossians 3:12-13).

Our old self was that disposition which rules us, with the capacity to serve Satan, self, and sin. But the new self, which the Holy Spirit has produced in us, gives us the capacity to serve God and people, and stand for what is right.

Sanctification involves putting to death the deeds of the old self, that is, our sinful actions (Colossians 3:5; Romans 8:13), so that we do not continue in sin. It also involves the principle of holy living that was implanted at regeneration. Out of this spiritual experience there flows a life characterized by faith in Jesus Christ; a new walk distinguished by new standards, goals, and motives; and a life that is sober, upright, and godly.

We might compare the ongoing process of spiritual growth to the sap which rises in a tree. As the sap rises, it crowds off the dead leaves which have stubbornly clung to the tree in spite of cold weather and raging storms. In the same way, the Holy Spirit crowds out the imperfections, earthly desires, and habits of the old self so that we may live lives of dedication and commitment to Christ.

1 Circle the letter in front of the correct example of the nature of sanctification.

a) John has died sufficiently to Satan, self, and sin so that he no longer is bothered by temptation and the demands of the old self.
b) Alfred has established Christ as the Lord of his life; therefore, since his new self is in control, he experiences a continual weakening of the old self.
c) Anthony, in one dramatic experience—regeneration—has become holy, pure, and perfect. And as a result, he lives on an exalted spiritual plane.

Meaning of Sanctification

Objective 2. *Recognize true statements concerning the meaning of* sanctification.

The New Testament teaching on sanctification rests upon the foundation of the work of Christ for and in us. This means that because He elected, called, regenerated, justified, and adopted us, we respond with upright living. We see, then, that sanctification is closely related to all the doctrines of salvation. It is the logical result of all of them.

Notice in Ephesians 2:8-10 the various doctrines we have considered:

> For it is by *grace* you have been saved, through *faith*—and this not from yourselves, it is the gift of God [election]—not by works [justification], so that no one can boast. For we are God's workmanship [election], created in Christ Jesus [regeneration] to do good works, which God prepared in advance [foreordination] for us to do.

2 Reread Ephesians 2:8-10 and state what should be the result of all these provisions.

....

....

The literal meaning of *to sanctify* is "to make holy or to consecrate." But the basic meaning of the words translated *sanctification* or *holiness* is "to separate or set apart," especially from what is profane or secular (worldly). The biblical words used refer to character, and this shows the very close relationship between being set apart and personal holiness.

When speaking of God's holiness some see a twofold separation. They see God as separate from and highly exalted over His creatures and creation (Exodus 15:11; Isaiah 40:25-26; 57:15). Though His handiwork appears in all creation, He is unlike anything else. And nothing may be compared to Him. That is why they refer to His *majestic holiness*, which speaks of His exaltation above all His creation. Then they see God as "separate from sin." He cannot tolerate sin in any form. Thus He requires that we obey His moral laws. If we would truly become His, then we must be pure in thought, word, and action (Psalm 24:3-4). This separation from sin refers to His *ethical holiness*, which signifies that He is altogether separate from sin.

3 Read Isaiah 6:1-5 and state whether it speaks of God's majestic holiness, His ethical holiness, or both.

....

4 According to the following Scriptures, what happens when a person draws near to God and recognizes His infinite holiness?

a Isaiah 6:1-5 ....

....

b James 4:8-9 ....

....

If you were to enter a room which was filled with intense lighting, every piece of your clothing would be highly visible. If you had on a white suit, and it had a spot on it, the spot would be seen by other people in the room. But if you were to leave that room and walk in the dark, who would know the difference? In the same way, the closer we draw to God the more we are aware of sin and the greater our desire will be to be *sanctified* or *set apart* for His service. It is this concept of ethical holiness that provides the basis for our understanding of the biblical teaching on sanctification. Sanctification is the work of God's grace in us by which we are renewed in our total being in the image of God. As this work of grace progresses, we are enabled to overcome our sinful nature more and more and to live uprightly.

We see, then, that while God is separate from sin, He did not remain apart from sinful people. He sent His Son, who became like man in order to redeem people. Therefore when Peter says that we are to sanctify the Lord in our hearts, we understand that we are to reverence Him as God and Lord (1 Peter 3:15). The basic meaning of the word *sanctification*, therefore, explains why it can be said of Christians—like it was said of the Corinthians who were guilty of serious failure—that they are saints or holy persons. Paul recognized that while the Corinthians were *set apart* by conversion, they needed to mature in the faith.

In the same way we can understand why lifeless *things* are sometimes called *holy*. They are holy because they are *set apart* for sacred use. We must remember that as it is used here, the meaning is that a person or thing is to be holy because it is set apart.

5 In each Scripture below note what is holy.

a Exodus 3:5; Joshua 5:15 ....

b Leviticus 11:44 ....

c Leviticus 27:14-16 ....

d Numbers 8:17 ....

e Isaiah 48:2 ....

Sanctification implies more than separation *from* sin and the things that corrupt. It speaks of dedication *to* God. One who is separated from the bondage of sin but who is not dedicated to God is like a ship that has broken loose from its moorings but which has no steering mechanism.

In sanctification we fully dedicate ourselves to fulfill the holy purposes for which we have been set apart. As we do this, we are progressively made holy. Included in the process of sanctification there is separation, dedication, and purification.

God is the author of the sanctifying process. It is because of His own holiness that we understand the need for sanctification. God intends to fully sanctify our whole being—spirit, soul, and body. His purpose for this is that we might be free from every fault at the coming of our Lord Jesus Christ (see 1 Thessalonians 5:23).

As we have seen, in sanctification we put off the old self and put on the new by the power of the Holy Spirit. This means that we bring our sinful and willful self-life into subjection. We "put to death" that part of us which rebels against God and holiness. And, in addition, we try to express the new life that we have received in Christ Jesus. This new life is the new self or new nature. What Paul calls *putting off* and *putting on* (Colossians 3:9-10) are ongoing experiences in our lives. They are not crisis experiences that occur "once for all" in a Christian's life.

6 Circle the letter of each TRUE statement below.
a Sanctification means separation from sin and nothing more.
b In sanctification a person dedicates himself to fulfill the holy purposes for which he has been set apart.
c God's purpose in sanctification is to prepare us for the coming of the Lord Jesus Christ.
d Sanctification involves both a putting *off* of the old self and the putting *on* of the new life we receive in Christ Jesus.

As you examine the scriptural teaching on sanctification, notice how it touches every area of your life and every relationship, both human and divine.

1. See how a person acts with respect to God. He acts with reverence (Proverbs 1:7) and love toward God (Matthew 22:37). He joyfully submits to the will of God, and he seeks to conform his will to the will of God (Hebrews 13:20-21). Furthermore, he longs for fellowship and communion with God (1 John 1:3), and he seeks to do everything for His glory (1 Corinthians 10:31).

2. As concerns Christ, sanctification results in self-denial as we acknowledge the Lordship of Christ (Matthew 16:24), and keep Him before us as our example (1 Peter 2:21). Like Paul, we must strive to be changed into His likeness (Philippians 3:8-10) more completely each day. Should we fail, however, we may come to Him for cleansing (1 John 1:9).

3. With respect to the Holy Spirit, sanctification involves living as the Spirit directs and walking under His control (Romans 8:4-5), being careful not to grieve Him (Ephesians 4:30) nor restrain Him (1 Thessalonians 5:19).

4. As concerns sin, sanctification produces in us a hatred for sin as well as sorrow for it (Romans 7:24). And as His grace operates in us, "It teaches us to say 'No' to ungodliness and worldly passions, and to live self-controlled, upright and godly lives in this present age" (Titus 2:12), and it also creates in us a desire to be totally free from sin.

5. Finally, in relation to others, sanctification enables us to manifest the fruit of the Spirit (Galatians 5:22-23). As one walks in the Spirit, then, he produces the fruit of this relationship.

7 Which is correct? We can say that sanctification most correctly
a) embraces every aspect of one's life, touching and affecting all relationships as well, as a person lives under the control of the Spirit.
b) is distinguished by a person's efforts to make himself holy, pure, acceptable to God on the basis of his own actions.
c) concerns the immediate death of the old self and the installment of the new self at the center of control in one's life, making him sinless.

A number of terms are used to describe sanctification. Among the more common descriptions, you will hear the process referred to as *the deeper life, the victorious life, life on the highest plane, holiness,* and *a pure heart,* among others. Here we must point out an important feature of the word *sanctification*: it does not mean the same thing to all groups. For example, some groups teach that sanctification is the same as the baptism in the Holy Spirit (or the filling of or receiving of the Holy Spirit). But as we shall see, these terms concerning the baptism of the Holy Spirit don't refer to sanctification.

8 Read the following Scriptures and indicate what the accompanying signs were as believers received or were baptized in the Holy Spirit.

a Luke 24:47-49 ....

b Acts 1:8 ....

c Acts 2:4; 4:31 ....

d Acts 19:1-6 ....

In none of these Scriptures is there any indication that the experience of receiving, being filled with, or being baptized in the Holy Spirit refers to sanctification. The Spirit baptism gives power to witness, spiritual boldness, and ability to preach effectively. It is accompanied by speaking in other tongues, which is a sign that the experience has taken place. The experience of being filled with the Holy Spirit will affect a person's separation to God and his conformity to the likeness of Christ. However, it is not the same experience as the progressive work of sanctification that is ongoing in the believer from the new birth until he stands in the presence of the Lord.

9 Below are statements concerning the meaning of sanctification. Circle the letter in front of each statement that is TRUE.

a Because of God's holiness, He cannot tolerate sin.

b To be sanctified means to be set apart for service to God.

c Sanctification means that we are not capable of committing sin.

d Sanctification includes both separation from sin and dedication to God's service.

e Sanctification is a spiritual process which does not involve an act of the will.

f Sanctification affects every aspect of our lives: our attitudes toward God, His Son, His Spirit, sin, and other people.

g Sanctification means that we are becoming more and more like Jesus.

h Sanctification involves allowing our new nature to take control over the old nature.

i As the process of sanctification takes place, our old nature dies out completely.

Two Aspects of Sanctification

Objective 3. *Differentiate between examples of positional and progressive sanctification.*

In this section we consider a most important concept in our study of sanctification. It is vitally important for us to understand that sanctification is both positional and experiential; that is, it is a position the believer occupies in relation to God, and it is also an ongoing experience in his life. Sanctification is both instantaneous (or sudden) and progressive. Positional or sudden sanctification is not related to a person's spirituality, and in it there are no degrees. For example, one person is not more sanctified positionally than another. *Positional* sanctification means a change of position by which a corrupt sinner is changed to a holy worshiper. It is one finished work, for Christ Jesus has become our holiness or sanctification (1 Corinthians 1:30). On the other hand, *progressive* sanctification is directly related to a person's spiritual development. Moreover, in progressive sanctification there are degrees: one person may be more sanctified than another.

10 For each of the following Scriptures, tell which of the two *aspects* of sanctification is discussed: positional or progressive. Also, state what the *means* of sanctification is in each. Use your notebook for this exercise.

a Romans 8:13
b Romans 12:2
c 1 Corinthians 1:2
d 1 Corinthians 6:11
e 2 Corinthians 3:18
f 2 Corinthians 5:14-15
g 2 Corinthians 7:1
h Ephesians 2:1-6
i Colossians 3:3-4
j Colossians 3:5
k 1 Thessalonians 3:12

11 Based upon the above Scripture references, when does positional sanctification occur?

....

These Scriptures make clear that *positional* sanctification is a position that God has provided in Christ for those who are born again. It is not presented as an experience we are encouraged to seek *after* our conversion, for it is part of the conversion experience.

Two Scripture portions present the complete biblical position on positional and progressive sanctification. In the first (1 Corinthians 6:9-20) Paul speaks of what the Corinthian believers were before they came to Christ. He reminds them that at the time of their conversion they were washed, sanctified, and justified (v. 11), which brought about the *necessity* for pure living as well as the *possibility* to live pure lives. Notice that he speaks of the washing, sanctifying, and justifying work in the past tense; for these actions were the result of their salvation experience. In Colossians 3:1-10, however, Paul links the believers' *position* with the finished work of Christ and asserts that this experience *must* result in godly living in contrast to their former life-style. Their new life-style, their walk according to the Spirit, is one marked by *progress* in Christlikeness as they move toward a more complete knowledge of God.

12 Identify the time when each of the experiences mentioned in the left column occurs by placing a **1** in front of those that occur "at the time of salvation" and **2** in front of those that occur "in a progressive way."

.... **a** "But grow in the grace and knowledge of our Lord" (2 Peter 3:18).	1) At time of salvation
.... **b** "We have been made holy (sanctified) through the sacrifice of the body of Jesus Christ once for all" (Hebrews 10:10).	2) In a progressive way
.... **c** "Christ Jesus . . . has become . . . our righteousness, holiness and redemption" (1 Corinthians 1:30).	
.... **d** "May the Lord make your love increase and overflow for each other and for everyone else" (1 Thessalonians 3:12).	

There are several implications of progressive sanctification. First, it is developmental, since the Christian is admonished to become progressively more Christlike. Second, since it is a progressive experience, the implication is that it is lifelong. Therefore, it does not lead to absolute perfection in this life.

13 Read the following Scriptures and name the particular aspect of Christian perfection being described.

a Hebrews 10:14 ....

b 1 Corinthians 2:6; 14:20 ....

c Galatians 3:3 ....

d Colossians 4:12; Matthew 5:48 ....

e Colossians 1:22; Philippians 3:12 ....

....

These Scripture references teach that perfection is both positional and progressive. We stand perfect or complete in Christ because of

His gracious provision. And we are counted perfect because we have a perfect Savior and perfect righteousness. But in our own experience we continually strive for perfection (Philippians 3:15; Hebrews 6:1).

In the New Testament we have the command of Jesus to be perfect (Matthew 5:48). If this refers to sinless perfection, then no one has reached that position. However, it is clear from the context that Jesus means for His followers to be like their Heavenly Father in showing love to friends and enemies alike. Notice the way Paul treats the idea of perfection in Philippians 3:12, 15. At one moment he says perfection is not possible, and then in the next he claims it. This is easily understandable when we recognize that *positionally* he was

perfect the moment he accepted Christ, but in his daily, ongoing experience he was still striving for perfection. Colossians 1:28, 4:12, and Hebrews 12:23 represent perfection as a future goal to be reached in the end, but not in this life.

14 Jesus' challenge to "be perfect" refers to
a) the necessity for us to become instantly and absolutely perfect now.
b) the need for Christians to demonstrate love for both friends and enemies as God does.
c) the need to seek an experience after conversion that will make us absolutely perfect.

Those who believe that man is capable of sinless perfection place too much emphasis on a person's ability to live perfectly. They also place too little emphasis on God's holiness and the seriousness of sin. They tend to treat sin as if it were something outside of us. But the Bible teaches that sin is primarily a result of the human spirit. My conviction is that we sin more by our ungodly thoughts and rebellious attitudes than we do by committing outward sins. Perfection is complete because we are in Him, but it is incomplete because we are still human. I believe that there are but two kinds of perfection: absolute and relative. What is absolutely perfect cannot be improved upon; therefore, only God can qualify for this type of perfection. But that which is relatively perfect simply fulfills the purpose for which it was designed. This type of perfection is possible for people.

15 Circle the letter of each TRUE statement.

a One who believes that a person can be absolutely perfect places too much confidence in man's ability to live perfectly and too low a value on God's holiness and the seriousness of sin.

b The people who believe in a person's ability to be absolutely perfect believe that sin is mainly internal and therefore less apparent and serious.

c As concerns perfection, God alone is absolutely perfect; however, people can be relatively perfect if they fulfill the purpose for which they were created.

Those Christian groups which hold that Christians can be absolutely perfect in this life believe that sanctification is a decisive experience. At some point in time following their conversion, they believe, Christians receive perfection instantaneously by faith and an accompanying confirmation by the witness of the Holy Spirit. They insist that in this experience the old nature is instantly destroyed. This view is known as *perfectionism*. It is based mainly on Romans 6. However, a careful examination of Romans 6:1-11 shows that this is the *positional* experience in which the believer is identified with Christ. If this were not so, why does the apostle Paul insist (6:11) that a person yet needs to consider himself dead to sin and alive to God? A person who is absolutely dead does not need to "consider" himself dead. He is dead apart from any "considering" or thinking.

In Romans 7, Paul reveals his own condition: as an unsaved man (vs. 7-13), and as a saved man (vs. 14-24). He finds victory over a life of defeat, not in the destruction of the old nature, but through the Lord Jesus Christ (7:25). In the eighth chapter, however, he shows that the Lord Jesus makes this victory real in the believer by means of the indwelling Spirit. (See especially 8:1-17.) First, the Holy Spirit delivers the believer from the law of sin and death, that is, from the control of the old sinful nature. And then he is able to "live in accordance with the Spirit" and to have his mind "set on what the Spirit desires" (v. 5). Victory over the law of sin and death, however, does not mean the total destruction of the old sinful actions by the power of the indwelling Spirit (v. 3). This is something that each believer has to do repeatedly—whenever the desires of the sinful nature arise to tempt him. "Putting to death" refers to the weakening of the power of sin. It also means putting to death our sinful actions so that we do not continue in habitual sin. For victory in this area the grace of God and the enablement of the Holy Spirit are necessary. (Compare Romans 8:13 with Colossians 3:5, 8-10.)

16 Place a **1** before examples of positional sanctification and a **2** before examples of progressive sanctification.

.... **a** Sarah, who was a defiled sinner, is now a holy worshiper.
.... **b** Philip has grown in his understanding of spiritual life and now teaches others.
.... **c** Paul described his life in the Spirit as a reaching forward or striving for excellence in his service to God and in the development of Christian love and grace.
.... **d** Paul said that Corinthians had been drunkards, immoral, thieves, and liars but that they had been purified from sin, dedicated to God, and put right with God by Jesus Christ so that he could address them as "saints" (1 Corinthians 6:9-11).
.... **e** John, after his new birth experience, stands complete in the finished work of Christ. He is ready to begin living for Christ.
.... **f** James is a conscientious Christian who strives to be open to the leading of the Holy Spirit so that he may fulfill the purpose for which he was created. He is obviously maturing in the things of the Spirit.

RECEIVERS OF SANCTIFICATION

Objective 4. *Identify those who can receive sanctification.*

The people who are sanctified are the chosen or elect of God. Those whom He chooses in eternity, He sanctifies in time. Those who are elected and redeemed are also sanctified. Those who are a chosen generation become God's holy people.

Sanctification involves the total person: intellect, emotions, and will (1 Thessalonians 5:23). "You were taught . . . to be made new in the attitude of your minds" (Ephesians 4:22-23); thus the renewed mind is progressively made more Christlike, upright, and holy. The *emotions* or *affections* are made holy: "Be devoted to one another in brotherly love" (Romans 12:10). And finally, the *will* is surrendered to the will of God and this gives the believer the power to achieve God's purpose, "For it is God who works in you to will and to act according to his good purpose" (Philippians 2:13). In addition, Paul exhorts the believers at Rome: "Do not offer the parts of your body to sin, as instruments of wickedness, but rather offer yourselves to God . . . and offer the parts of your body to him as instruments of righteousness" (Romans 6:13). Sanctification is for all those who make up the church. As the bride of Christ, the church is the subject of this work: "Christ loved the church and gave himself up for her to make her holy, cleansing her by the washing with water through the word" (Ephesians 5:25-26). This was fitting and proper so that he might present the church to Himself in all its beauty—"radiant . . . without stain or wrinkle or any other blemish, but holy and blameless" (v. 27).

17 The receivers of sanctification may be identified as
a) all human beings; that is, sanctification is for everyone.
b) those who are especially worthy to be set apart for God's use.
c) all those who accept Christ, who make up His church.

EXPERIENCE OF SANCTIFICATION

Objective 5. *Choose a statement which correctly states the purpose of sanctification.*

The Bible clearly teaches that the baptism in the Holy Spirit is an experience which normally follows regeneration (Acts 2:38). We see a variation to this pattern in Acts 10:44-46, however, in which the household of Cornelius experienced both on the same occasion. The purpose of the baptism in the Spirit is to give power for service (Acts 1:8). In contrast to this, the purpose for sanctification is to produce in a person the kind of right living that reflects his relationship to God and causes him to grow spiritually.

Some people, however, view sanctification as a separate *crisis* experience which occurs in a person's spiritual nature. They believe that some time after the new birth a person is made instantly perfect from all sin. They claim that this experience, which involves a *decision* to be sanctified, brings the soul into a state of perfected holiness, and includes freedom from sin and corruption, and perfect dedication to God. They insist that this instant perfection is the result of the baptism in the Holy Spirit (which they say is the same as sanctification). Let's examine their claims.

These "perfectionists" refer to 1 John 3:8-9 in support of their position. Read this Scripture reference. It is clear that John is speaking about a person who continues in or repeatedly practices sin. No true Christian can possibly do this. But John does not say that a Christian *never* sins. By comparing this Scripture with 1 John 1:8—2:2 we see what John meant. John's purpose is to challenge Christians to walk in the light and to strive for an obedient and purposeful relationship with God. As if to prevent any misunderstanding, John says to his Christian audience: "If we claim we have not sinned, we make him out to be a liar" (1 John 1:10). And in 1 John 2:1-2, he notes that "Jesus Christ, the Righteous One . . . is the atoning sacrifice for our sins, and not only for ours but also for the sins of the whole world." (Note that John includes himself with other believers.)

We see, then, that sanctification is neither a decisive crisis experience, nor an experience in which the believer is made perfectly sinless. And it is not empowerment for service. The purpose of sanctification is to bring the believer ever closer to the state in which his nature will be conformed to the likeness of Christ. As he walks with the Lord, the believer continues to grow and develop, and the Holy Spirit continually gives him light (1 John 1:7). As he walks in the light, the blood of Jesus purifies him from every sin. As the glory of

BEING CHANGED INTO HIS IMAGE

the Lord is reflected from him, gradually he is changed. For he is in the process of being transformed in His likeness in an ever greater degree of glory (2 Corinthians 3:18). So we might say that sanctification is not a certain *experience*, as is the baptism in the Spirit, but it is a *process* in which our new nature develops in us a likeness to Christ.

18 The purpose of sanctification is to
a) empower believers for service and destroy their sinful nature in a crisis experience.
b) bring about a change in the believer by which he becomes progressively more Christlike.
c) produce Christians who reach absolute perfection in this life.

Means of Sanctification

Objective 6. *Describe the means of sanctification.*

Two parties are involved in a person's sanctification: God and man. From the divine side, God the Father sanctifies (1 Thessalonians 5:23; 1 Peter 5:10). The Son also sanctifies (Hebrews 2:10-11; 10:10;

13:12). And we are sanctified by His Holy Spirit (1 Peter 1:2; Romans 8:13) and He produces in us the fruit of the Spirit (Galatians 5:22-23). From the human side, man cannot sanctify himself. Paul declares that even in the believer God takes the first step (Philippians 2:13). Nevertheless, there are definite means a person may employ in the work of sanctification. First, a person must place his faith in Christ (Acts 26:18). When one believes in Christ, he is sanctified *positionally*. This occurs at the moment of regeneration, for Christ is made unto us sanctification (1 Corinthians 1:30).

The next step is to pursue holiness. We are solemnly warned that without a holy life we cannot see God (Hebrews 12:14). The pursuit of holiness will lead us to the Word of God, for it will reveal the state of our hearts and point out the remedy for failure (John 17:17). The preached Word also has its part in pointing out the need of holiness (Ephesians 4:11-13) and challenging believers to pursue it (1 Peter 1:15-16). The surrender of our life to God is the supreme condition for practical sanctification (Romans 6:13, 19-22; 12:1). To surrender completely to God means that a person must separate himself so that "he will be an instrument for noble purposes, made holy, useful to the Master and prepared to do any good work" (2 Timothy 2:21).

Another means God uses to purify us is affliction (Hebrews 12:10-11; Psalm 119:67, 71). God sometimes permits painful experiences to overtake us. Yet when these times of difficulty are over, we see that they have quietly produced the fruit of real goodness in us as we accept them in the right spirit. God does it, the writer says, "for our good, that we may share his holiness" (Hebrews 12:10).

19 Answer these questions in your own words without looking back at the preceding section.

a Who is involved in a person's sanctification?

....

b What two things are necessary for a person to experience sanctification?

....

....

c How does God's Word help us in the process of sanctification?

....

....

d What is involved in a complete surrender to God?

....

e In what way do times of difficulty help us in our sanctification process?

....

Sanctification brings about increasing victory over sin. This in turn results in greater power in our life and greater fruitfulness. But we must cooperate in maintaining the spiritual progress. We must abide in Christ in obedience and devotion. Sanctification is not a concept but it involves a living person, Jesus Christ, and our continuing relationship with Him. As we remain in fellowship with Him, we are to continue to progress in sanctification.

A little chorus that we sometimes sing expresses what happens as we allow God's Spirit to take control of our lives and conform us into the image of Christ. Let's make this our prayer to conclude this lesson.

Let the beauty of Jesus be seen in me,
All His wonderful passion and purity.
O, thou, Spirit divine,
All my nature refine,
Till the beauty of Jesus be seen in me.

self-test

TRUE-FALSE. Circle the number in front of the statements which are TRUE.

1 The purpose of sanctification is to produce in Christians the kind of right living that reflects their relationship to God and causes them to grow spiritually.

2 The nature of sanctification is such that it represents not only separation from the world but also separation unto God.

3 Sanctification refers to a decisive or crisis experience in a believer in which the *old self* is destroyed and the *new self* totally controls his life.

4 Sanctification is the work of God's grace in us by which we are renewed in our total being in the image of God.

5 As the Holy Spirit performs His work in our lives, we are enabled to overcome our sinful nature more and more and to live uprightly.

6 What Paul refers to as "putting off the old self" and "putting on the new self" are crisis experiences which occur *once for all* in a Christian's life.

7 Sanctification produces in us love for God, Christlikeness, a walk in the Spirit, hatred of sin, and issues forth in the fruit of the Spirit in our relationship to others.

8 Positional sanctification refers to the change of position that occurs at regeneration when a corrupt sinner becomes a holy worshiper.

9 Progressive sanctification is linked to a person's position before God at the moment of justification.

10 It is possible to be perfect positionally in Christ because of our regeneration experience and yet to strive for perfection in our own ongoing experience with God.

11 The doctrine of those who claim that people are capable of being sinlessly perfect in this life is known as *perfectionism.*

12 Some Christian *groups* teach that sanctification is a decisive experience in which Christians achieve instantaneous perfection.

13 Certain Christian groups teach that sanctification is the same thing as the baptism in the Holy Spirit.

14 The apostle Paul found victory over a life of defeat through the destruction of his old nature.

15 The process by which the believer is sanctified includes the surrender of his life to the control of the Holy Spirit and the active pursuit of holiness.

answers to study questions

10

Aspect	Means
a Progressive	The Holy Spirit
b Progressive	God transforms one by the renewing of his mind
c Positional	Union with Christ Jesus
d Positional	In the name of the Lord Jesus
e Progressive	The Holy Spirit
f Positional	Our death with Christ
g Progressive	Living in reverence for God
h Positional	Our death with Christ
i Positional	Our death and life with Christ
j Progressive	Putting to death earthly desires
k Progressive	The Lord's help

1 b) Alfred has established Christ as the Lord of his life...

11 It takes place when we accept Christ, because of our identification with Him in His death and resurrection.

2 The result is good deeds. These deeds are only "good" in God's eyes in the life of one who is pure in motives and behavior—one who is being changed progressively (gradually) into the likeness of Christ.

12 **a** 2) In a progressive way.
b 1) At time of salvation.
c 1) At time of salvation.
d 2) In a progressive way.

3 Both aspects of God's holiness are reflected in this example.

13 **a** Positional perfection in Christ.
b Spiritual maturity as contrasted with spiritual immaturity.
c Progressive perfection.
d Maturity and complete obedience in the will of God.
e Ultimate perfection in heaven.

4 **a** Isaiah reacted to God's majestic holiness with a sense of his own insignificance or worthlessness. Moreover, he felt in an even greater way the sense of his own sin in the presence of God's ethical holiness and purity.
b As one draws near to God and comes near to him, he has a deep sense of sin and great sorrow for it.

14 b) the need for Christians to demonstrate love for both friends and enemies as God does.

5 **a** The ground in that place was holy.
b The human body.
c A house or land dedicated to the Lord.
d The firstborn sons and animals.
e The holy city (Jerusalem).

15 **a** True.
b False.
c True.

6 **a** False.
b True.
c True.
d True.

16 **a** 1) Positional.
b 2) Progressive.
c 2) Progressive.
d 1) Positional.
e 1) Positional.
f 2) Progressive.

7 a) embraces every aspect of one's life, touching and affecting all relationships as well, as a person lives under the control of the Spirit.

17 c) all those who accept Christ, who make up His church.

8 **a** Power to preach.
b Power to witness.
c Speaking in tongues and boldness to preach.
d Speaking in tongues.

18 b) bring about a change in the believer by which he becomes progressively more Christlike.

9 **a** True.
b True.
c False.
d True.
e False.
f True.
g True.
h True.
i False.

19 **a** God, through His Holy Spirit, and the individual believer.
b He must believe in Christ to receive a new nature, and he must then make an effort to live a holy life, allowing his new nature to take control over his old, evil nature.
c The Word shows us the condition of our heart, and it shows us how we can overcome failure. It also shows the need to be holy.
d Separation from sin and unto God, being always ready to do that which is right and good.
e They purify us when we accept them in the right spirit.

for your notes

LESSON 10

The Completion of Man's Salvation: Glorification

From the time of Creation, man has tried to create ideal conditions of life for himself. Adam and Eve started this effort when they tried to bridge the gap between God and themselves by eating the forbidden fruit (Genesis 3). Still later, men built the Tower of Babel in an effort to provide security against natural disaster (Genesis 11).

More recent history records the search of one man for the "Fountain of Youth" whose waters, it was said, would keep people from growing old and dying. Governments have carried out many experiments to create perfect conditions of equality in the law. Attempts have been made to produce perfect health and freedom from sickness and pain. But none of these attempts has been successful, for it is written in God's Word: "Man is destined to die once, and after that to face judgment" (Hebrews 9:27).

Nevertheless, what people have always longed for but have been unable to attain for themselves, God freely offers. In this lesson we shall see that what God offers to those who accept His salvation He will bring to completion at their *glorification*. It is at our glorification that we will see an end to sin, sickness, disease, pain, death, poverty, wars, injustice, and so much more. In place of these things, the glory

of God shall cover the earth and fill the hearts and minds of the redeemed. Knowing this should cause us to serve God expectantly as we await our glorification.

lesson outline

Review of Salvation
Definition of Glorification
Basis of Glorification
Assurance of Glorification
Nature of Glorification

lesson objectives

When you finish this lesson you should be able to:

- Relate the other doctrines of salvation to the doctrine of glorification.
- Explain what our assurance of future glorification rests upon.
- Discuss the nature of glorification.
- Eagerly anticipate the completion of your salvation experience.

learning activities

1. Read Romans 8:18-25 through several times. Read also 2 Corinthians 5:1-5 and 1 Corinthians 15:1-57, and other Scripture references as they are given.
2. Look over the key word list for any words that are unfamiliar to you. Be sure to look up their definitions in the glossary at the back of this book.
3. When you have completed the lesson development, take the self-test as usual.
4. Review the material you have studied in Unit 3, and answer the questions for Unit 3 in your Unit Student Report booklet. Follow the directions given in the booklet.

key words

carnal
chain reaction
climactic
condemnation
depreciated
glorification
humiliation
incriminating
intercession
perverted
transcendent

lesson development

REVIEW OF SALVATION

Objective 1. *Match terms and definitions of the concepts involved in the salvation experience.*

In the preceding lessons we have compared salvation to a chain reaction—that is, when a sinner bows in repentance for his sins and acknowledges his faith in Christ to forgive his sins, all of the other events involved in the salvation experience take place. As we have pointed out, it is only for the purpose of systematic study that we have examined the doctrines of salvation in a certain order. Before we consider the final event involved in salvation, let's briefly review our study up to this point.

1. We learned that in the eternal counsel of God, even before Creation, God willed that people through their union with Christ should be His, and that they should become holy and blameless before Him. This is the doctrine of ***election***, or ***foreordination***. We saw that this was God's purpose for us because of His grace and love.

2. When in time God created people, He created them with a will that was free to respond to His love and grace, or to refuse them. When Adam disobeyed God, exercising his free will, he fell from his position of fellowship with God.

3. We examined the results of sin: separation from God, spiritual death, and condemnation. In fact, it was precisely because of Adam's sin that salvation was necessary, for his sin affected him and his wife, and corrupted all of his descendants also.

4. We learned that God made a way for His righteousness to be maintained through the *atonement*—as a penalty for the sinner was paid by a worthy and acceptable substitute. For Christ became the substitute for people's sin: both for their sinful nature inherited from Adam, and for the sins which they commit.

5. God's gracious *salvation*, therefore, fully meets the spiritual needs of people:

a. It covers their sins.
b. It turns away God's anger against their sin.
c. It reconciles them to God.
d. It satisfies the righteousness of God.
e. It pays the penalty for sin.
f. It removes condemnation from the repentant sinner.

These highlights from Lessons 1 and 5 give us the background of salvation and reveal God's will in salvation.

1 Circle the letter of each TRUE statement in the following exercise, keeping in mind what we learned in Lessons 1 and 5.

a In eternity past God elected people through Christ to be His without fault and to be holy.

b In eternity past God determined which people should be saved and which should be lost.

c Salvation is based upon the grace of God apart from any worthiness in people.

d While all people have inherited their disposition to sin (sinful nature) from Adam, not everyone is personally guilty of sin.

e The atonement provides covering for sin, appeasement of God, reconciliation between God and the sinner, redemption of the sinner, and restoration of fellowship between God and people.

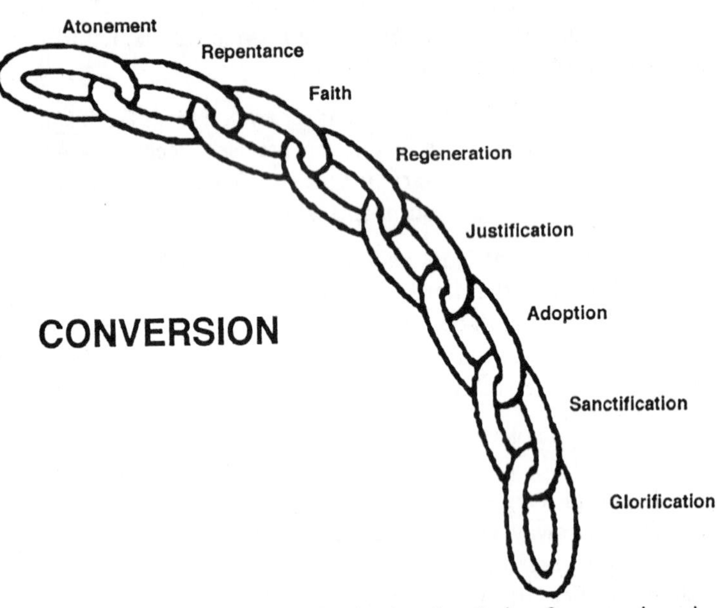

Repentance, as we have seen, begins the chain of conversion. As a person recognizes his sin and turns from it, confessing it to God, he gives evidence of true repentance. The next link in the chain is *faith in Christ*. Faith, we learned, is the voluntary act and attitude of a person by which he places his complete confidence in a trusted object, allowing that object to control his actions. Repentance involves *turning from sin*, and faith involves *turning to God*. When a person does these things (turns *from* sin *to* God), he experiences *conversion*. We studied these doctrines in Unit 1 under *What God Requires*.

In Unit 2 we examined *What God Provides*, which included *regeneration*, *justification*, and *adoption*. Regeneration, you recall, is the act of God which gives spiritual life to the repentant sinner as he receives the Lord Jesus Christ. This instant, supernatural change which is brought about by the Holy Spirit in the life of the one who believes is called the *new birth*. And even as this change is occurring, God justifies the believer by an act of free grace, pardoning all his sins and accepting him as righteous in His sight. The justified one receives a new standing: not guilty.

God does this, as we saw, by reckoning to the repentant sinner the righteousness of Christ (which is received by faith alone). But this is not all, for in addition our Heavenly Father by *adoption* places us in His family as sons with all the rights and privileges that accompany sonship. Thus we saw that . . .

- In **regeneration** a person receives a *new nature*.
- In **justification** he receives a *new standing*.
- In **adoption** he receives a *new position*.

In our last lesson we discussed the doctrine of *sanctification*. We saw that because of Christ's work in us, we are called to respond in holy living. Sanctification refers to our need to be "set apart" from sin and to be "set apart" unto God in complete dedication. We learned that when we were born again, we received a position of sanctification which God provided in Christ. Consequently, our new life-style involves walking according to the Spirit, and this experience (or walk) is to be marked by progress in Christlikeness as we move toward a more complete knowledge of God.

And finally, in this present lesson we consider our eventual destiny as we are gathered together in the presence of our Savior. This is the concluding aspect of salvation which all creation eagerly awaits—our *glorification* (Romans 8:18-25).

2 Identify the basic concepts involved in salvation by matching each doctrine (left) with its appropriate description or completion (right).

. . . . **a** Glorification
. . . . **b** Conversion
. . . . **c** Adoption
. . . . **d** Repentance
. . . . **e** Election and foreordination
. . . . **f** The atonement
. . . . **g** Faith
. . . . **h** Regeneration
. . . . **i** Sanctification
. . . . **j** Justification

1) A new standing
2) Turning to God
3) Covering for sin
4) Process of becoming like Christ
5) A new position
6) To make a complete turnabout
7) Turning from sin
8) God's activity in eternity past
9) A new nature
10) The final goal

DEFINITION OF GLORIFICATION

Objective 2. *Select from several statements the correct definition of* glorification.

As we have considered the chain of salvation link by link, we have been aware that what God has begun must surely be carried forward to completion. The indwelling of the Holy Spirit simply represents the down payment, the beginning of life eternal, which will be completed in the life to come. Paul says he is "confident . . . that he who began a good work in you will carry it on to completion until the day of Christ Jesus" (Philippians 1:6). Thus, glorification, the final link, will be added on the Day of Christ Jesus as the final, crowning act in God's work of redemption. That day lies ahead, and with its arrival our whole being will be set free and all creation will be liberated as well (Romans 8:21-23).

What is this *Day of Christ Jesus*? It is the day when Christ returns for His own, His church, those who have been redeemed and who are trusting in Him. We read these words in 1 Thessalonians 4:16—5:2:

> For the Lord himself will come down from heaven, with a loud command, with the voice of the archangel and with the trumpet call of God, and the dead in Christ will rise first. After that, we who are still alive and are left will be caught up with them in the clouds to meet the Lord in the air. And so we will be with the Lord forever. Therefore encourage each other with these words. Now, brothers, about times and dates we do not need to write to you, for you know very well that the *day of the Lord* will come like a thief in the night. (Italics mine.)

We read further about this day of the Lord in 1 Corinthians 15:51-52, and 58:

> Listen, I tell you a mystery: We will not all sleep, but we will all be changed—in a flash, in the twinkling of an eye, at the last trumpet. For the trumpet will sound, the dead will be raised imperishable, *and we will be changed*... Therefore, my dear brothers, stand firm. Let nothing move you. Always give yourselves fully to the work of the Lord, because you know that your labor in the Lord is not in vain. (Italics mine.)

Also, we read these words in Philippians 3:20-21:

> But our citizenship is in heaven. And we eagerly await a Savior from there, the Lord Jesus Christ, who, by the power that enables him to bring everything under his control, *will transform our lowly bodies so that they will be like his glorious body.* (Italics mine.)

As surely as creation was a historical event, even so glorification will be a climactic historical event. It *will* take place and we shall be changed, glorified in His presence (1 Corinthians 15:54). *Glorification* then, may be defined as the work that God will perform by which He will complete our salvation, making us morally perfect for eternity, and bringing us into His presence in a body like Christ's glorious body (Philippians 3:21). Not only have we longed for this event which Paul spake of nearly two thousand years ago to Roman Christians (Romans 8:18-25), but also we, like Hebrew Christians have "tasted... the powers of the coming age" (Hebrews 6:5). Like a powerful magnet the attraction of this coming age turns our hearts and minds "homeward."

3 When does the Day of the Lord take place?

....

4 What will happen to us who are Christians on the Day of the Lord?

....

....

5 From the following statements select the one which gives the correct definition of *glorification.* Glorification is

a) a term which describes the nature of people's salvation experience.
b) the act by which God decrees that the redeemed of the earth are to take their place in heaven.
c) the act of God by which He completes His redeeming work in us through Christ, making us morally ready for eternity in His presence.

BASIS OF GLORIFICATION

Objective 3. *Choose a statement which correctly states the basis of glorification.*

We have seen that each aspect of salvation rests on the atoning work of Christ. Our future glorification is also guaranteed by His *death*, *resurrection*, and *intercession.*

His death, which is the final effective solution for the problems caused by people's sin, has made the following provisions:

1. God's righteousness is established (Romans 3:25).
2. Reconciliation is made between God and people (2 Corinthians 5:18-21).
3. Purification of sins is accomplished (Hebrews 1:3).
4. Redemption is effected (Ephesians 1:7).

Christ's ***resurrection*** indicates God's satisfaction with His work. In his classic chapter on resurrection, 1 Corinthians 15, the apostle Paul proclaims that because Christ has been raised from the dead, believers shall be also.

Christ's work in our behalf did not end with his death and resurrection. He shows His concern for us by His ***intercession*** in our behalf before His Father in heaven (Romans 8:34; Hebrews 7:25). Jesus Himself assured us that He would intercede for us. (Read Luke 22:32, John 14:16, and John 17:9.) Christ's intercession is effective in preserving His blood-bought people from falling and in preparing them to be in His presence forever.

6 Answer the following questions based on the preceding paragraphs.
a What assurance do we have that we will be raised from the dead to be with Christ forever?

....

b State in your own words briefly how Christ's death made it possible for us to be glorified.

....

....

c When Christ said He would intercede for us (believers) what did He mean?

....

7 Circle the letter of the statement which correctly states the basis of glorification.

a) Glorification rests upon the faithfulness of the believer and results from his complete sanctification.

b) The basis of glorification is the death, resurrection, and intercession of Christ.

c) Glorification results from the works of believers and is based upon the idea of merit.

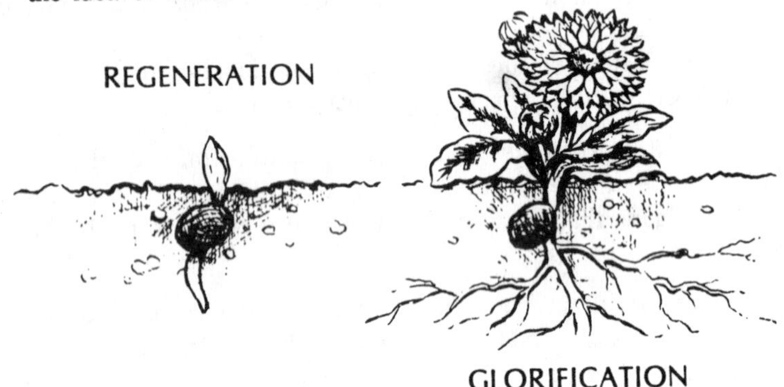

ASSURANCE OF GLORIFICATION

Objective 4. *Match biblical terms which give an assurance of glorification with their meanings.*

While the fact of our glorification is based upon the objective work of Christ in history, our assurance of future glorification is based upon certain terms which arise out of the work of Christ as it applies to us as believers.

8 Read the following sets of Scripture verses, and list in your notebook the term in each which gives us assurance of glorification.

a Titus 1:2; 1 John 2:25

b 1 Corinthians 15:20, 23

c 2 Corinthians 1:22; 5:5; Ephesians 1:14
d 2 Corinthians 1:22; Ephesians 1:13; 4:30
e Ephesians 1:14, 18; 5:5; Colossians 3:24; Hebrews 9:15; 1 Peter 1:3-4

9 Notice how the terms in the preceding verses give us an assurance of future glorification. This exercise will help you to see more fully the significance of the terms. Match each term (right column) with the definition which best describes it (left column).

. . . . **a** Speaks of ownership and security, guaranteeing that the day of full redemption will come
. . . . **b** Gives the idea of a down payment which is a guarantee that full payment will eventually be made
. . . . **c** Implies a future fulfillment
. . . . **d** Implies something to be received in the future
. . . . **e** Implies a full crop; simply the beginning of what will be a great harvest

1) Promise
2) Firstfruits
3) Earnest or deposit
4) Seal
5) Inheritance

These terms indicate that our salvation looks toward the future for complete fulfillment. Our present salvation experience, then, is only the beginning of what will be brought to completion on the day of Christ Jesus (Philippians 1:6).

NATURE OF GLORIFICATION

Objective 5. *Identify true statements concerning the nature of glorification.*

Perfecting of the Soul

Glorification speaks primarily of moral perfection. Of this John says, "We shall be like him" (1 John 3:2). This does not mean that we will be God as He is God, but we shall be like Him in moral perfection.

As we stand glorified in His presence, we shall not be able to sin. Glorification removes forever the possibility of our falling into sin again. Glorified, we shall be like Him (sinless) forever.

The following verses of Scripture explain something of the fulness of perfection we shall have. I have included in parentheses the words used in the original language of the New Testament (Greek) to indicate the degree of our perfection. Read each of these Scripture verses carefully.

1. **Ephesians 1:4; 5:27; Colossians 1:22** (*amomos*)—indicates that we shall be without spot or moral blemish.
2. **Colossians 1:22** (*hagios*)—suggests that glorification consists in our being made holy in Christ to such a degree that we will perfectly satisfy the holiness of God.
3. **Philippians 1:10** (*aproskopos*)—implies the absence in us of any cause of stumbling, so that we arrive at our destination morally uninjured and unworthy of any blame.
4. **Philippians 1:10** (*eiliknines*, used with *aproskopos*)—gives the idea of that which is pure, without spot, and therefore immaculate.
5. **1 Corinthians 1:8** (*anegkletos*)—speaks of that which is free from any incriminating charge. Because of this, on the Day of Christ Jesus we shall all stand in God's presence free from all moral objections.
6. **1 Thessalonians 3:13; 5:23** (*amemptos*)—indicates that we shall stand in the presence of the Father faultless in every part of our being—spirit, soul, and body.
7. **Ephesians 5:25-27** (*spilos* and *rhutis*)—teaches that the church shall be "without spot or wrinkle or any other imperfection."

Taken together these expressions give us some idea of the perfection we shall have. It is the moral perfection for which mankind has longed ever since the Fall of man in the garden of Eden (Genesis 3). Moreover, the society we shall enjoy will be a perfect one, for it will be populated by perfect human beings. With paradise restored, our eternal state will be wonderful beyond our greatest dreams. For with no disease, crime, poverty, and political disharmony, the enlightened hearts and minds of the redeemed will be free to enjoy the wonders of an infinite creation and glorify the One who makes it all possible.

10 Circle the letter of each TRUE statement in the following exercise.

a When John declares, "We shall be like Him," he means that eventually people become God.

b Glorification is an experience or event that takes place on the Day of Christ, after which there is no possibility of our falling into sin again.

c The Greek words which speak of moral perfection indicate the absence of moral blemish, blamelessness, being immaculate, free from any charge, faultless, spotlessness, and being sufficiently holy in Christ to satisfy God's holiness.

d Our future state will include a society that is morally perfect.

Participation in Eternal Life

Glorification will bring about our *full participation* in eternal life. At the present time we have eternal life (John 5:24), but the fullness of this life is still to be realized. Perhaps the following example will illustrate this a bit better. At regeneration the implanted seed of eternal life begins to grow, but it does not produce fruit until it reaches maturity on the *Day of Christ Jesus.*

Eternal life includes two aspects: 1) a superior quality of life, and 2) unending life. When we were restored to our proper relationship with God through Christ Jesus, we entered a new life. This life is in harmony with the life of God Himself. It is a life greatly superior to the life we previously lived. It is truly an abundant life. Glorification is the giving of the total measure of eternal life to us—a perfect relationship with God that has a transcendent quality about it. It surpasses all that our finite minds can comprehend about it, for it is perfect, and therefore infinite, whole, and ideal. And this full measure of eternal life shall be ours forever.

11 When we say that glorification will bring about *full participation* in eternal life we mean that

a) believers do not now possess eternal life in any degree.

b) Christians now have eternal life, but the fullness of this life is yet to be realized.

c) eternal life is something a person grows into when he becomes spiritually mature.

Full Realization of Freedom

Salvation produces something that is contrary to what would normally be expected: as Christians submit themselves to Christ they become free. Jesus said, "You will know the truth, and the truth will set you free" (John 8:32). He added, "If the Son sets you free, you will be free indeed" (John 8:36). The truth, as revealed in the Word that became flesh (Christ Jesus), is what makes people truly free.

Freedom is the very thing people want; and what they want, God promises. But those people who will not give up their own will in submission to God remain in bondage. They will forever be enslaved to sin, hopelessness, and death.

Glorification includes the full realization of freedom. Among other things, we shall be *free from sin. Now* our freedom from sin is partial (John 8:32-36; Romans 6-8; Galatians 5:1, 13), but it will be complete on the Day of Christ. At the present time we struggle against carnal desires, but then this struggle will be over. And we shall have freedom to do what is good.

Glorification will also bring us *freedom from the Law.* In Christ we are free from the Law insofar as justification and sanctification are concerned. At the present time God's moral law provides guidelines for our conduct, but in the eternal state there will be no need for such law (Matthew 5:17-18).

And finally, glorification will bring *freedom from death.* While at present Christians have not been freed from the experience of dying, they have been shielded from its power to hurt (1 Corinthians 15:51-56). As a result of Christ's death and resurrection, we no longer need to fear death (Hebrews 2:14-18). And at glorification we shall finally triumph, for death shall be no more!

We will enjoy the full realization of our freedom in Christ at our glorification. (See Romans 8:18-25; 2 Corinthians 4:16-18). We are *now* "children of God" (1 John 3:2) and we are trying to be like our Lord; however, *then* we shall be perfectly conformed to the likeness of the Son (Romans 8:29-30). When we are glorified our humanity is perfected into the perfect likeness of the perfect human nature of our Lord Jesus Christ.

12 Glorification brings about many glorious changes. Complete the following statements which concern various aspects of our glorification.

a Glorification will end people's agelong dream of having complete

....

b The liberty of Christians comes about as a result of ....

....

c Christians will be free from ....,

.... and ....

d The manhood (humanity) of Christians will be perfected into the likeness of the perfect human nature of ....

Perfecting of the Body

Since glorification involves the whole person, it includes the perfecting of the body. The Bible gives true dignity to the human body, and nowhere is the body depreciated or called sinful. In fact, we are told in Genesis 1:26-30 that the whole person was made in the image of God. Adam, you will recall, was included in Creation when God reviewed it and declared that it was very good (Genesis 1:31).

In the New Testament where the term *flesh* is used, it refers most frequently to the sinful nature, the carnal self, the "old man." The New Testament speaks of the body as the physical part of people's being. People have eyes, ears, hands, feet, and other physical members, and they are not sinful. The normal bodily functions themselves are not evil. It is only when these functions are perverted that there is moral wrong. Thus, the body itself will share in the glory, since it is a vital part of what we are. Remember, we are a unity: body-soul-spirit beings.

13 Read 2 Corinthians 5:1-5 and answer the following questions.

a Paul says that in our eternal existence, we shall be clothed with an

....

so that we shall not be *without* a body.

b At the present time we groan, not to be rid of our earthly body, but

to have our ....,
so that what is mortal may be changed into that which is eternal.

c God is the one who has prepared us for this change, and He gave us

the .... as the
deposit, or guarantee, of all that He has in store for us.

In these verses Paul asserts that the body is an important part of people's wholeness, even in eternity. Although many ancient pagans believed that the body was the prison of the soul, Paul viewed it as a temple appropriately created to be the dwelling place of the Holy Spirit (1 Corinthians 6:19).

Some have been misled by the word translated *vile* in the King James translation of Philippians 3:21: "who shall change our *vile* body." However, newer translations render this more properly as "Who . . . will transform our *lowly* bodies" (NIV). It is true that at the present time, because of the influence of sin, it is the body of our *humiliation* (margin reference for Philippians 3:21, KJV). As a result, it is yet subject to the curse of sin, with its pain, sickness, suffering, and death. But in glorification, the body will be changed and made like Christ's glorious body (Philippians 3:21; 1 John 3:2).

14 Read 1 Corinthians 15:51-57 carefully and answer the following questions.

a When will living Christians reach their glorified state?

....

b When will those who have died in Christ reach their glorified state?

....

The resurrection of the dead and the transformation of the living are miraculous events which stagger our imagination. Our limited minds just can't grasp what a glorious, universe-shaking event the Day of Christ will reveal. Like John, we don't know precisely what the nature of the glorified body will be (1 John 3:2). To this question Paul answers that God will clothe us with a body of His choosing. He adds:

> So it will be with the resurrection of the dead. The body that is sown is perishable, it is raised imperishable; it is sown in dishonor, it is raised in glory; it is sown in weakness, it is raised in power; it is sown a natural body, it is raised a spiritual body. And just as we have borne the likeness of the earthly man, so shall we bear the likeness of the man from heaven (1 Corinthians 15:42-44, 49).

Paul compares the resurrection of the body to the growth of a plant from a seed planted in the ground. The stalk of grain that comes up is not exactly the same as the seed. As the glory of the grain stalk outshines the lowliness of the seed, so the resurrected body is more glorious than the body that was buried. The resurrected body is not an exact copy of the old body that was buried. The important thing is that Christ's resurrection is a guarantee that those who die in Him shall be raised to life eternal (1 Corinthians 15:20).

BURIAL RESURRECTION

15 Circle the letter preceding TRUE statements concerning the nature of glorification.

a Glorification speaks primarily of physical perfection.

b When we stand glorified in God's presence, we shall no longer be able to sin.

c Every part of our being—body, soul, and spirit—will be faultless when we are glorified on the Day of Jesus Christ.

d Glorification is that process by which we gradually become more and more like Christ, until we are exactly like Him.

e When the Bible says that we shall be like Him, it means that we shall be sinless like Him.

f Glorification not only includes participation in eternal life, but also full realization of freedom.

g Glorification will bring freedom from sin, the Law, and death.

h In the glorified state we will no longer have a physical body.

i Part of the change that we will experience at glorification will be a change in our physical body.

j Our eternal life will be both never-ending and superior to our present life.

At our glorification, therefore, we shall undergo the greatest change that people have experienced since Creation and Calvary, as God brings us into His presence forever. All creation will share in this glorious freedom as it is set free from decay (Romans 8:19-23). There will be a new earth. Death and dying shall be no more, neither grief, nor crying, nor pain. All tears shall be wiped away forever. The God of creation and redemption is the one who glorifies us and makes His home with us—forever. And with Paul we may rejoice in the confidence the future holds for us, sure that God who began this good work will carry it on to completion (Philippians 1:6).

self-test

1 Glorification is related to the other doctrines of salvation

a) in that it represents the final completion of the work of salvation in the lives of Christians.

b) as one of the stages of growth in people's spiritual development before they stand in Christ's presence.

c) but since it deals with the believer's future status, it receives little or no mention in the Bible.

2 The believer's assurance of glorification rests upon certain factors which arise out of Christ's work as it applies to his life. These factors indicate that

a) the believer's assurance of glorification rests primarily on hope.

b) believers are now fully God's *sons*, and they can expect little change in their experience at glorification.

c) our salvation looks toward the future for complete fulfillment.

3 In discussing the nature of glorification we can note that it includes primarily

a) physical change.

b) spiritual change.

c) moral perfection.

4 Which of these is NOT a part of glorification?

a) A complete change of the body

b) A state of sinlessness achieved in this life

c) A superior quality of eternal life and unlimited freedom

5 The Lord has not just made statements about the future blessed state we shall enjoy and then left us to trust His Word. In addition, He has

a) sent regular trustworthy messengers to tell us about the eternal state to keep our hopes alive.

b) provided an experience for us that results in the indwelling of the Holy Spirit, who guarantees what is to come.

c) placed the gift of prophecy in the church to inform Christians of His intentions concerning the future.

6 The terms *promise, firstfruits, earnest* or *deposit, seal,* and *inheritance* serve the purpose of

a) giving us assurance that our salvation looks forward to complete fulfillment.
b) demonstrating that our present salvation is final and complete and needs no further fulfillment.
c) making us familiar with biblical terms which describe redemption.

7 Our study of seven Greek words which deal with our future perfection leads us to the conclusion that

a) glorified people will be equal with God.
b) redeemed people will possess moral perfection that will fit them for eternal life.
c) glorification concerns individual Christians but will not affect the society of the eternal state.

8 The basis of glorification, like that of the other doctrines of salvation, is the

a) degree of cooperation which people give to the work of God.
b) maturity of believers: the more mature have quality, the less mature do not.
c) death, resurrection, and intercession of Christ.

9 Glorification may be defined as the act of God by which He

a) saves a person who puts his trust in Him.
b) completes His redeeming work in people, making them morally ready for eternity.
c) raises a select group of redeemed ones from the earth to heaven at the beginning of the judgment of the wicked nations.

10 We have seen that at our glorification

a) our spirits are primarily in view, since moral perfection deals mainly with this side of our being.
b) we will be liberated from our bodies as we enter the eternal state.
c) every part of us: body, soul, and spirit—the whole person—will be changed.

Be sure to complete your unit student report for Unit 3 and return the answer sheet to your ICI instructor.

answers to study questions

8 a It is called a *promise.*

b Christ is called the *firstfruits* of our salvation in most modern translations, although the TEV uses the word *guarantee.*

c The Holy Spirit is called the *earnest* (KJV), *deposit* (NIV), or *guarantee* of our full and final salvation.

d The Holy Spirit *seals* us.

e Salvation is called an *inheritance.*

1 a True.
b False.
c True.
d False.
e True.

9 a 4) Seal.
b 3) Earnest or deposit.
c 1) Promise.
d 5) Inheritance.
e 2) Firstfruits.

2 a 10) The final goal.
b 6) To make a complete turnabout.
c 5) A new position.
d 7) Turning from sin.
e 8) God's activity in eternity past.
f 3) Covering for sin.
g 2) Turning to God.
h 9) A new nature.
i 4) Process of becoming like Christ.
j 1) A new standing.

10 a False.
b True.
c True.
d True.

3 No one knows, but Scripture, as we have seen, says that Christ will come as a thief in the night.

11 b) Christians now have eternal life . . .

4 We will be raised, whether we are living or dead, to meet Him in the air, and we will be changed—we will receive our glorified bodies which will be like His.

12 **a** freedom.
b their submission or bondage to Christ.
c sin, the Law, death.
d Christ.

5 c) the act of God by which He completes...

13 **a** eternal body
b heavenly body
c Holy Spirit

6 **a** Christ's own resurrection gives us assurance of our resurrection.
b Christ's death removed the barriers between us and God (sin, separation, and unholiness).
c He meant that He would pray to the Father in our behalf, so that we might receive strength to live a holy and victorious life.

14 **a** Living Christians shall be changed at Christ's coming.
b Those Christians who have died will be changed as they are resurrected.

7 b) The basis of glorification is the death...

15 **a** False. (This is part of it, but the most important aspect is moral perfection.)
b True.
c True.
d False.
e True.
f True.
g True.
h False.
i True.
j True.

for your notes

Glossary

The right-hand column lists the lesson in the study guide in which the word is first used.

		Lesson
abandon	— to withdraw protection, support, or help from	3
accountable	— responsible, answerable	5
acquits	— releases or frees from an obligation or accusation	8
alien	— foreign; outside; belonging to another person, place, or thing	3
apostasy	— the act of forsaking completely a previous loyalty, such as a religious faith	4
appease	— to bring to a state of peace; pacify; conciliate	1
appropriate	— to take for oneself; use as one's own	7
appropriation	— the act of taking possession of something for a specific use	7
arbitrary	— selected at random or without reason; selected without a plan, purpose, or pattern	5
assent	— agreement	3
atonement	— reconciliation of God and man through the sacrificial death of Jesus Christ	1
belittle	— to cause a person or thing to seem little or less	1
cancellation	— the act of destroying, of bringing to nothingness	7

GLOSSARY

carnal	— relating to or given to bodily pleasures and appetites; fleshly; relating to man's lower nature	10
chain reaction	— a series of events so related to each other that each one initiates the next	10
citizen	— an inhabitant; a resident; a person who owes his loyalty to a government and receives protection from it	3
climactic	— of or relating to a major turning point	10
compassion	— sympathetic awareness of another's distress with a desire to lessen or relieve it	1
compromise	— to make a shameful or disreputable concession	3
concept	— something conceived in the mind; idea; notion; a class of objects or events	1
condemnation	— blame; the act of pronouncing guilty	10
conditional	— dependent upon the terms of an agreement	3
conditioned	— brought or put into a specified state; produced by conditioning	3
confrontation	— the clashing of forces or ideas; a face-to-face meeting	4
consequences	— results; effects	2
consuming	— using up; wasting; doing away with completely	6
conversion	— the act of turning from sin to the Lord Jesus for forgiveness of sins, which includes a complete turnabout involving every part of a person's being	4

converted — one who has experienced conversion is said to have converted; in this sense, one who has changed from unbelief to faith in the Lord Jesus for salvation has converted 3

conviction — the act of convincing a person of error; a strong persuasion or belief 7

corruption — decay; departure from what is pure or correct 6

credit — the balance in a person's favor; something entrusted to another 7

crisis — an emotionally significant event or radical change in a person's life 6

decisive — marked by determination or firmness; implies the ability or intent to settle an undecided matter once and for all 4

depreciated — spoke slightingly of; belittled; disparaged 10

destined — that which is decreed beforehand; predetermined; that which is set apart for a specific purpose or end 6

destiny — something to which a person or thing is destined; predetermined course of events held by some to be an irresistible power or agency 5

deterministic — view which holds that God determined in eternity past that some should be saved and have eternal life and some should be eternally lost 5

disembodied — separated from the body 8

dominant — most powerful or influential; controlling; governing 5

GLOSSARY

doomed	— condemned to eternal punishment: separated from God's presence and consigned to hell	5
down payment	— part of the full price paid at the time of purchase or delivery, with the balance to be paid later	8
dynamic	— active; marked by energy; forceful	3
earnest (noun)	— money given or something done at the time of a bargain as a pledge that the bargain will be carried out; thing that shows what is to come; pledge; token	8
elect (the)	— refers to those who are selected by God for special office, work, honor	5
election	— refers to the divine choice of nations or communities for the possession of special privileges with reference to the performance of special services; the divine choice of individuals to a particular office or work; the divine choice of individuals to be the children of God, and therefore heirs of eternal life	5
elements	— the basic parts of which anything is made up	3
endurance	— the ability to withstand hardship, adversity, or stress; power to put up with, bear, or stand	3
enlightened	— freed from ignorance and misinformation; based on a full comprehension of the problems involved	4
ethical	— having to do with standards of right and wrong; of ethics or morals	9

exalt	— make high in rank, honor, power, character, or quality; elevate	1
externally	— on the outside; coming from without	8
fatalism	— a doctrine that events are fixed in advance for all time in such a manner that human beings are powerless to change them; a belief in or attitude determined by this doctrine	5
fatalistic	— accepting things and events as inevitable; of or having to do with fatalism or fatalists	
fate	— one's lot or fortune; final outcome; destiny	7
foreordain	— means to decide upon beforehand	5
foreordination	— refers to God's determination in eternity to carry out His purpose to save those who accept His Son and the offer of salvation; an ordaining beforehand	5
forfeit	— lose or have to give up by one's own act, neglect, or fault; loss or giving up of something as a penalty	8
forsake	— to renounce (as something once cherished) without intent to recover or resume	2
glorification	— the work that God will perform by which He will complete our salvation, making us morally perfect for eternity, and bringing us into His presence in a body like Christ's glorious body (Philippians 3:21)	10
Graeco-Roman	— having characteristics that are partly Greek and partly Roman	8

grief	— great sadness caused by trouble or loss; heavy sorrow	2
grieve	— feel grief; be very sad	2
heir	— person who receives or has the right to receive someone's property or title after that one dies; person who inherits property	8
humiliation	— a lowering of pride, dignity, or self-respect; state or feeling of being humiliated	10
idolatry	— the worship of a physical object as a god; immoderate attachment or devotion to something	2
implantation	— instilling or fixing securely or deeply; to set permanently in the consciousness or habit patterns	6
imputation	— the act of imputing	7
impute	— to credit to a person or cause: attribute; to lay responsibility or blame for, often falsely or unjustly	7
incarnate	— embodied in flesh; in Christian theology the union of divine nature and human nature in the person of Jesus; the Son of God taking upon Himself human form	1
incriminating	— the kind of evidence that indicates involvement in a fault or crime	10
inheritance	— to get as one's own a possession, condition, or trait from past generations; something that is or may be inherited	8
intellect	— power of knowing, understanding; mind; the power of knowing as distinguished from the power to feel and to will	3

intellectual — of or relating to the intellect or its use; developed or chiefly guided by the intellect rather than by emotion or experience 3

intercession — the act of interceding; prayer, petition, or entreaty in favor of another 10

internally — inside; inside the body 8

irresistible — impossible to resist successfully; overwhelming; too great to be withstood 4

irresponsible — said or done with no sense of responsibility; untrustworthy; unreliable 5

judicial — of or by judges; having to do with the administration of justice 8

justification — the act of God's free grace by which He pardons sin and declares that the repentant sinner is righteous on the basis of Christ's righteousness 7

liable — obligated according to law or equity; responsible; exposed or subject to usually adverse action 8

liberation — the state of being liberated 8

majestic — having or exhibiting majesty; stately; sublime; glorious 9

merit — something that deserves praise or reward; commendable quality 5

meritorious — deserving of reward or honor; having merit; worthy; commendable 7

moral — of or relating to principles of right and wrong in behavior 9

motivating	— providing with a motive or incentive; inducing one to act	5
motivation	— the act or process of furnishing with an incentive or inducement to action	6
negative conversion	— refusal to follow any further one's religious faith or moral principles; abandonment of previous loyalty; desertion	4
objective standard	— refers to the use of the Bible to verify the reality of one's conversion experience; involves the use of scriptural facts rather than personal feelings or prejudices to judge spiritual experiences	4
obstacle	— something that stands in the way or stops progress	3
offenders	— persons who do wrong or break the law; those who transgress the divine or moral law	7
passive	— being acted on without itself acting; not acting in return; not resisting; yielding or submitting to the will of another	6
passively	— inactive; inert; submissive	3
paternal	— of or like a father, fatherly; received or inherited from one's father	8
patriarchal period	— the period of Abraham, Isaac, and Jacob	8
penalty	— punishment imposed by law; disadvantage attached to some act or condition; something forfeited by a person if an obligation is not fulfilled	1

persecutor — one who annoys others with persistent or urgent approaches; one who harasses others in a manner designed to injure, grieve or afflict them: specifically because of their beliefs 4

perverted — corrupted; those who have been turned away from what is true, desirable, good, or morally right 10

philosophy — study of the truth or principles underlying all real knowledge; study of the most general causes and principles of the universe 4

pilgrimages — journeys to sacred places as acts of religious devotion; long journeys 7

positional — of, having to do with, or depending on the position a believer occupies in relation to God; in sanctification, referring to the change of position by which a corrupt sinner is changed into a holy worshiper. 9

potential — capable of coming into being or action; possible as opposed to actual 3

predestined — that which has been destined, decreed, determined, appointed or settled beforehand; foreordained 5

predicament — a difficult, perplexing, trying, or dangerous situation 1

profane — not sacred; worldly; secular; not holy because unconsecrated, impure, or defiled 9

progressive — of, relating to, or characterized by progression; moving forward or onward: advancing; developing 9

propitiation	— the act of reducing the anger of, winning the favor of, appeasing one who has been offended	1
quicken	— to make alive: revive; to cause to be enlivened intensely	6
ransom	— price paid or demanded before a captive is set free	1
rebellion	— opposition to one in authority or dominance; resistance against any power or restriction	1
reconciliation	— a reconciling; bringing together again in friendship; settlement or adjustment of differences	1
re-creation	— the act of creating anew; thing created anew	6
redemption	— deliverance from certain evil by the payment of a price	1
renovation	— act of restoring to life, vigor, or activity: revive	8
repentance	— may be defined as the experience in which one recognizes that he has sinned, feels sorry about his sins, turns from them, and gives them up completely	2
resources	— supplies that will meet needs; stocks or reserves upon which to draw when necessary	3
restitution	— act of making good any loss, damage, or injury; reparation; amends; restoration of something to its rightful owner	2
restrain	— hold back; keep in check or keep within limits: repress, curb	9

righteousness	— condition of one who does right, behaves justly and acts virtuously; one whose actions are proper, just, and right	1
rites	— prescribed forms or manners governing the words or actions for ceremonies	7
ritual	— form or system of rites; a prescribed order of performing a ceremony or rite	7
sacraments	— formal religious acts that are sacred as signs or symbols of spiritual reality; something especially sacred; baptism and communion are two sacraments with which most Christians are familiar	6
sacrificial	— having to do with or used in sacrifice	1
sanctifies	— makes holy; makes legitimate or binding by a religious sanction; sets apart as sacred	5
secular	— not religious or sacred: worldly	9
sovereign	— above all others; supreme; greatest; very excellent or powerful	1
sovereignty	— supreme power or authority	2
subjection	— bringing under some power or influence; condition of being under some power or influence	9
symbolize	— to serve as a symbol of; to represent, express, or identify by a symbol	6
transcendent	— surpassing ordinary limits; excelling; superior; extraordinary	10
transformation	— condition brought about in a thing or a person because of a thoroughgoing or fundamental change in appearance, shape, or nature	4

unconditional	— not limited: absolute, unqualified	3
unmerited	— not merited; undeserved; unearned	1
unreconciled	— not reconciled; not restored to friendship; state in which differences between two or more parties have not been adjusted	7
unregenerate	— not born again spiritually; not turned to the love of God; wicked; bad	6
upright	— good; honest; righteous	9
uprightness	— state of being good, honest, and righteous	7
verdict	— the finding or decision of a judge or jury on a matter submitted for trial	7
verify	— prove to be true; check for accuracy; confirm	8
vitality	— strength or vigor of mind or body; energy	3
yoke	— something that holds people in slavery or submission; rule; dominion	2
zeal	— eager desire or effort; earnest enthusiasm; fervor	2

Answers to Self-Tests

Lesson 1

1 **a** True.
b True.
c False.
d True.
e False.

2 **a** True.
b False
c True.
d True.
e True.
f False.
g True.

3 **a** True.
b False.
c True.
d True.
e False.
f True.

Lesson 2

1 a) is the first step in a return to God.

2 b) recognizing sin, feeling sorry . . .

3 c) those who do not repent now will one day weep . . .

4 a) every part of our being is concerned . . .

5 c) there is a full development of the teaching . . .

6 b) Christians who fail God . . .

7 b) goodness of God. And the means He uses . . .

8 a) all people are guilty of sin.

9 b) heaven rejoices with the sinner who turns to God.

10 b) it gives this message to the world: the one making restitution has changed.

11 **a** 2) Emotional.
b 1) Intellectual.
c 3) An act of the will.
d 3) An act of the will.
e 1) Intellectual.
f 2) Emotional.

Lesson 3

1 True.

2 False.

3 True.

4 False.

5 True.

6 True.

7 True.

8 False.

9 False.

10 True.

11 False.

12 True.

13 False.

14 True.

15 False.

ANSWERS TO SELF-TESTS

Lesson 4

1 a) in a very close way, for they are steps . . .

2 b) acts that touch people at every point of their being . . .

3 a) man's response to the ministry of the Word . . .

4 c) responsibility of man, *primarily*, for God commands it . . .

5 b) preaching of the gospel.

6 **a** 1) Result of conversion.
b 1) Result of conversion.
c 2) Not a result of conversion.
d 1) Result of conversion.
e 1) Result of conversion.
f 1) Result of conversion.
g 2) Not a result of conversion.
h 1) Result of conversion.

Lesson 5

1 b) describes the process by which the believer is to become ever more like his Lord.

2 c) Christ Jesus.

3 a) those who respond to God's offer of salvation.

4 b) God's foreknowledge.

5 c) John 14:1-3.

6 a) faith.

7 c) both of the above, a) and b).

8 a) does not fix either people's salvation or destruction.

9 b) proclaim the gospel message by every means possible to all creatures.

10 c) a deep sense of appreciation for God's grace . . .

Lesson 6

1 birth from above or born again.

2 reborn spiritually.

3 Christ.

4 Everyone in the world.

5 You may include any two of the following: awareness of new life within, a new desire for living, new purpose, new values, new outlook on life, witness of the Spirit in our life as He leads and directs, love for God, God-centered life and love for others.

6 b) a person is regenerated by baptism.

7 c) holy nature of God.

8 a) corrupt nature of people.

9 b) each sinner who is lost in the desert of sin . . .

10 c) The work of regeneration occurs in a mysterious . . .

Lesson 7

1 b) in love God provided a just way through the cross . . .

2 c) declared righteous because Christ's righteousness . . .

3 c) brings the benefits of both a) and b).

4 a) faith alone apart from works . . .

5 b) grace of God and the cross of Christ.

6 b) no more of our own merit than is the beggar's act . . .

7 c) mercy. (If they received justice, as in a), they would personally pay the penalty for their sins.)

8 a) righteousness of people which results from good deeds.

9 c) "Just as if I'd never sinned."

10 b) is limited to those who appropriate it . . .

Lesson 8

1 b) placed as sons in God's family . . .

2 c) those who have received the adoption of adult sons . . .

3 b) believe in the Lord Jesus and receive Him.

4 c) receives us, adopts us as His own, and gives us the Holy Spirit . . .

5 a) has eternally been part of God's redemptive plan.

6 d) Status as legal bondservants.

7 b) the Graeco-Roman custom of adoption.

8 b) is begun in time and will be completed in eternity future.

9 c) bodies, making us completely fit . . .

10 **a** 3) Adoption.
b 1) Regeneration.
c 2) Justification.

Lesson 9

1 True.

2 True.

3 False.

4 True.

5 True.

6 False.

7 True.

8 True.

9 False.

10 True.

11 True.

12 True.

13 True.

14 False.

15 True.

Lesson 10

1 a) in that it represents the final completion . . .

2 c) our salvation looks toward the future . . .

3 c) moral perfection.

4 b) A state of sinlessness achieved in this life.

5 b) provided an experience for us that results . . .

6 a) giving us assurance that our salvation looks forward . . .

7 b) redeemed people will possess moral perfection . . .

8 c) death, resurrection, and intercession of Christ.

9 b) completes His redeeming work in people, making them morally ready for eternity.

10 c) every part of us: body, soul, and spirit . . .

CS3231

Alive in Christ

A STUDY OF SALVATION

UNIT STUDENT REPORTS
AND
ANSWER SHEETS

DIRECTIONS

When you have completed your study of each unit, fill out the unit student report answer sheet for that unit. The following are directions how to indicate your answer to each question. There are two kinds of questions: TRUE-FALSE and MULTIPLE-CHOICE.

TRUE-FALSE QUESTION EXAMPLE

The following statement is either true or false. If the statement is

TRUE, blacken space A.
FALSE, blacken space B.

1 The Bible is God's message for us.

The above statement, *The Bible is God's message for us,* is TRUE, so you would blacken space A like this:

MULTIPLE CHOICE QUESTION EXAMPLE

There is one best answer for the following question. Blacken the space for the answer you have chosen.

2 To be born again means to
a) be young in age.
b) accept Jesus as Savior.
c) start a new year.
d) find a different church.

The correct answer is b)*accept Jesus as Savior,* so you would blacken space B like this:

2 A ■ C D

STUDENT REPORT FOR UNIT ONE

Answer all questions on Unit Student Report Answer Sheet 1. See the examples on the **DIRECTIONS** *page which show you how to mark your answers.*

PART 1—TRUE-FALSE QUESTIONS

The following statements are either true or false. If the statement is
TRUE, blacken space a space A.
FALSE, blacken space B.

1 I have carefully read all of the lessons in Unit One.

2 Repentance is necessary because all are guilty of sinning.

3 Repentance is mainly an intellectual activity.

4 Repentance is produced by the ministry of the Word and by a fresh vision of God.

5 Faith is vitally important to us, for it affects every aspect of our lives.

6 Faith is composed of but one element, assent, for it basically involves emotions.

7 Repentance and faith equal conversion.

8 The only measure for true conversion is the Word of God.

PART 2—MULTIPLE-CHOICE QUESTIONS

There is one best answer for each of the following questions. Blacken the space on your answer sheet for the answer you have chosen.

9 The results of repentance are that
a) the entire community rejoices at the sinner's action.
b) the family of the repentant sinner rejoices.
c) heaven rejoices with the sinner who turns to God.
d) people of the world rejoice because of the good change.

10 When people feel sorry for their sins, this affects their
a) intellect.
b) emotions.
c) will.

11 The aspect of repentance involved in decision making is
a) the physical aspect.
b) the emotional aspect.
c) the intellectual aspect.
d) the act of the will.

12 For a sinner to recognize he has offended God means that
a) the intellect is involved in repentance.
b) an emotional problem exists in the sinner.
c) the sinner lives in an enlightened society.
d) sinners are hearing a message of judgment, not love.

13 Simply stated, we might say that faith is
a) an act by which we express our confidence in God and begin to hope in His grace.
b) the act of grasping firmly some truth we have heard and relying on this.
c) the act by which we place our confidence in God, allowing Him to direct our actions.
d) simply a blind leap toward that which we desire.

14 Living faith, which pleases God, is shown by
a) the complete commitment of our lives to Christ.
b) simple trust in God, and no accompanying actions or works.
c) its believing something about Jesus.
d) its reliance on the intellect, not on the emotions or will.

15 One of the qualities of living faith is good actions which
a) are instrumental in saving a person.
b) give evidence of the health and vitality of one's faith.
c) show that a sinner is worthy of salvation.
d) should be demonstrated to impress the unbelieving world.

16 By degrees of faith, we understand that
a) one always has little faith which will increase in time.
b) one moves from a lesser degree of faith to a greater.
c) having received greater faith, one can never have less.
d) faith is living and growing, and can mature in everyone.

17 Repentance and faith are related to conversion
a) only in that all are part of the salvation experience.
b) in a very small sense, since all three are related to the Holy Spirit's work in people.
c) because each is related to an aspect of salvation.
d) directly, for they prepare the sinner for conversion.

18 Conversion is brought about as a result of
a) self-knowledge, showing one has not met a moral standard.
b) a curious mind seeking an unknown Savior.
c) man's response to the ministry of the Word, and the activity of the Spirit.

19 Which of the following is NOT the result of conversion?
a) We receive eternal life and are saved from eternal death.
b) Our sins are blotted out.
c) We are instantly perfect, with full spiritual knowledge.
d) We have new relationships with God and people.

20 Repentance, faith, and conversion
a) affect our total being: emotions, intellect, and will.
b) are exclusively the work of God; we have no part in these.
c) are words which have no difference in meaning.
d) are the irresistible work of God.

END OF REQUIREMENTS FOR UNIT ONE. Follow the remaining instructions on your answer sheet and return it to your ICI Instructor or office in your area, then begin your study of Unit Two.

STUDENT REPORT FOR UNIT TWO

Answer all questions on Answer Sheet for Unit Two. See the examples on the **DIRECTIONS** *page which show you how to mark your answers.*

PART 1—TRUE-FALSE QUESTIONS

The following statements are either true or false. If the statement is
TRUE, blacken space A.
FALSE, blacken space B.

1 I have carefully read all of the lessons in Unit Two.

2 The need for regeneration is universal, for all have sinned.

3 In regeneration, God gives spiritual life to the repentant one and he is born again.

4 Justification is faith plus the observance of the Law.

5 As guilty sinners stand condemned before a holy God they need justice.

6 Justification is an objective work that takes place before the throne of God.

7 In adoption a person receives a new position.

8 One of the great benefits of adoption is the witness of the Spirit who verifies our sonship.

PART 2—MULTIPLE-CHOICE QUESTIONS

There is one best answer for each of the following questions. Blacken the space on your answer sheet for the answer you have chosen.

9 In the Bible regeneration is presented as
a) a change which affects only a person's attitudes and beliefs.
b) creating new values in one wanting a better life.
c) arising from sincere convictions of good people.
d) birth from above or by the Spirit.

10 Regeneration is necessary because
a) people have guilt feelings as a result of their sin.
b) pressure is placed upon the sinner by his family.
c) of the nature of people and the nature of God.
d) of the expectations of society.

11 One commonly wrong idea about regeneration is that
a) it is the same as conversion.
b) a person is regenerated by baptism.
c) this experience is essentially a change of one's mind.
d) the requirements vary from one culture to another.

12 The experience of regeneration is one in which
a) sinners lost in the desert of sin come to Christ, the oasis, as the only solution for their problems.
b) sincere people struggle up the mountain by different paths, and all these eventually lead to the same place.
c) one changes by his own efforts, education, and knowledge.

13 The righteousness of God is upheld even as sinners are declared "not guilty," because in justification
a) God's declaration is sufficient without payment for sin.
b) a person's good works are payment for his sins.
c) our sins are transferred to Christ and His righteousness is transferred to us.

14 Scripture teaches that a person is justified by
a) faith alone, not by works, penances, or personal merit.
b) a combination of the Law, faith in Christ, and good works.
c) progressive growth in spiritual life.

15 We can most easily support the statement—people are justified by faith alone—by using which of the following Scriptures?
a) Romans 8.1
b) Galatians 3:5
c) Titus 3:5
d) Romans 4:5

16 Justification rests upon the
a) pity which God feels for lost sinners.
b) grace of God and the cross of Christ.
c) need of lost people for an easy way to escape justice.
d) yearning of people's hearts to be put right with God.

17 Adoption is an act of God's grace by which we are
a) born again into God's family.
b) placed as sons in God's family, with a natural son's rights.
c) freed from the penalty of sin, being declared righteous.
d) given a new nature in Christ.

18 Adoption, which is closely related to justification and regeneration, is the change of a person's
a) rank and position, giving him privileges as a son of God.
b) nature and deals primarily with his new birth experience.
c) standing before God and concerns his personal merit.
d) attitudes and actions that are affected by conversion.

19 The means of adoption as set forth in the New Testament is
a) the effort and desire of all to respond to God's love.
b) the irresistible grace of God towards the elect.
c) God's grace receiving us when we receive Christ.
d) Christ, the fulfillment of the written and moral law.

20 Which one of the following is NOT a benefit of adoption?
a) The Father's love, care, and understanding
b) Needs supplied, protection, instruction, and correction
c) Boldness to come into His presence as His heirs
d) An inheritance never to be lost, however we may live

END OF REQUIREMENTS FOR UNIT TWO. Follow the remaining instructions on your answer sheet and return it to your ICI instructor or office in your area, then begin your study of Unit Three.

STUDENT REPORT FOR UNIT THREE

Answer all questions on Answer Sheet for Unit Three. See the examples on the **DIRECTIONS** *page which show you how to mark your answers.*

PART 1—TRUE-FALSE QUESTIONS

The following statements are either true or false. if the statement is
TRUE, blacken space A.
FALSE, blacken space B.

1 I have carefully read all of the lessons in Unit Three.

2 Sanctification is being separated from sin unto God.

3 Relative perfection means that we simply fulfill the purpose for which we were made.

4 Sanctification is to put off the old man and put on the new.

5 One who believes that a person can live perfectly has a limited concept of God's holiness and man's sin.

6 Glorification, our future state, is unrelated to the other doctrines of salvation.

7 We are assured of glorification by biblical references which show that salvation involves future fulfillment.

8 Glorification concerns primarily our judicial standing.

PART 2—MULTIPLE-CHOICE QUESTIONS

There is one best answer for each of the following questions. Blacken the space on your answer sheet for the answer you have chosen.

9 The purpose of sanctification in the believer's life is to
a) bring to present perfection his experience in Christ.
b) bring him to full spiritual maturity by one experience.
c) make him progressively more Christlike.
d) give him standing as a holy one in God's sight.

10 The experience of sanctification brings about
a) a decisive crisis experience.
b) a change in us, conforming us to the image of Christ.
c) a complete and final state of sinlessness in us.
d) an empowerment for service.

11 The kind of sanctification one receives as he is born again is
a) positional.
b) progressive.
c) relative.
d) conditional.

12 Those who believe that Christians can become sinlessly perfect view sanctification as the
a) complete destruction of the carnal nature.
b) baptism in the Holy Spirit, which is given for the purpose of empowered service.
c) same as regeneration.
d) final experience which Christians can expect.

13 Pentecostals believe that the baptism in the Holy Spirit is
a) the same as sanctification.
b) only possible for those who are spiritually mature.
c) received when the new birth is experienced.
d) an experience which gives the believer power for service.

14 Sanctification gives believers
a) an experience which will end all struggles with their carnal natures.
b) the motivation to excel in the use of spiritual gifts.
c) the desire to seek holiness and to dedicate themselves increasingly to God.

15 Glorification is related to the other doctrines of salvation
a) in an indirect way, since it concerns the future.
b) as the final link in the chain; it represents the completion of salvation.
c) since it concerns the ultimate perfection of the saints at sanctification.
d) in no certain way, as the Bible does not deal with it.

16 God has placed glorification before us, and this promise is specifically guaranteed to us by
a) the prophets.
b) Christian tradition.
c) ordinances which Jesus gave.
d) the gift of the Holy Spirit.

17 By nature glorification primarily concerns
a) moral perfection.
b) judicial standing.
c) legal status.
d) family position.

18 The work of glorification rests primarily on the
a) degree of response in each of us to God's grace.
b) merit of each one, based upon our good works.
c) death, resurrection, and intercession of Christ.
d) spiritual maturity of believers.

19 At our glorification that which will be affected is our
a) spirit.
b) soul.
c) intellect.
d) entire being.

20 We may define glorification as the act by which God
a) gives a new nature to those who repent.
b) completes His redemptive work in people, making them ready for eternity.
c) accepts as pure and righteous those who trust him.
d) translates the living saints to heaven.

END OF REQUIREMENTS FOR UNIT THREE. Follow the remaining instructions on your answer sheet and return it to your ICI instructor or office in your area. This completes your study of this course. Ask your ICI instructor to recommend another course of study for you.

ALIVE IN CHRIST

ANSWER SHEET FOR UNIT ONE

CS3231

Congratulations on finishing your study of the lessons in Unit One! Please fill in all the blanks below.

Your Name ....KAREN.....NEWELL..

Your ICI Student Number ....

(Leave blank if you do not know what it is.)

Your Mailing Address ..33...BROWNSTOWN.....ROAD.............

City PORTADOWN.................... Province or State ..Co. ARMAGH

Country ..N. IRELAND..

Age ..23..... Sex .....F.......... Occupation ..SINGLE.....MOTHER

Are you married? ..NO.. How many members are in your family? ..2..

How many years have you studied in school? ....

Are you a member of a church? ....YES..

If so, what is the name of the church? ..VICTORY.....PRAISE.......

What responsibility do you have in your church? ....

....

How are you studying this course: Alone? ....

In a group? ✓ ....

What other ICI courses have you studied? ....BASIC..................

....

....

ANSWER SHEET FOR UNIT ONE

Blacken the correct space for each numbered item. For all questions, be sure the number beside the spaces on the answer sheet is the same as the number of the question.

	A	B	C	D	8	A	B	C	D	15	A	B	C	D
	A	B	C	D	9	A	B	C	D	16	A	B	C	D
	A	B	C	D	10	A	B	C	D	17	A	B	C	D
	A	B	C	D	11	A	B	C	D	18	A	B	C	D
	A	B	C	D	12	A	B	C	D	19	A	B	C	D
	A	B	C	D	13	A	B	C	D	20	A	B	C	D
	A	B	C	D	14	A	B	C	D					

Write below any questions you would like to ask your instructor about the lessons.

....

....

....

Now look over this student report answer sheet to be sure you have completed all the questions. Then return it to your ICI instructor or office in your area. The address should be stamped on the copyright page of your study guide.

For ICI Office Use Only

Date .... **Score** ....

ALIVE IN CHRIST

ANSWER SHEET FOR UNIT TWO

CS3231

We hope you have enjoyed your study of the lessons in Unit Two! Please fill in all the blanks below.

Your Name ....

Your ICI Student Number ....

(Leave blank if you do not know what it is.)

Your Mailing Address ....

City .... Province or State ....

Country ....

ANSWER SHEET FOR UNIT TWO

Blacken the correct space for each numbered item. For all questions, be sure the number beside the spaces on the answer sheet is the same as the number of the question.

1	A	B	C	D	8	A	B	C	D	15	A	B	C	D
2	A	B	C	D	9	A	B	C	D	16	A	B	C	D
3	A	B	C	D	10	A	B	C	D	17	A	B	C	D
4	A	B	C	D	11	A	B	C	D	18	A	B	C	D
5	A	B	C	D	12	A	B	C	D	19	A	B	C	D
6	A	B	C	D	13	A	B	C	D	20	A	B	C	D
7	A	B	C	D	14	A	B	C	D					

Write below any questions you would like to ask your instructor about the lessons.

....

....

....

Now look over this student report answer sheet to be sure you have completed all the questions. Then return it to your ICI instructor or office in your area. The address should be stamped on the copyright page of your study guide.

For ICI Office Use Only

Date .... **Score** ....

ALIVE IN CHRIST

ANSWER SHEET FOR UNIT THREE

CS3231

We hope you have enjoyed your study of the lessons in Unit Three! Please fill in all the blanks below.

Your Name ....

Your ICI Student Number ....

(Leave blank if you do not know what it is.)

Your Mailing Address ....

City .... Province or State ....

Country ....

REQUEST FOR INFORMATION

The ICI office in your area will be happy to send you information about other ICI courses that are available and their cost. You may use the space below to ask for that information.

....

....

....

ANSWER SHEET FOR UNIT THREE

Blacken the correct space for each numbered item. For all questions, be sure the number beside the spaces on the answer sheet is the same as the number of the question.

A	B	C	D	8	A	B	C	D	15	A	B	C	D
A	B	C	D	9	A	B	C	D	16	A	B	C	D
A	B	C	D	10	A	B	C	D	17	A	B	C	D
A	B	C	D	11	A	B	C	D	18	A	B	C	D
A	B	C	D	12	A	B	C	D	19	A	B	C	D
A	B	C	D	13	A	B	C	D	20	A	B	C	D
A	B	C	D	14	A	B	C	D					

Please write below one specific comment about the unit:

....

....

....

CONGRATULATIONS!

You have finished this Christian Service course. We have enjoyed having you as a student and hope you will study more courses with ICI. Return this unit student report answer sheet to your ICI instructor or office in your area. You will then receive your grade on a student score report form along with a certificate or seal for this course in your program of studies.

Please print your name below as you want it on your certificate.

Name ....

For ICI Office Use Only
Date .... **Score** ....

Christian Service Program